Good-Bye Hegemony!

Good-Bye Hegemony!

POWER AND INFLUENCE IN THE GLOBAL SYSTEM

Simon Reich
Richard Ned Lebow

PRINCETON UNIVERSITY PRESS

PRINCETON AND OXFORD

Library of Congress Cataloging-in-Publication Data

Reich, Simon.
Good-bye hegemony! : power and influence in the global system / Simon Reich,
Richard Ned Lebow.
pages cm
Includes bibliographical references and index.
ISBN 978-0-691-16042-9 (hardcover : alk. paper)—ISBN 978-0-691-16043-6 (pbk. :
alk. paper) 1. Balance of power—History—21st century. 2. World politics—21st
century. 3. International relations—History—21st century. I. Lebow, Richard
Ned. II. Title.
JZ1310.R45 2013
327.1′1—dc23
2013018206

British Library Cataloging-in-Publication Data is available

This book has been composed in Palatino

Printed on acid-free paper. ∞

Printed in the United States of America

1 3 5 7 9 10 8 6 4 2

To the Ballard family and la famiglia Forlatti

With love and gratitude transcending the decades

Contents

List of Tables

Preface

American leaders had contradictory goals in the decades following World War II. They wanted to foster democracy and economic development, but were opposed to left-wing parties and governments. They wanted the order they associated with hierarchy and to preserve the United States' extraordinary position in 1945 as far and away the world's most powerful country. Policy makers sometimes made trade-offs among these goals, as they did by consistently supporting right-wing dictatorships over their democratic opponents in the name of anticommunism. More often than not they denied trade-offs, convincing themselves they could pursue all these goals simultaneously.

American academics catered to this illusion by developing the concept of hegemony. It made it appear that hierarchy in the form of American hegemony was beneficial to democracy and development and was welcomed by major actors everywhere outside the Soviet bloc. Americans considered Moscow's opposition to US hegemony as opposition to global order and thus a sign of aggressive intentions. A growing bloc of neutrals who also expressed their disquiet, with India as its most vocal spokesmen, were dismissed as misguided, or even as dupes of Moscow. Instead of speaking truth to power, international relations scholars, with few notable exceptions, became spokesmen, therapists, and propagandists on behalf of the burgeoning national security establishment for the assumptions that undergirded American foreign policy.

Almost seventy years later, American realists and liberals continue to defend hegemony in theory and practice. They ignore the evidence that hegemony was only partial and short-lived and that American efforts to maintain order (e.g., in Vietnam, Afghanistan, and Iraq) were a primary source of disorder in the international system. Despite ample evidence to the contrary, they delude themselves into believing that most of the world welcomes American leadership and that its policies invariably engender stability.

We challenge this orthodoxy and offer what we believe is a more plausible and constructive view of America's role in a posthegemonic world. It recognizes the limitations to American leadership, but seeks to enhance its interests and to reflect its values in the context of a rapidly evolving world. As scholars we engage not only the empirical claims associated with hegemony but its conceptual foundations. The latter are ambiguous, inconsistent, and err in equating material capabilities with power and power with influence. America is unequivocally powerful but only occasionally influential.

Our project has multiple sources of inspiration. Scholars and friends like Hans Morgenthau and Susan Strange influenced our thinking. They retained both the notion that international relations should be transformative and rejected the tendency of theorists to reflect, rather than challenge, the dominant orthodoxy of their societies.

Our paths crossed many years before we became coauthors. It was in the early 1980s, when Simon was a graduate student and Ned a professor at Cornell University. We worked in different areas of the discipline, one in political economy and the other in security, and continued our separate ways even as colleagues at the University of Pittsburgh. Our agendas finally converged as we both shook our heads in amazement at the continuing fixation on hegemony of so many of our US colleagues.

Several dozen oysters washed down by a good Sancerre on the rue Cler led to a commitment to coauthor a book. We received sustained support from our wives, Ariane and Carol, the usual distraction from Simon's children (Jamie, Melissa, and Amanda) and helpful feedback from Ned's three children and son-in-law (scholars in their own right). We also received professional interest, support, and guidance from Chuck Myers, then executive editor at Princeton University Press, and his successor, Eric Crahan, who brought this book to fruition. We wish Chuck well in his new position.

Simon Reich wishes to thank Karie Gubbins and M. J. Kronfeld, who provided him with research assistance, and Ann Martin for her support and friendship. Guonan Ma, Barry Naughton, and Tom Rawski proved very helpful in tracking down the data on China, for which we are grateful. Simon also acknowledges the financial support of both the Graduate School and the Division of Global Affairs at Rutgers–Newark, and the School of Politics and International Relations at Australian National University (ANU), where he was a visiting fellow. He particularly thanks Adam Graycar.

In addition to giving lectures on the basis of this work at ANU, Simon presented aspects of this research at the Diplomatic Academy in Vienna; the Air Force University in Montgomery, Alabama; the Centre d'Études et de Recherches Internationales at Sciences Po in Paris; the German Marshall Fund in Washington, D.C.; Kings College London's Department of War Studies, and the International Studies Association conferences in Edinburgh and San Diego. Simon also wishes to thank

Shaun Breslin, Carla Norrlof, and—most notably—Bruce Jentleson; they provided valuable comments on all or part of the manuscript.

Simon dedicates this book to the Ballard Family: to Peter, the angel with a dirty face, with deep respect for his love and dedication; and to Ruth for her love, humor, and continuing support.

Ned thanks Simon for bringing the project to his attention and inviting him to be coauthor. He is grateful to the Swedish National Research Council and the University of Lund for awarding him the Olof Palme Professorship and hosting him for the 2011–12 academic year. This allowed him to work full-time on this book and other projects. He must also thank Mervyn Frost and the War Studies Department at King's College for a most stimulating postretirement professorship, and colleagues at Pembroke College, University of Cambridge, for electing him a Bye-Fellow.

Ned dedicates this book to Laura Forlatti-Picchio, Zeno Forlatti, and their four daughters, sons-in-law, and grandchildren. In the course of thirty-plus years of friendship Laura and Zeno and their family have become his family, and he and Carol and his children are deeply grateful for their friendship and many kindnesses.

London and Paris, February 2013

Good-Bye Hegemony!

Chapter 1

//

The Wall Has Fallen

In the film *Good Bye Lenin!*, an East Berlin mother has a heart attack and falls into a coma. When she revives, many months later, the Berlin Wall has fallen and East Germany is history. The children want to bring her back to their apartment but the doctors are reluctant to let her leave the hospital, as any shock could trigger another infarction. The children promise to provide as unthreatening an environment as possible; they conspire to prevent their mother, who was content under the communist regime, from learning about its demise. They go to increasing lengths to establish and maintain this conceit; they remove their new furniture and return their apartment to the way it once was, scour the city for the old brand of pickles she loved and have a friend produce news programs that purport to be from the now defunct German Democratic Republic. Once, by mistake, real television news fills the screen and the mother watches old clips of the Berlin Wall being breached. She becomes agitated, but is reassured by her children that while this is true, it is Westerners who have broken through the Wall to seek asylum in the East. Suitably reassured, the mother insists that it is their patriotic duty to take in some Western refugees. Word about the make-believe apartment gets around, and elderly people, unable to adapt to change, come around to enjoy its anachronistic ambience and reinforce one another's nostalgia for the old life. Their rosy reminiscences bear little relationship to former realities.

International relations scholars responsible for the burgeoning literature on hegemonic decline are like the elderly visitors in *Good Bye Lenin!*. They are unreconciled to change and nostalgic for a world that is long since gone. Their memories of its glories are just as distorted. More troubling still, some scholars and many policy makers and their advisers more closely resemble the poor mother. They believe they live in a world in which America is still the hegemon and are convinced of its manifold advantages to themselves and everyone else. Analogous to the mother, they engage in sterile debates among themselves about what can be done to preserve American dominance.

What is hegemony? The definition and consequence is a source of great debate among liberals and realists. Michael Doyle understands it to mean "controlling leadership of the international system as a whole."[1] Michael Mastanduno contends that hegemony exists when one political unit has the "power to shape the rules of international politics according to its own interests."[2] Stuart Kaufman, Richard Little, and William Wohlforth describe hierarchy, which they all but equate with hegemony, as the political-military "domination" of a single unit "over most of the international system."[3] John Ikenberry and Charles Kupchan insist that such influence ultimately rests on material power, and "it is most effectively exercised when a hegemon is able to establish a set of norms that others willingly embrace."[4]

In reality, American hegemony was short-lived and a feature of the country's extraordinary economic primacy in the mid-twentieth century in a world devastated by history's costliest and most destructive war. At the time, relatively few welcomed American hegemony as a source of political stability and economic reconstruction. Certainly, the rapid comeback of Western Europe and Japan, and later the economic development of the Pacific Rim, were greatly assisted by American aid, loans, and markets. Yet, success made hegemony superfluous and Charles Kindleberger posited that hegemony had run its course by 1963, and was certainly history by the 1970s.[5] Americans nevertheless convinced themselves that their hegemony was alive and well—and benign. Given the Soviet threat, which policy makers, think tank analysts, and scholars grossly exaggerated, American hegemony was also described as in the common Western interest. Following the Cold War and the collapse of the Soviet Union, the United States remained "the

[1] Michael W. Doyle, *Empires* (Ithaca, NY: Cornell University Press, 1986), 40.

[2] Michael Mastanduno, "Hegemonic Order, September 11, and the Consequences of the Bush Revolution," *International Relations of the Asia Pacific* 5 (2005): 177–96.

[3] Stuart J. Kaufman, Richard Little, and William C. Wohlforth, *The Balance of Power in World History* (New York: Palgrave Macmillan, 2007), 7.

[4] G. John Ikenberry and Charles A. Kupchan, "Socialization and Hegemonic Power," *International Organization* 44, no. 3 (1990): 283–315.

[5] See Charles P. Kindleberger, "Dominance and Leadership in the International Economy: Exploitation, Public Goods, and Free Rides," *International Studies Quarterly* 25, no. 2 (1981): 242–54, especially 248, and Charles P. Kindleberger, *Manias, Panics and Crashes: A History of Financial Crises* (New York: Basic Books, 1978), 202.

indispensable nation," in the words of former secretary of state Madeleine Albright.[6] President Barack Obama would say something similar in a presidential debate prior to his reelection.[7]

POWER VERSUS INFLUENCE

American hegemony eroded during the postwar decades as other nations regained their economic strength and political stability. Of equal importance, the postwar world witnessed movements and developments over which the United States could exert little to no control, such as Third World nationalism and the rise of China. Efforts by Washington to maintain a puppet regime in South Vietnam and futile efforts to block Beijing from taking China's seat in the UN Security Council darkened America's image and publicized its impotence. The decline of the dollar accelerated this trend. Yet American foreign policy still embraces hegemony and has not effectively adjusted to the reality. It is an unrealistic and counterproductive aspiration. The glaring discrepancy between America's self-image and goals on the one hand, and others' perception of them, may explain one of the principal anomalies of contemporary international relations (IR): *the extraordinary military and economic power of the United States and its increasing inability to get other states to do what it wants.* Examples of this phenomenon abound. In Iraq, the administration of President George W. Bush claimed to have created "a coalition of the willing," but in practice, the intervention was opposed by some of America's closest allies and the support of lesser states had to be purchased. In trade, the United States sought a critical Group of Twenty (G20) consensus on how to manage the Great Recession of 2008, only to be rebuffed by Asians and Europeans alike. In this book we will show how American attempts to shape and manage globalization, the principal economic development of the current age, have also failed.

To quote Alice, our story becomes "curiouser and curiouser." Although American hegemony has not existed for some time, prominent American IR scholars believe it does, but periodically worry that it is

---

[6] Michael Dobbs and John M. Goshko, "Albright's Personal Odyssey Shaped Foreign Policy Beliefs," *Washington Post*, 6 December 1996.

[7] Barack Obama, in the third presidential debate on foreign policy, proclaimed, "America remains the one indispensable nation. And the world needs a strong America." Transcript and Audio: "Third Presidential Debate," 22 October 2012, http://www.npr.org/2012/10/22/163436694/transcript-3rd-obama-romney-presidential-debate (accessed 3 June 2013).

about to disappear. In the aftermath of the Cold War, Charles Krauthammer famously proclaimed that the long-awaited "unipolar moment" had arrived. Like-minded realists predicted that American hegemony would remain unchallenged for decades to come. Other realists began worrying about immediate threats. George Friedman, who runs *Stratfor*, a respected and widely read realist-oriented newsletter, predicated a war in the near future with Japan.[8] Realists are still divided among themselves. Michael Mandelbaum, among others, thinks it essential that the United States cut back on its foreign policy commitments, but that this will result in greater disorder, leading other countries to look back with nostalgia on American hegemony. More optimistic realists like William Wohlforth contend that America can finesse this transition and remain dominant.[9] For most realists, the key question is how the US will face the expected challenge from a rising China. Some believe that a power transition of this kind will almost certainly lead to war.[10]

Liberals come in as great a variety of hues as do realists. They share certain attributes with realists: a rationalist approach in which power and influence are conflated; a focus on states as key actors; a research program focused on American hegemony; and an analytic approach in which the functions of hegemony are conflated. There are important differences among liberals as to the form and longevity of American hegemony, which we will discuss in chapter 2. Liberals nevertheless

---

[8] George Friedman, *The Coming War with Japan* (New York: St. Martins, 1991).

[9] See James Traub, "Wallowing in Decline," *Foreign Policy*, 24 September 2010, http://www.foreignpolicy.com/articles/2010/09/24/wallowing_in_decline?page=0,1 (accessed 27 December 2010); Stephen M. Walt, "The Virtues of Competence," *Foreign Policy*, 22 September 2010, http://walt.foreignpolicy.com/posts/2010/09/22/the_virtues_of_competence (accessed 27 December 2010); Aaron L. Freidberg, "The Future of US-China Relations: Is Conflict Inevitable?" *International Security* 30, no. 2 (2005): 7–45; Michael Mandelbaum, *The Frugal Superpower: America's Global Leadership in a Cash-Strapped Era* (Philadelphia: Public Affairs, 2010), especially 3–5. For critics, see Stephen G. Brooks and William C. Wohlforth, *World out of Balance: International Relations and the Challenge of US Primacy* (Princeton, NJ: Princeton University Press, 2008); William C. Wohlforth, "The Stability of a Unipolar World," *International Security* 24, no. 1 (1999): 5–41; William C. Wohlforth, "US Strategy in a Unipolar World," in G. John Ikenberry, ed., *America Unrivaled: The Future of the Balance of Power* (Ithaca, NY: Cornell University Press, 2002): 98–120. For a summary of realist views, see Christopher Layne, "The Waning of US Hegemony—Myth or Reality?" *International Security* 34, no. 1 (2009): 147–72.

[10] Charles Glaser, "Will China's Rise Lead to War? Why Realism Does Not Mean Pessimism," *Foreign Affairs*, March/April 2011, http://www.foreignaffairs.com/articles/67479/charles-glaser/will-chinas-rise-lead-to-war (accessed 3 June 2011); Steven W. Mosher, *Hegemon: China's Plan to Dominate Asia and the World* (San Francisco: Encounter, 2000); Stefan Halper, *The Beijing Consensus: How China's Authoritarian Model Will Dominate the Twenty-First Century* (New York: Basic Books, 2010).

share a fundamental optimism that American hegemony will survive in some form. Their greatest concern, pace realists, is that a global system without a hegemon would become unstable and more war prone.[11]

Realists and liberals frame hegemony as a question of power. Realists in particular assume that material capabilities constitute power and that power confers influence. These categories are related in more indirect and problematic ways. Material capabilities are only one component of power. Power also depends on the nature of a state's capabilities, how they developed, and how they are used. Perhaps the most graphic illustration of this political truth is offered by the US and Soviet (now Russian) nuclear arsenals. These weapons and their delivery systems were expensive and all but unusable in any scenario. The principal one they were designed for—all-out war—would have constituted mutual, if not global, suicide. Intended to deter the other superpower, these weapons became a cause of their conflict.[12] For the Soviet Union, its nuclear arsenal and conventional forces also became its principal claim to superpower status. Extravagant expenditure on the military in the context of a stagnating economy is generally understood to have been one of the causes of the Soviet collapse.

Nuclear weapons could rarely, if ever, be used to make credible threats. The utility of conventional forces has also become increasingly restricted. In an era of nationalism, people are less willing to be coerced by foreign powers. The wars in Vietnam and Afghanistan became competitions in suffering, which the foreign powers were bound to lose. The ability to inflict pain—the mechanism on which military power depends—can be offset by the ability of the weaker side to absorb it. The US-Mexican relationship offers a different window into this problem. Repeated efforts by successive American administrations to exploit its greater power to act unilaterally in violation of its agreements with Mexico led to Mexican resistance. America needs to renegotiate because new agreements gained less, not more, for Washington.[13]

Attempts to translate power directly into influence rest on carrots and sticks. Such exercises, even when successful, consume resources

[11] Robert O. Keohane, *After Hegemony: Cooperation and Discord in the Modern World* (Princeton, NJ: Princeton University Press, 1984); G. John Ikenberry, *Liberal Leviathan: The Origins, Crisis, and Transformation of the American World Order* (Princeton, NJ: Princeton University Press, 2011); Joseph S. Nye Jr., "The Future of American Power," *Foreign Affairs* 89, no. 6 (2010): 2–12; Bruce Russett and John Oneal, *Triangulating Peace: Democracy, Interdependence and International Organizations* (New York: Norton, 2001).

[12] For elaboration, see Richard Ned Lebow and Janice Gross Stein, *We All Lost the Cold War* (Princeton, NJ: Princeton University Press, 1994), chap. 14.

[13] David Bohmer Lebow and Richard Ned Lebow, "Mexico and Iraq: Continuity and Change in the Bush Administration," in David B. MacDonald, ed., *The Bush Leadership, the Power of Ideas and the War on Terror* (Farnham, Surrey, England: Ashgate, 2012), 91–112.

and work only so long as the requisite bribes and threats are available and effective. More often than not, they fail. The Anglo-American invasion of Iraq offers a dramatic example. Raw power was ineffective when applied in a politically unsophisticated way and at odds with prevailing norms and practices. It eroded, not enhanced, American influence. Failures in Iraq and Afghanistan are anomalies for most realist and liberal understandings of power, but not for an approach that disaggregates influence from power and directs our attention to its social as well as material basis. Such a shift grounds the study of influence in the shared discourses that make it possible. It builds on Thomas Hobbes's understanding in *Behemoth* that "the power of the mighty hath no foundation but in the opinion and belief of the people."[14]

Effective influence rests on persuasion; it convinces others that it is their interest to do what you want. Persuasion depends on shared values and acceptable practices, and when it works, helps to build common identities that can make cooperation and persuasion more likely in the future. Influence of this kind also benefits from material capabilities but is not a function of them. It is restricted to common goals and requires considerable political skills. It depends on sophisticated leaders and diplomats, shared discourses with target states, advocacy of policies that build on precedent, and a willingness to let others help shape and implement initiatives. Suffice it to say here that power, by which we mean primarily economic and military capabilities, is a raw material that can be used to gain influence. By *influence* we mean the ability to persuade others to do what one wants, or refrain from doing what one does not want.

A POSTHEGEMONIC WORLD

The focus on power obscures the ways in which the international system has been evolving. Hegemony can nevertheless provide insight into these changes. In this section we will unpack the concept. By identifying the ways in which hegemony is thought to make global order possible, we can disaggregate these functions from the role and ask if it is possible to fill them in other ways. We believe this is eminently feasible—and more realistic in today's world.

The first responsibility of hegemony is *normative*. Much of what liberals conceive as "leadership" is the capacity to shape the policy agenda

---

[14] For a related approach, see Thomas Hobbes, *Behemoth* (Chicago: University of Chicago Press, 1990), 16; Steven Weber and Bruce W. Jentleson, *The End of Arrogance: America in the Global Competition of Ideas* (Cambridge, MA: Harvard University Press, 2010).

of global institutions or ad-hoc coalitions.[15] It requires knowledge and manipulation of appropriate discourses.[16] It also requires insight into how other actors define their interests, what they identify as problems, and what responses they consider appropriate. In contrast to the realist emphasis on material power, constructivist scholars emphasize persuasion over coercion, and maintain that the former is most effectively achieved by shaping policy debates through agenda setting and an appeal to shared norms. Power is important, but understood as embedded in institutional and normative structures. Normative influence is heavily dependent on political skill, and all the more so in a world in which so many, if not most, important initiatives are multilateral.

The second constituent of hegemony is economic management. In the posthegemonic era this function is primarily *custodial*. We elaborate on the meaning of the term, ask who performs this role, and how well it is performed. Above all else, custodianship entails the management of risk through market signaling (information passed, intentionally or not, among market participants) and intergovernmental negotiations in a variety of venues. The intent, according to Charles Kindleberger, the progenitor of hegemonic stability theory, is to stabilize and undergird the functions of the global economic system.[17] This formulation has become foundational for his realist and liberal successors as they seek to justify the global need for continued American hegemony. Many American international relations theorists nevertheless ignore the evidence that America has either willingly contravened, or is increasingly incapable of performing, these functions. Somewhat paradoxically, while overlooking the declining performance of the United States as a manager of the global system, these theorists' understanding of a hegemon has expanded to include additional functions: the provision of liberal, multilateral trading rules; the sponsorship of international institutions; and the promotion of liberal democratic values.[18]

[15] See Michael Barnett and Raymond Duvall, "Power in International Politics," *International Organization* 59, no. 1 (2005): 39–75; and Ian Manners, "Normative Power Europe: A Contradiction in Terms?" *Journal of Common Market Studies* 40, no. 2 (2002): 235–58, especially 239.

[16] Barnett and Duvall, "Power in International Politics," 56–57.

[17] In more formal terms these economic functions consist of maintaining an open market for distress goods, providing countercyclical lending, policing a stable system of exchange rates, ensuring the coordination of macroeconomic policies, and acting as a lender of last resort. Charles P. Kindleberger, *The World in Depression, 1929–1939* (Berkeley and Los Angeles: University of California Press, 1973), 305.

[18] G. John Ikenberry, "Grand Strategy as Liberal Order Building," paper prepared for the conference "After the Bush Doctrine: National Security Strategy for a New Administration," University of Virginia, 7–8 June 2007, 3.

The third and final element of hegemony is enforcement of global initiatives, what we call *sponsorship*. Sponsorship ultimately depends on capabilities. They may be military, economic, or knowledge-based. In part, sponsorship reflects what IR theorists consider essential to the creation and maintenance of international institutions and of the enforcement of global regulations or norms. We argue, however, that material resources, while necessary, are insufficient for a functioning sponsorship strategy. To be effective, sponsorship requires dialogue, negotiation, and the use of regional or global institutions as venues. Above all, it requires agreed-upon goals and procedures to confer legitimacy on any initiative and achieve a division of responsibilities. Sponsorship is not the same as leadership, as defined by either realists or liberals. It is neither unilateralism nor "a first among equals" in a traditional multilateral forum or alliance. Rather, it entails a capacity to listen, and then a selective willingness to use a variety of capabilities to implement consensual goals that are consistent with self-interest.

All three functions of hegemony require contingent forms of influence rather than the blunt exercise of power. Their application is becoming increasingly diffused among states, rather than concentrated in the hands of a hegemon. These functions are performed by multiple states, sometimes in collaboration with nonstate actors. Global governance practices are sharply at odds with the formulations of realists and liberals alike. Western Europeans have made consistent efforts to extend their normative influence by promoting agendas well beyond those with which they are traditionally associated. These include environmental and human rights initiatives, but also security issues and corporate regulation. Asian states—most notably China—have increasingly assumed a custodial role, albeit embryonic at this point, quite at odds with the neomercantilist or rising military power depicted by realists. Under President Obama, the United States has continued to pursue a bipartisan sponsorship role that runs parallel to its more conventional efforts at leadership.

THE PURPOSE OF THIS BOOK

Hans Morgenthau maintained that international relations theory should be transformative in its goals. Rather than justifying the status quo, or making it easier for policy makers to function within it, theory should enlighten them to the potential of positive change and describe the modalities of using power and influence toward this end. We offer our book with this aim in mind. Our starting point is a reformulation of the concepts of power and influence and an elaboration of their complex relationship. We illustrate how different actors have gravitated toward distinct, albeit mixed, roles in the international system and describe some of the most important implications of this differentiation. We examine the changing role of the United States, and the key problems it faces or is likely to confront in the course of this decade, and offer thoughts about its appropriate role in this rapidly changing environment. We seek to make related theoretical and substantive contributions to the study of international relations and the practice of foreign policy. Our emphasis on influence, its sources and practice, is a sharp contrast to the realist and liberal emphasis on power. In our judgment, it offers more insight into how the world works and the choices open to key states.

The major foreign policy challenge, in the security and economic spheres, is responding to China's phenomenal rise in power. It is the primary security issue faced by the West that has the potential to lead to a catastrophic war. We do not think this at all likely, but there are powerful forces in both countries that see the other as a dangerous rival who must be constrained. Their Cassandra-like warnings are reinforced by "devil images" that arise from the conceptual foundations and worst-case analysis that each side so often uses to make sense of the other and its foreign policy goals.[19] The general perception of China as an enemy is widespread. A search of newspaper articles, journals, dissertations, trade publication articles, book reviews, books, and e-books revealed 192,532 related references. A more refined search of "China as an enemy to the US" brought 69,141 total hits, 3,201 for 2011 alone.[20]

We intend to show how and why these conceptions are inappropriate and offer new ones in their place. Our argument rests on the assumption—at odds with many representations of realism—that there is nothing structural about Sino-American conflict. We show that China has accepted greater custodial responsibilities as it has become increasingly invested in the post–Cold War global order. With better conceptual frames of reference on both sides, this relationship could be managed intelligently and successfully.

When we turn to US economic relations, with China and the rest of the world, we argue that liberals often invoke inappropriate frameworks. We reject the conventional view that emphasizes America's

[19] Barack Obama, *National Security Strategy* (Washington, DC: White House, May 2010), http://www.whitehouse.gov/sites/default/files/rss_viewer/national_security_strategy.pdf (accessed 21 January 2013). China is mentioned nearly a dozen times in this guiding strategic document, and US preparedness for China's military improvement is specifically discussed, albeit in diplomatic language (see 43).

[20] Bryan Patridge, "Constructivism—Is the United States Making China an Enemy?" (Carlisle, PA: United States Army War College, 2012).

structural position in the global economy, or its capacity to leverage its market access using crude instruments of power.[21] Instead, we argue that the US role in the global economic world can best be understood in terms of the three roles we identify—agenda setting, custodianship, and sponsorship—and that success in each relies on differing combinations of material and social power. Influence in all three domains is subtle and contingent. Our intent is to develop, at best, a new conceptual vocabulary for thinking through a series of problems, one that is also based on divorcing influence from power and putting more emphasis on mutually acceptable goals than capabilities.

At this point let us provide two examples of how important conceptions are in foreign relations. Until the late eighteenth century and the writings of Adam Smith, and later of David Ricardo, the world's wealth was thought to be finite. This made interstate relations a zero-sum game in which an increase in wealth for any state was believed to come at the expense of others.[22] Once political elites learned that the division of labor could augment the total wealth, mechanical sources of energy, and economies of scale, international economic cooperation became attractive and came to be considered another means of generating wealth. Trade and investment, and the economic interdependence to which this led, did not prevent war, as many nineteenth and early twentieth century liberals hoped, but it did more or less put an end to wars of material aggrandizement.

In the security sphere, the United States relied on deterrence throughout the Cold War, convinced that it was the appropriate strategy for coping with an aggressive adversary. International relations scholars developed deterrence theory to provide an underpinning for US national security policy. They imposed, improperly, a rationalist framework on the problem, assuming that leaders conducted a careful cost calculus before acting, that their preferences were transitive and apparent to outside actors, and that they could best be influenced by raising the expected costs of the action deterrence sought to prevent. None of these assumptions turned out to be valid. Leaders before, during, and after the Cold War were often moved to challenge adversaries by a combination of foreign and domestic problems. To the extent that a challenge was perceived as necessary, they convinced themselves it would succeed, and misinterpreted, explained away, or downright denied evidence to the contrary. When threatened by adversaries, leaders often

[21] Stephen G. Brooks, G. John Ikenberry, and William C. Wohlforth, "Don't Come Home America: The Case against Retrenchment," *International Security* 37, no. 3 (2012–13): 7–51.

[22] Jacob Viner, "Power vs. Plenty as Objectives of Foreign Policy in the 17th and 18th Centuries," *World Politics* 1, no. 1. (1948): 1–29.

reframed the problem, with the goal of not giving in and demonstrating resolve taking precedence over any interests at stake. In the Soviet-American rivalry, the strategy of deterrence, characterized by major arms buildups, forward deployments, and bellicose rhetoric, had the unintended effect of provoking the very crises—like that of Cuba—that it was intended to avoid.[23]

These examples indicate that the conceptual frameworks we use to understand the world determine the problems we identify and often the range of responses we consider appropriate to them. The broader goal of our book is to offer a more sophisticated framework for thinking about the world by concentrating on influence in lieu of power. Our framework is relatively parsimonious and universal in nature, but its application must always be context dependent. It is theory in the tradition of Thucydides and Morgenthau, intended to offer a first cut into a problem and to help scholars and policy makers work their way through it by combining general insights with specific contextual knowledge. We will apply our framework in a general way to US relations with China and Europe, and collective efforts to manage ever more closely connected economic relations within and across the regions of the world.

OUTLINE OF THE CHAPTERS

In chapter 2 we develop our formulation of influence. We examine the relationship, but also the important distinctions, between material capabilities and power, and between power and influence. We highlight alternative sources of power and sources of influence that do not depend, at least directly, on material capabilities. Our approach is constructivist in its emphasis on values and discourses, but it does not ignore material capabilities, strategic thinking, or implementation. We are careful to distinguish between the universal relevance of our formulation and its context-dependent application. We show how it works in practice when applied to understanding globalization, financial crises, and civilian protection.

Chapter 3 examines Europe's efforts at agenda setting. It demonstrates the importance of persuasion as a form of influence. Robert Kagan, a noted American realist, argues that Europeans recognize complexity and rely on diplomacy because they are weak and lack Ameri-

[23] Richard Ned Lebow, *Between Peace and War: The Nature of International Crisis* (Baltimore: Johns Hopkins University Press, 1981); Robert Jervis, Richard Ned Lebow, and Janice Gross Stein, *Psychology and Deterrence* (Baltimore: John Hopkins University Press, 1984). Lebow and Stein, *We All Lost the Cold War.*

ca's material power.[24] We dispute this claim. Europeans could easily spend more on their military but choose not to do so. This is an effective policy if their goal is to exercise influence. The norms of regional and international systems are undergoing significant shifts that deprive military power of much of its political utility while enhancing other forms of influence. To sustain our argument, we offer case studies of successful European efforts to manage globalization and bring about a treaty that bans landmines. European initiatives on both fronts were opposed by the economically and militarily more powerful United States.

Chapter 4 documents the embryonic shift in custodial economic functions from the United States to Asia. Whether measured in terms of the purchasing of government and private debt, or the provision of foreign direct investment and overseas aid, the United States plays a diminishing role in sustaining global capitalism. Asian countries—most notably China, and to a lesser extent, Japan—have increasingly assumed this role because their leaders see it in their national interest. As holders of trillions of dollars of US debt, these countries arguably provide more stability to the global system than Washington does. The United States is the largest debtor in the world, and contrary to any claims of hegemony, is now a great source of economic *instability*.[25] It suffers from insufficient savings, huge levels of private and public debt, and underinvestment, as corporations shift production abroad in search of lower tax rates. The liberal emphasis on structural power, associated with the dollar and the size of the US market, is increasingly misplaced because it is a questionable source of influence.[26] Such a reading also ignores the increasingly important roles of China, other countries in the Organisation for Economic Co-operation and Development and aspiring economies in stabilizing the global economic system.

Chapter 4 also examines China's expanding custodial role. Realists characterize its economic policies as mercantilist. In 2005, World Bank President Robert Zoellick encouraged the People's Republic of China to become a "responsible stakeholder." We do not deny that Chinese behavior is self-serving, but we see no evidence that China is any more economically irresponsible than any other major power or committed to seeking hegemony.[27] We begin by addressing the security question.

[24] Robert Kagan, "Power and Weakness," *Policy Review* 113 (June–July 2002), http://www.newamericancentury.org/kagan-20020520.htm (accessed 16 February 2011).

[25] Herman Schwartz, *Subprime Nation: American Power, Global Capital, and the Housing Bubble* (Ithaca, NY: Cornell University Press, 2009).

[26] Carla Norrlof, *America's Global Advantage: US Hegemony and International Cooperation* (Cambridge: Cambridge University Press, 2010): 5–6.

[27] Robert B. Zoellick, "Whither China: From Membership to Responsibility?" Remarks

American realists in the academy and government routinely invoke power transition theory as the appropriate lens to analyze the consequences of China's rise to great power status. There is no historical support for power transition theory—quite the reverse. Evidence indicates that transitions occur mostly as a result of wars rather than causing them. It also indicates that rising and dominant powers rarely if ever fight each other.[28] Chinese security policy, we argue, seeks regional *hēgemonia* and not global hegemony, an analytic distinction we make in chapter 2. The goal is consistent with, even possibly supportive of, US and Western security.

The second section of chapter 4 turns to economic issues. We analyze the issue of custodianship through a series of lenses. We use macrolevel data, including global economic imbalances and their relationship to shifting savings and consumption rates in Asia, a factor many economists regard as key to addressing the issue of global economic stabilization. We then examine cross-national and domestic-level data, including China's purchase of US Treasuries and European government bonds, its purchase of US bank stocks at the nadir of the financial crisis, and the reshaping of development assistance through the Chinese Development Bank and Import-Export Bank. The evidence indicates that Chinese leaders understand that performing custodial functions enhances their influence.

Chapter 5 draws on our conceptual and empirical analysis to rethink America's posthegemonic role in the world. While guided by self-interest, the United States should pursue a strategy that helps to implement policies that are widely supported and are often mooted or initiated by others. It should generally refrain from attempting to set the agenda and lead in a traditional realist or liberal sense. Drawing on Simon Reich's work on global norms, we look at the success Washington has had in sponsoring—that is, in backing—initiatives originating elsewhere.[29] We examine the successful provision of military assistance to NATO's campaign in Libya, which offers a stark contrast to the US approach to Iraq. We then offer counterfactual cases of US drug policy in Mexico and efforts to keep North Korea from going nuclear in which we contrast leadership and sponsorship strategies.

In chapter 6 we revisit the concept of hegemony. Drawing on our empirical findings, we contend that hegemony is no longer applicable

---

to the National Committee on United States–China Relations, New York City, 21 September 21 2005, http://2001-2009.state.gov/s/d/former/zoellick/rem/53682.htm (accessed 16 June 2013).

[28] Richard Ned Lebow and Benjamin A Valentino, "Lost in Transition: A Critique of Power Transition Theories," *International Relations* 23, no. 3 (2009): 389–410.

[29] Simon Reich, *Global Norms, American Sponsorship and the Emerging Patterns of World Politics* (Basingstoke, England: Palgrave Macmillan, 2010).

to international affairs, as its constituent functions are widely shared and exercised more by negotiation than fiat. This constellation requires a new conceptualization of influence. It points to a new research agenda for the present century based on the recognition that we now live in a multipowered world—where actors combine social and material power to gain influence in varying ways—and not a unipolar world.

Chapter 2

Power and Influence in the Global System

In the 1950s and '60s, Hans Morgenthau repeatedly criticized international relations (IR) theory for failing to speak truth to power. In his view, the close links among universities, foundations, and government made it relatively easy to co-opt the discipline's principal spokesmen and to substantially reward those who said and wrote what those in power wanted to hear.[1] There is a more benign explanation for this phenomenon: scholars are products of the same culture as policy makers and are likely to share worldviews. For this latter reason, we believe, many American IR theorists and foreign policy and national security analysts have a normative commitment to American world leadership. Theorists have developed the concept of hegemony to justify and advance this project. It rests on a particular understanding of power and its superordinate importance in world politics.

We offer a conceptual and empirical critique of hegemony. We contend that postwar American hegemony was a short-lived phenomenon and that efforts to preserve it were and are illusory and counterproductive. The perceived benefits of hegemony, and failure to recognize that it was a passing moment, have reinforcing ideological and intellectual causes. The former pertains to the nearly universal belief among Americans that their country is special, that it is morally and politically superior and the rightful leader of the world community. The latter has to do with the way power and its utility are understood by American policy makers and academics. We demonstrate the inadequacy of these con-

---

[1] Hans J. Morgenthau, *Scientific Man vs. Power Politics* (Chicago: University of Chicago Press, 1946); Hans J. Morgenthau, *Truth and Power: Essays of a Decade, 1960–1970* (New York: Praeger, 1970): 14–15; Robert J. Myers, "Hans J. Morgenthau: On Speaking Truth to Powers," *Society* 29, no. 2 (1992): 65–71.

ceptions and the ways in which they blind those who share them to the realities of the post–Cold War world.

Our critique of power lays the foundation for a reconstruction of theory and policy. In contrast to most realists and liberals, we see more to power than material capabilities and, more important, distinguish power from influence, as the former does not necessarily confer the latter. We recognize different kinds of power and the diverse ways in which power might be translated into influence. We also unpack and critique the concept of hegemony; we argue that it rests on the false assumption that it is necessary to sustain a functioning global economy and polity. By rejecting hegemony as an organizing concept, we can offer a more realistic account of the international system and reframe our understanding of the foundations of security and prosperity. Having defined the three components of hegemony (agenda setting, custodianship, and sponsorship), we describe the domains to which they are appropriate, analyze the ways in which they work, and characterize the kinds of power on which they depend. Our analysis makes it abundantly clear that no hegemon is necessary to manage the system; that it has the potential to work successfully without one.

Hegemony is difficult to reconcile with democracy. Leading intellectuals and political leaders have frequently proclaimed that democracy and pluralism in government and decentralization in economics are not only more effective means of governing than hierarchy and centralization but important ends in their own right. A commitment to democracy and pluralism is equally applicable to international relations, which makes it enigmatic and indefensible for scholars and policy makers to embrace hegemony and the undemocratic hierarchy it aspires to impose and maintain.

HEGEMONY

As understood by American IR scholars, hegemony is international leadership provided by a state whose power is grossly disproportionate to that of other actors in the system. Realists and liberals alike maintain that the United States has been a hegemon since 1945, although only a partial hegemon during the long Cold War because of the opposition of the powerful Soviet Union and its allies. At the end of that conflict and the collapse of the Soviet Union, the United States, in their view, became closer to a global hegemon as bipolarity supposedly gave way to unipolarity.

Realists and liberals differ somewhat in their understanding of hegemony. Many realists contend that America's unrivaled military power enables it to impose its leadership, which they openly acknowledge as a form of domination. Stephen Brooks and William Wohlforth assert, "No system of sovereign states has ever contained one state with comparable material preponderance."[2] Judging by the numbers, Robert Jervis concludes that they are certainly correct.[3] The United States accounts for well over 40 percent of the world's military spending and is the source of one quarter of its economic activity; its share of the world's gross domestic product (GDP) is larger than that of the EU and three times that of China, and some 65 percent of the world's currency reserve is held in US dollars.[4] This understanding of hegemony describes it as the relatively straightforward outcome of the material dominance of one state.[5]

An alternative formulation, and to our way of thinking, a more sophisticated one, conceives of hegemony as the result of legitimacy as well as power.[6] Drawing on the theories of Antonio Gramsci, Roger Simon describes hegemony as a relation "not of domination by means of force, but of consent by means of political and ideological leadership."[7] Theorists differ about whether consent is a function of self-interest (it is better to bandwagon than oppose the dominant power) or legitimacy (the hegemon protects and advances shared norms, values, and policies).[8] Neorealists John Mearsheimer and Christopher Layne emphasize material interests because they see power at the core of all international relations.[9] The ideational explanation appeals to construc-

---

[2] Stephen G. Brooks and William C. Wohlforth, *World out of Balance: International Relations and the Challenge of American Primacy* (Princeton, NJ: Princeton University Press, 2008).

[3] Robert Jervis, "The Remaking of a Unipolar World," *Washington Quarterly* 29, no. 3 (2006): 7–19.

[4] Carla Norrlof, *America's Global Advantage: US Hegemony and International Cooperation* (Cambridge: Cambridge University Press, 2010): 19–21.

[5] Christopher M. Dent, "Regional Leadership in East Asia: Towards New Analytical Approaches," in Christopher M. Dent, ed., *China, Japan and Regional Leadership in East Asia* (Cheltenham, England: Edward Elgar, 2008), 275–304; Brooks and Wohlforth, *World out of Balance*, 28. For critiques, see Lavina R. Lee, *US Hegemony and International Legitimacy: Norms, Power and Followership in the Wars in Iraq* (London: Routledge, 2010); and Ian Clark, *Hegemony in International Society* (Oxford: Oxford University Press, 2011).

[6] Roger Simon, *Gramsci's Political Thought: An Introduction* (London: Lawrence and Wishart, 1982); Mark Haugard, "Power as Hegemony in Social Theory," in Mark Haugard and Howard H. Lentner, eds., *Hegemony and Power: Consensus and Coercion in Contemporary Politics* (Lanham, Md.: Lexington, 2006), 50; Richard Ned Lebow, *The Tragic Vision of Politics: Ethics, Interests and Orders* (Cambridge: Cambridge University Press, 2003), 283–84; Clark, *Hegemony in International Society*, 18–23.

[7] Simon, *Gramsci's Political Thought*, 21.

[8] Lebow, *The Tragic Vision of Politics*, 283–84; Ian Hurd, "Making and Breaking Norms: American Revisionism and Crises of Legitimacy," *International Politics* 44, nos. 2–3 (2007): 194–213; Clark, *Hegemony in International Society*, 23–28.

[9] John G. Mearsheimer, *The Tragedy of Great Power Politics* (New York: Norton, 2001),

tivists, and those like us who distinguish influence from power. Scholars who stress the normative aspects of hegemony note that great power and hegemonic status rest on the recognition of rights and duties and are therefore quasi-judicial categories. In practice, powerful states like Russia that have not met their responsibilities in the eyes of other actors are denied the standing and respect conferred by great power status.[10]

Liberals tend to conceive of hegemony as a mix of power and norms. Robert Keohane observes that hegemony rests on the twin premises that "order in world politics is typically created by a single hegemonic power" and "the maintenance of order requires stability."[11] Offering a quintessential liberal formulation, he argues that it is more fruitful to think of it as leadership by a single state, although not necessarily by military means.[12] Drawing on their economic might and so-called soft power, hegemons construct regimes that facilitate cooperation.[13] Keohane's conception of hegemony emphasizes norms, rules, and decision-making processes over coercion and bribery, but leaves unclear how institutions, norms, and their procedures are related to or dependent on economic or military power.

In his most recent book John Ikenberry suggests that for five decades the American-led liberal, rule-based hegemonic order "has been remarkably successful." The United States has championed multilateralism, built global institutions, provided services, and security and open markets as "the "owner and operator" of the liberal capitalist political system.[14] Hegemony has "provided a stable foundation for decades of Western and global growth and advancement."[15] Through hegemony and a series of strategic partnerships, the United States was able to orchestrate a relatively benign leadership, distinct from an "imperial hegemonic order." It helped to foster Western prosperity, democracy

---

40; Christopher Layne, *The Peace of Illusions: American Grand Strategy from 1940 to the Present* (Ithaca, NY: Cornell University Press, 2006), 11–12.

[10] Lebow, *The Tragic Vision of Politics*, 283–84; Gerry Simpson, *Great Powers and Outlaw States: Unequal Sovereigns in the International Legal Order* (Cambridge: Cambridge University Press, 2004); Hurd, "Making and Breaking Norms"; Andrew Hurrell, *On Global Order: Power, Values, and the Constitution of International Society* (Oxford: Oxford University Press, 2007); Clark, *Hegemony in International Society*, 23–28.

[11] Robert O. Keohane, *After Hegemony: Cooperation and Discord in the Modern World* (Princeton, NJ: Princeton University Press, 1984), 31; see also David A. Lake, "Leadership, Hegemony, and the International Economy: Naked Emperor or Tattered Monarch with Potential?" *International Studies Quarterly* 37, no. 4 (1993): 459–89, especially 480.

[12] Keohane, *After Hegemony*, 39–40.

[13] Ibid., 136.

[14] G. John Ikenberry, *Liberal Leviathan* (Princeton, NJ: Princeton University Press, 2011), 2.

[15] Ibid.

elsewhere, and a peaceful end to the Cold War. This is "a remarkable achievement."[16]

According to Ikenberry, the current crisis is one "of authority *within* the old hegemonic organization of liberal order, *not* a crisis in the deep principles of the order itself. It is a crisis of governance." As a result, "the character of rule in world politics has been thrown into question."[17] Although American leadership has been challenged, the liberal international order remains resilient. As "an organizational logic of world politics" it is, however, a victim of its own success. A new bargain needs to be struck between the United States and emergent actors. It will still rest on a unipolar distribution of power, and with it, "constituencies that support a continued—if renegotiated—American hegemonic role" within a liberal hegemonic order. Ikenberry believes that the United States will have to surrender some rights and privileges and strike the kind of deal that will allow it to remain a "liberal leviathan." Under such a new arrangement, the United States would still qualify as a hegemon.[18]

Another prominent liberal, Joseph Nye Jr., deliberately and explicitly shies away from terms such as *unipolarity* and *hegemon* in his more recent work. He nevertheless de facto defines American military power in those terms. Nye warns that "mistaken beliefs in decline—at home and abroad—can lead to dangerous mistakes in policy." He is relatively optimistic about American retrenchment and capacity for renewal; he acknowledges the potential of a Chinese threat, domestic economic decline, and a decline in the dollar through rising debt, but insists, "Despite these problems and uncertainties, it seems probable that with the right policies, the U.S. economy can continue to produce hard power for the country."[19]

More than Ikenberry, Nye emphasizes the role of agency and the need to make the right policy choices, and calls for "a new narrative about the future of U.S. power." He dismisses realist fears of war based on power transition, arguing that it is not applicable to the US-China relationship because the United States "is not in absolute decline, and in relative terms, there is a reasonable probability that it will remain more powerful than any single state in the coming decades." Unlike Rome, the United States will not decay to "be surpassed by another state, including China."[20]

[16] Ibid., 3.

[17] Ibid., 6, 8; emphasis in the original.

[18] Ibid., 2–10.

[19] Joseph S. Nye Jr., "The Future of American Power: Dominance and Decline in Perspective," *Foreign Affairs* 89, no. 6 (2010): 3.

[20] Ibid.

In contrast to many realists, Nye recognizes that power does not in itself determine outcomes; policy choices and implementation also matter. He distinguishes modes of power: economic versus military, and soft versus hard. He nevertheless remains resolute in his belief of the centrality of American values and power to the global order. He warns, "The coming decades are not likely to see a post-American world, but the United States will need a smart strategy that combines hard- and soft-power resources." Toward this end, Nye advocates, as he has for some time, a liberal approach emphasizing multilateralism, bargaining, and the promotion of American values through globalization.[21]

Realists and liberals share much in common. They maintain a state-centric view of the world and evaluate states in terms of their relative power. Much of their writing analyzes the polarity of the world on the assumption that important consequences flow from it. Realists and liberals concur in understanding that any change from unipolarity to multipolarity is the result of the decline of the United States and the rise of other countries. These alarms have a familiar ring. Back in the 1970s, realists and liberals alike worried that hegemony was fast disappearing in light of America's seeming economic decline and the rise of Japan and Germany. Some even worried about war with Japan![22]

Today, the threat is China, which pessimistic realists expect to challenge the United States for world leadership within a decade or two.[23] Many realists and liberals portray the United States as a declining power.[24] This fear found an official voice in President Barack Obama's 2010 *National Security Strategy*.[25] The differences among realists as to whether the United States is a secure or declining hegemon reflect differences in judgments about power and its relative distribution. They indicate just how subjective any such estimates inevitably are. For liberals, who tend to stress so-called soft as well as hard power, this discrepancy is more understandable.[26]

---

[21] Ibid.

[22] George Friedman, *The Coming War with Japan* (New York: St. Martins, 1991).

[23] See Christopher Layne, "The Waning of US Hegemony—Myth or Reality? A Review Essay," *International Security* 34, no. 1 (2009): 147–72, especially 148; Aaron L. Freidberg, "The Future of US-China Relations: Is Conflict Inevitable?" *International Security* 30, no. 2 (2005): 7–45; John J. Mearsheimer, *The Tragedy of Great Power Politics*, 400; Michael H. Hunt, *The American Ascendancy: How the United States Gained and Wielded Global Dominance* (Chapel Hill, N.C.: University of North Carolina Press, 2007), 322; Michael Cox, "Is the United States in Decline—Again? An Essay," *International Affairs* 83, no. 4 (2007): 261–76; and Fareed Zakaria, *The Post-American World* (London: Allen Lane, 2008).

[24] Hunt, *American Ascendancy*, 322; Cox, "Is the United States in Decline—Again?"; Zakaria, *The Post-American World*.

[25] US National Security Council, *US National Security Strategy 2010*, http://www.whitehouse.gov/nscnss/2010, 43 (accessed 25 February 2013).

[26] Hunt, *American Ascendancy*, 322; Inderjeet Parmar and Michael Cox, eds., *Soft Power*

Realists and liberals share a common normative agenda: the preservation of American hegemony. In his 2010 study, Michael Mandelbaum, a well-known realist, warned of the "chaos" that would result in the absence of US hegemony. Like John Mearsheimer, he worries that US decline and Chinese ascendancy would result in a hegemonic war.[27] Liberals are just as committed as realists to preserving what they believe to be America's preeminent position in the global system, conceiving of the United States as "exceptional and indispensible" to the system's stability.[28] They disagree among themselves about the proper mix and relative importance of power projection, economic dominance, institutions, and cultural influence as appropriate means toward this end but still find enough in common to collaborate on major books and articles.[29] In one recent major article, Brooks, Ikenberry, and Wohlforth, two liberals and a realist, assert that American hegemonic leadership is benign because it provides political and economic benefits for the United States and its partners that outweigh its costs. These include the "reduction of transaction costs, establishment of credible commitments, facilitation of collective action, creation of focal points [and] monitoring." Hegemony thus produces many public goods, notably system stability, although the United States, they concede, benefits disproportionately from its preeminence.[30]

Brooks, Ikenberry, and Wohlforth offer the binary choice of engagement and disengagement, and are committed to the former. By focusing on the extreme alternative of near-total disengagement, they find it cor-

and US Foreign Policy; Theoretical, Historical and Contemporary Perspectives (Abingdon, England: Routledge, 2010).

[27] Michael Mandelbaum, *The Frugal Superpower: America's Global Leadership in a Cash-Strapped Era* (Philadelphia, Public Affairs, 2010): 3–8; Roger C. Altman and Richard N. Haass, "American Profligacy and American Power," *Foreign Affairs* 89, no. 6 (2010): 25–34.

[28] Michael Dobbs and John M. Goshko, "Albright's Personal Odyssey Shaped Foreign Policy Beliefs," *Washington Post*, 6 December 1996; Madeleine K. Albright, interview on *The Today Show* with Matt Lauer, 19 February 1998; Daniel Deudney and G. John Ikenberry, *Democratic Internationalism: An American Grand Strategy for a Post-Exceptionalist Era* (New York: Council on Foreign Relations, 2012), 1.

[29] G. John Ikenberry, Michael Mastanduno, and William Wohlforth, eds., *Unipolarity and International Relations Theory* (New York: Cambridge University Press, 2011); G. John Ikenberry and Joseph Grieco, *State Power and World Markets: The International Political Economy* (New York: Norton, 2003); G. John Ikenberry and Michael Mastanduno, eds., *International Relations Theory and the Asia-Pacific* (New York: Columbia University Press, 2003); G. John Ikenberry, David A. Lake, and Michael Mastanduno, eds., *The State and American Foreign Economic Policy* (Ithaca, NY: Cornell University Press, 1988); G. John Ikenberry and Charles A. Kupchan, "Socialization and Hegemonic Power," *International Organization* 44, no. 3 (1990): 283–315; Stephen G. Brooks, G. John Ikenberry, and William C. Wohlforth, "Don't Come Home, America: The Case against Retrenchment," *International Security* 37, no. 3 (2012/13): 7–51.

[30] Brooks, Ikenberry, and Wohlforth, "Don't Come Home, America," 12.

respondingly easier to make the case for engagement in the form of hegemony, another extreme position. They offer a one-sided reading of the early Cold War in their claim that US hegemony was "largely an empire by invitation."[31] Elsewhere, Ikenberry proclaims that "American global authority was built on a Hobbesian contract—that is, other countries, particularly in Western Europe and later in East Asia, handed the reigns of power to Washington, just as Hobbes's individuals in the state of nature voluntarily construct and hand over power to the Leviathan."[32] This remarkable claim ignores the unsanctioned stationing of US troops in the defeated Axis powers, the threats and coercion against communists in France and Italy, and efforts, in Europe and elsewhere, to impose US political and economic preferences—actions that have led critics to characterize America's efforts to assert authority as an "imperial project."[33] In Latin America and Asia, US efforts at hegemony were often achieved through support of right-wing dictatorships, coups against democratically elected governments and outright military intervention. The description Brooks, Ikenberry, and Wohlforth offer of benign American paternalism hardly tallies with historical fact or the way in which America is perceived abroad, even among moderates in pro-Western countries.

We come down on the side of engagement, but define it differently from these authors. They believe hegemony exists and is beneficial; we do not. They emphasize the abiding value of the US military instrument to both security and nonsecurity issues; we do not. They ignore the variety of important ways in which the United States has violated the responsibilities and roles assigned to a hegemon. We highlight

[31] Geir Lundstadt, *The American "Empire"* (Oxford: Oxford University Press, 1990); Charles S. Maier, "Alliance and Autonomy: European Identity and US Foreign Policy Objectives in the Truman Years," in Michael Lacey, ed., *The Truman Presidency* (Cambridge: Cambridge University Press, 1991), 273–98; John Lewis Gaddis, *We Now Know: Rethinking Cold War History* (New York: Oxford University Press, 1997); Thomas F. Madden, *Empires of Trust: How Rome Built—and America Is Building—a New World* (London: Plume, 2009).

[32] Ikenberry, *Liberal Leviathan*, 10.

[33] Walden Bellow, *Dilemmas of Domination: The Unmaking of the American Empire* (New York: Metropolitan, 2005); Chalmers Johnson, *Blowback: The Costs and Consequences of the American Empire* (London: Time Warner, 2002); Chalmers Johnson, *Dismantling the Empire: America's Last Best Hope* (New York: Metropolitan Books, 2010). For American intervention in European domestic politics, see Tony Judt, *Postwar: A History of Europe Since 1945* (New York: Penguin, 2005); Michael Cox and Caroline Kennedy-Pipes, "The Tragedy of American Diplomacy? Rethinking the Marshall Plan," *Journal of Cold War Studies* 7, no. 1 (2005): 97–134; Michael J. Hogan, *The Marshall Plan: America, Britain and the Reconstruction of Western Europe, 1947–1952* (Cambridge: Cambridge University Press, 1987); Alan Milward, *The Reconstruction of Western Europe, 1945–1951* (London: Methuen, 1984); and William Appleman Williams, *The Tragedy of American Diplomacy* (New York: Norton, 1988).

these departures and characterize the United States as constituting as much a threat to global order and stability as it is a possible pillar of its preservation.[34]

Our criticism of the hegemonic discourse is therefore twofold. First and foremost, we maintain, the claim of hegemony is empirically false. By definition, it requires both economic and military dominance and leadership. The American hegemony of the immediate postwar period eroded quickly. It was based on the extraordinary and short-lived economic and military power of the United States in comparison to the rest of the noncommunist world. In 1944, the US GDP peaked at 35 percent of the world total, a figure that had dropped to 25 percent by 1960 and 20 percent by 1980.[35] Western Europe and Japan not only rebuilt their economies but also regained much of their self-confidence; both developments reduced the need and appeal of American leadership. The Korean War stalemate in the early 1950s demonstrated the limits of this supposed hegemony, as did the failure of intervention in Indochina in the 1960s and 1970s and the delinking of the dollar from the gold standard in 1971. In the 1980s, the United States systematically reneged on its own liberal trading rules by introducing a variety of tariffs and quotas instead of bearing the costs of any economic adjustments.[36] More recently, imperial overstretch was evident in the interventions in Afghanistan and Iraq. In each instance, America's capacity was found wanting and its strategic objectives were frustrated. The supposed 'unipolar moment' of US power in the early 1990s was accompanied by an unprecedented number of intrastate wars, with the United States unable to impose solutions consistent with hegemony.[37]

Hegemony rests on legitimacy as well as power, and here, too, the US position has seriously eroded. Public opinion in Europe was extremely

[34] For a variant approach to global engagement, also rooted in a more pragmatic and less ideological and paradigmatic approach to foreign policy, see Steven Weber and Bruce W. Jentleson, *The End of Arrogance: America in the Global Competition of Ideas* (Cambridge, MA: Harvard University Press, 2010).

[35] Angus Maddison, *Monitoring the World Economy, 1820–1992* (Paris: Organisation for Economic Co-operation and Development, 1995). Even Robert Gilpin, renowned proponent of hegemonic stability theory, acknowledges the fact that US global dominance was fleeting; see Robert Gilpin, *War and Change in World Politics* (New York: Cambridge University Press, 1987): 173–75.

[36] On this point, see, for example, Charles P. Kindleberger, "Dominance and Leadership in the International Economy: Exploitation, Public Goods, and Free Rides," *International Studies Quarterly* 25, no. 2 (1981): 242, 248; and Simon Reich, *Restraining Trade to Invoke Investment: MITI and the Japanese Auto Producers: Case Studies in International Negotiation* (Washington, DC: Institute for the Study of Diplomacy, 2002).

[37] Andrew Mack, "The Changing Face of Global Violence (Part 1)," in *The Human Security Report 2005* (Oxford: Oxford University Press, 2005), http://www.humansecurity report.info/HSR2005_PDF/Part1.pdf (accessed 5 February 2013).

sympathetic to the United States after 9/11, but then reversed itself and came to consider the United States a greater threat to world peace than North Korea.[38] In Britain, those with favorable opinions of the United States dropped from 83 percent in 2000 to 56 percent in 2006. In other countries, the United States suffered an even steeper decline.[39] This evaluation had not changed much by 2007, when an opinion poll carried out for the BBC World Service in twenty-seven countries found that 51 percent of respondents regarded the United States negatively, a figure surpassed only by their negative evaluations of Iran and Israel, at 54 and 56 percent, respectively. By comparison, North Korea was regarded negatively by only 48 percent of respondents.[40] Since the onset of the Iraq War, the United States has undergone a shift in its profile from a status quo to a revisionist power.[41]

While the election of Obama had a positive effect on these ratings, the United States still trails other advanced industrial states in popularity. Among Western nations, no country generated as many *negative* responses as the United States (34 percent) in terms of global influence.[42] Even the "Obama bump did not last, global opinion about his policies declining significantly by the spring of 2012."[43] A global survey in 2013 confirmed this trend, with the level of those expressing a "mainly positive" opinion of the United States declining by 2 percent while the percentage of those holding a mainly negative view was unchanged.[44] Edward Snowden's subsequent revelation in the early summer of 2013—that the United States had been spying on its friends as well as its enemies—did incalculable damage to America's reputation and to

[38] Steve Schifferes, "US Names Coalition of the Willing," *BBC News*, 18 March 2003, http://news.bbc.co.uk/2/hi/americas/2862343.stm (accessed 5 February 2013); "Biggest Threat to Peace," *Time Europe*, 2 June 2003, http://www.time.com/time/europe/gdml/peace2003.html.

[39] Pew Global Attitudes Project, "America's Image Slips, but Allies Share US Concerns over Iran, Hamas," 13 June 2006, http://www.pewglobal.org/2006/06/13/americas-image-slips-but-allies-share-us-concerns-over-iran-hamas (accessed 25 February 2013).

[40] BBC World Service, "Israel and Iran Share Most Negative Ratings in Global Poll," 6 March 2007, http://news.bbc.co.uk/2/shared/bsp/hi/pdfs/06_03_07_perceptions.pdf (accessed 5 February 2013).

[41] Christian Reus-Smit, "Unipolarity and Legitimacy," unpublished manuscript.

[42] BBC World Service, *Global Views of United States Improve While Other Countries Decline*, 10 April 2010, http://www.worldpublicopinion.org/pipa/pipa/pdf/apr10/BBC Views_Apr10_rpt.pdf (accessed 1 July 2013).

[43] Pew Global Attitudes Project, "Global Opinion of Obama Slips, International Policies Faulted," 13 June 2012, http://www.pewglobal.org/2012/06/13/global-opinion-of-obama-slips-international-policies-faulted (accessed 17 August 2012).

[44] "BBC Poll: Germany the Most Popular Country in the World," 23 May 2013, http://www.bbc.co.uk/news/world-europe-22624104 (accessed 29 May 2013).

President Obama's "moral standing" among key allies, particularly in Europe. It threatened to subvert any American prospects for exerting leadership and efforts at multilateral cooperation in numerous policy initiatives.[45] The American IR literature either ignores or minimizes the significance of these views or seeks to explain them away as somehow aberrant to a general trend that has allegedly sustained American power and its acceptance by others.

The second element of our critique concerns the inconsistency and even contradictions of the hegemonic literature. Realists and liberals have long associated the distribution of power with the distribution of functions in the global system. But they have never developed an adequate metric for measuring power, which accounts for the enormous variations in their assessments and forecasts. Such a metric is impossible to formulate, in any case, because power is a composite of so many different factors, among them territory, population, geographic location, economic development, robustness of the economy, level of technology, military strength, system of government, and quality of leadership. Most of these categories in turn are composites, as are the factors that compose them! Consider military power. Among other things, it is based on modern weaponry, skilled personnel, good strategic plans and leadership, and appropriate deployments. Weaponry varies in its capability, maintenance, and relevance to strategic and tactical challenges. Each of these criteria can only be assessed relatively and in context. The more we look into the question of power, the murkier the concept becomes.

HEGEMONY REDUX

Policy makers and academics are engaged in a new round of debate about saving American hegemony and staving off its decline. Recommendations on how to avert this decline and respond to China's rise fill pages in books, journals, popular magazines and newspapers. Writing at the outset of the first Obama administration, Christopher Layne observed, "Since the Soviet Union's downfall, the maintenance of the United States' preeminence in a unipolar system has been the overriding grand strategic goal of every administration, beginning with that of President George H. W. Bush. Early indications are that Barack Obama's administration—the key foreign policy positions of which are largely

---

[45] "World from Berlin: 'Obama Owes His Allies an Explanation,'" *Spiegel Online International*, 1 July 2013, http://www.spiegel.de/international/world/german-press-snowden-affair-and-nsa-eu-spying-revelations-a-908723.html (accessed 1 July 2013).

staffed by veterans of the Bill Clinton administration—will be just as equally wedded to preserving U.S. hegemony."[46]

On one side of this debate are optimists, drawn from both the realist and liberal communities, who believe that America can sustain its global leadership. They consider the international situation largely stable and interpret most economic and security indicators as favorable to American hegemony.[47] The pessimists, or "declinists," fear that the United States is in the final stages of its role as global leader and must take dramatic action if it is to sustain its hegemonic role.[48] In between we find numerous gradations. Yet they share the belief that any shift in the global distribution of power toward multipolarity would be destabilizing. For a few, this observable shift is less a function of US decline than it is of the rise to power of other states, most notably China.[49] Either way, the principal concern among these policy makers, analysts, and academics is how to restore, maintain, or strengthen American hegemony.[50]

---

[46] Layne, "The Waning of US Hegemony—Myth or Reality?"

[47] Examples of optimists include Mortimer Zuckerman, "A Second American Century," *Foreign Affairs* 7, no. 3 (1998): 18–31; Walter Russell Mead, *Power, Terror, Peace and War: America's Grand Strategy in a World at Risk* (New York: Knopf, 2004); Stephen G. Brooks and William C. Wohlforth, *World Out of Balance: International Relations and the Challenge of US Primacy* (Princeton, NJ: Princeton University Press, 2008); William C. Wohlforth, "The Stability of a Unipolar World," *International Security* 24, no. 1 (1999): 5–41; William C. Wohlforth, "US Strategy in a Unipolar World," in G. John Ikenberry, ed., *America Unrivaled: The Future of the Balance of Power* (Ithaca, NY: Cornell University Press, 2002): 98–120; and Ikenberry, *Liberal Leviathan*, 4.

[48] James Traub, "Wallowing in Decline," *Foreign Policy*, 24 September 2010, http://www.foreignpolicy.com/articles/2010/09/24/wallowing_in_decline?page=0,1 (accessed 27 December 2010); Stephen M. Walt, "The Virtues of Competence," *Foreign Policy*, 22 September 2010, http://walt.foreignpolicy.com/posts/2010/09/22/the_virtues_of_com petence (accessed 27 December 2010).

[49] Zakaria, *The Post-American World*.

[50] Richard Haass, "The Age of Nonpolarity: What Will Follow US Dominance?" *Foreign Affairs* 87, no. 3 (2008): 44–56; Layne, "The Waning of US Hegemony—Myth or Reality?" For data, see National Intelligence Council, *Global Trends 2025: A Transformed World* (Washington, DC: US Government Printing Office, 2008), http://www.dni.gov/nic/PDF_2025/2025_Global_Trends_Final_Report.pdf (accessed 25 May 2013). For non-American perspectives, see Dilip Hiro, *After Empire: The Birth of a Multipolar World* (New York: Nation Books, 2009); Giovanni Grevi, *The Interpolar World: A New Scenario*, Occasional Paper 79 (Paris: European Union Institute for Security Studies, 2009); Luis Peral, ed., *Global Security in a Multipolar World* Chaillot Paper 118 (Paris: European Union Institute for Security Studies, 2009); Thomas Renard, *A BRIC in the World: Emerging Powers, Europe and the Coming Order* (Brussels: Academic Press for the Royal Institute of International Relations, 2009); Álvaro de Vasconcelos, "Multilateralising Multi-Polarity II: Between Self-Interest and a Responsible Approach," in Luis Peral, ed., *Global Security in a Multi-polar World*, Chaillot Paper 118 (Paris: European Institute for Security Studies, 2009), 5–14; and Kishore Mahbubani, *The New Asian Hemisphere: The Irresistible Shift of Global Power to the East* (New York: Public Affairs Press, 2008).

Those who worry about America's decline are likely to portray China as selfish, mercantilist, strident, and opposed to human rights at home and abroad.[51] The European Union, by contrast, is characterized as benign, and on the whole American policy makers, foreign policy analysts, and academics have welcomed the European convergence spearheaded by the euro, foreign policy coordination, and military reforms. They are nevertheless quick to point out the European Union (EU) is beset by domestic challenges, including high unemployment, chronic public debt, and bloated welfare states.

Realists and liberals have a vested interest in keeping this debate going in the public eye because so many of their respective research programs are rooted in the concept of hegemony. These include, but are not limited to, hegemonic stability theory, power transition theory, regime theory, democratic peace theory, and much work in international political economy.

American policy makers are invested in hegemony because their policies remain largely state-centered and predicated on US leadership. Of equal importance, it provides a justification for extraordinary defense spending. For most members of the American foreign policy elite, alternatives to US global leadership are, if not unthinkable, extremely distasteful. For the general public, fed on a steady diet of American exceptionalism and superiority, they are unacceptable. Almost every major policy speech on foreign policy invokes the superiority of American values, its messianic role in the world and how responsible leaders everywhere welcome it.[52] The only alternative to leading, the American people are told, is following—and that is unpalatable. So US foreign policy remains focused on retaining something that no longer exists.

POWER AND INFLUENCE

First-generation realists Nicholas J. Spykman, E. H. Carr, Hans J. Morgenthau, and Frederick Schuman argued that power should be the

---

[51] Shirong Chen, "China Defends Africa Economic and Trade Role," 23 December 2010, http://www.bbc.co.uk/news/mobile/world-asia-pacific-12069624?SThisEM (accessed 23 December, 2010); Martin Wolf, *Fixing Global Finance: How to Curb Financial Crisis in the 21st Century* (New Haven, CT: Yale University Press, 2008). On human rights, see "China Rejects US Criticism of Human Rights Record," 11 May 2011, http://www.bbc.co.uk/news/world-asia-pacific-13358081 (accessed 11 May 2011).

[52] For one prominent example, see The White House, Office of the Press Secretary, "Remarks by the President in State of Union Address," 25 January 2011, http://www.whitehouse.gov/the-press-office/2011/01/25/remarks-president-state-union-address (accessed 29 January 2011).

guiding concept of international relations theory and the leading objective of foreign policy.[53] Morgenthau defined power as "anything that establishes and maintains the control of man over man."[54] He recognized that power was relational and thus context dependent; physical or moral resources that allowed leaders to influence one government might not work when deployed against another. As a close reader of Thucydides, Morgenthau understood that the exercise of power is likely to provoke resistance because it compels those who bend their wills in the face of it to recognize their inferior status. Subordination is an uncomfortable mental state, and an increasingly unacceptable one in an age in which equality and justice are the dominant political values. Power has to be masked to be effective. Even in circumstances involving coercion or bribery, leaders had to pretend that they were acting on the basis of consensus and conspire with those they coerced or bribed toward this end. This might be accomplished by making some face-saving concessions to others, using language that appeals to mutually shared values, and implementing policies through institutions in which others have representation and some real chance of influencing policy.[55]

Morgenthau attempted to develop a nuanced description of power that included its material bases, but also national character, popular morale, and the quality of leadership. Yet he conflated *power* and *influence*, terms he sometimes used interchangeably. This seems odd, as he was clear that power does not automatically translate into influence. Other IR theorists have sought to improve on Morgenthau. We briefly critique three such efforts: those of Thomas Schelling, Kenneth Waltz, and Joseph Nye Jr. The first two are realists and emphasize material capabilities. The liberal Nye, while not discounting material capabilities, stresses the importance of a globalizing world in which America's way of life has great international appeal.

Schelling, an economist, enlarged our understanding of power by focusing on the importance of signaling and commitments. He maintained that the will to use power was as important as the capability, and

---

[53] Nicholas Spykman, "Geography and Foreign Policy 2," *American Political Science Review* 36, no. 4 (1938): 213–36; Edward Hallett Carr, *The Twenty Year's Crisis, 1919–1939: An Introduction to the Study of International Relations* (London: Macmillan, 1940); Hans J. Morgenthau, *Politics among Nations: The Struggle for Power and Peace* (New York: Knopf, 1948); Frederick Lewis Schuman, *International Politics: An Introduction to the Western State* (New York: McGraw-Hill, 1958).

[54] Hans J. Morgenthau, *Politics in the Twentieth Century: The Impasse of American Foreign Policy* (Chicago: University of Chicago Press, 1962), 141.

[55] John Ikenberry argues that the founding fathers of American Cold War policy understood this principle well and it was a principal reason for the early successes of American hegemony. G. John Ikenberry, *After Victory: Institutions, Strategic Restraint, and the Rebuilding of Order after Major Wars* (Princeton, NJ: Princeton University Press, 2001).

that it is essential to demonstrate credibility by always honoring commitments. Reputation could be lost by failure to honor even a peripheral commitment.[56] Evidence from the Cold War indicates that this proposition was not only wrong but also bordered on the paranoid, as did the greatly exaggerated concern for credibility within the national security community.[57]

Schelling sought to devise an approach to power and strategic bargaining that was universally applicable. To do so, he focused on tacit bargaining, undeniably the most original part of his approach. However, like American policy of that era, his efforts represented yet another attempt to find a technical solution to a cultural and political problem. His discussion of "natural" boundaries—which led him to compare the Rio Grande to the Yalu—is a case in point. It fails to recognize how subjective such gestalts really are. They take on meaning not from their location on a map but from the political and cultural assumptions that opposing sides use to read these maps. Mexico and China understood these river boundaries differently from the United States, and in almost diametrically opposed ways. The same problem applies to seemingly clever signals, which also only take on meaning in context. Richard Ned Lebow has demonstrated how signals are often dismissed as noise or misinterpreted when understood as signals. A classic example is Soviet premier Nikita Khrushchev's Friday night letter to US president John F. Kennedy at the height of the Cuban missile crisis. It was intended to signal willingness to withdraw the missiles and end the crisis, but the president and his advisers read it as an act of escalation indicating a hardening of the Soviet will. More astonishing was Kennedy's trip to church on Sunday morning after being informed of Khrushchev's radio broadcast that effectively ended the crisis. He told his brother that he would attend in order to thank God for this deliverance. The KGB—the Soviet security agency—tailed him and cabled Moscow that war was now more likely as the president was going to church to build up his courage to launch a nuclear attack against the Soviet Union.[58]

Schelling followed Morgenthau in his emphasis on material capabilities, but ignored all of the latter's caveats of the limitations of trans-

[56] Thomas Schelling, *The Strategy of Conflict* (Cambridge, MA: Harvard University Press, 1960); Thomas Schelling, *Arms and Influence* (New Haven, CT: Yale University Press, 1966).

[57] Richard Ned Lebow and Janice Gross Stein, *We All Lost the Cold War* (Princeton, NJ: Princeton University Press, 1994); Ted Hopf, *Peripheral Visions: Deterrence Theory and American Foreign Policy in the Third World, 1965–1990* (Ann Arbor: University of Michigan Press, 1994).

[58] Richard Ned Lebow, *The Art of Bargaining* (Baltimore: Johns Hopkins University Press, 1996); Lebow and Stein, *We All Lost the Cold War*, chap. 6.

forming power into influence. His approach to the war in Indochina is revealing. Schelling was absolutely convinced that Washington could compel Hanoi to restrain the Vietcong and agree to respect the existence of a US puppet regime in South Vietnam. The US Air Force and Navy could deliver more ordnance than all Allied bombers had dropped on Germany in World War II. Schelling ignored the context in which this power was to be deployed—especially the absence of high-value targets, which would render bombing costly and ineffective. He failed to consider that coercive bargaining is an equation with terms on both sides: against the power to inflict punishment is the ability to absorb it. Here the Vietnamese had a decided advantage because of their greater morale. Many Vietnamese regarded the conflict with the southern regime and the Americans as a war of national liberation and were willing to die for this goal. Increasingly, the American public came to see the war as a distant conflict in which they had no stake and in which draftees were dying for no defensible purpose. This Indochina war offers a powerful illustration of the difficulties of equating material capabilities with power and power with influence.

Schelling's approach to power and its applications in Vietnam were amoral; for him, military power and threats to use it were just another instrument of politics. His only reference to morality concerns the French in Algeria, and is intended to highlight the differences between that conflict and the Vietnam War. The Algerian rebels waged a war of terror against their French and Algerian opponents. The French Army opposed them with force and sought to eliminate their military capability. When this strategy failed, the French turned to terror, with no greater effect. Algeria showed that relying on coercive terror in return might prove not only degrading but also incompatible with the purpose it is intended to serve. Schelling was naively confident that this would not happen in Vietnam because the United States had found a way to coerce the North Vietnamese government without using force against its population.[59] Hans Morgenthau insisted that both the ends and the means of foreign policy had to be consistent with the prevailing moral code—for ethical and practical reasons. Schelling's brand of realism—and American military intervention then and now—dispensed with all morality on the grounds that it had no place in a dangerous world populated by cutthroat adversaries and frightened allies. In doing so, Schelling and American policy makers lost sight of the limitations of power and the ways in which its exercise can diminish a country's standing and influence.

Kenneth Waltz's writings reveal a different face of power, and with it different problems in using it as an analytical concept. His starting

---

[59] Thomas Schelling, *Strategy of Conflict*, 174.

point is Morgenthau, whose formulation of power he attempts to make more robust and scientific. At the outset, he offers a *tour d'horizon* of the components of power that is almost identical with Morgenthau's. For reasons that are never really justified, he then rejects this complex assessment of power in favor of a unidimensional one based on the ability to develop and exploit technically sophisticated forms of military power. Such a definition, he maintains, has the advantage of parsimony, and readily allows one to determine the polarity of the international system.[60] Waltz insists, for the same reason, that we reject the notion of power as relational. In effect, he rejects any distinction between power and influence—the former simply confers the latter—and reduces power to a narrow understanding of material capabilities.

These several analytical moves allow Waltz to build a parsimonious theory, but one that has little relevance to the real world and cannot be made operational. His definition of power is inadequate for the same reason as Schelling's: it stresses the ability to inflict pain and ignores a willingness to absorb it. By his formulation of power, the United States should have easily triumphed in Vietnam, and both the United States and the USSR should have had easy victories in Afghanistan. The key to Waltz's theory is polarity, as it is the putative determinant of the war-proneness of the system. His definition of power is so vague that realists, who rely on it, disagree among themselves when the world became bipolar and whether it became multi- or unipolar when the Soviet Union collapsed.[61]

The conceptual confusion of realism stems from its tendency to conflate power and influence in order to reduce both, as far as possible, to material capabilities. This cramped and faulty understanding of power is not accidental. It reflects and panders to a particular American approach to the world that emphasizes power over persuasion and the material attributes of power over moral and psychological ones. This orientation attempts to reduce politics to a technical problem, in keeping with a long-standing and broader American tradition. In this sense, the conceptions of power developed by postwar realists and liberals reflect the culture of America and its scholarship, and strengthen its hold over a younger generation.

[60] Kenneth N. Waltz, *Theory of International Politics* (Reading, MA: Addison-Wesley, 1979).

[61] Kenneth N. Waltz, "The Emerging Structure of International Politics," *International Security* 18, no. 2 (1993): 44–79; Charles A. Kupchan, "After Pax Americana: Benign Power, Regional Integration, and the Sources of Stable Multipolarity," *International Security* 23 (1998): 40–79; William C. Wohlforth, "The Stability of a Unipolar World," *International Security* 24 (1999): 5–41; G. John Ikenberry, *America Unrivaled: The Future of the Balance of Power* (Ithaca, NY: Cornell University Press, 2002).

In practice, material capabilities and power are related in indirect, complex, and often problematic ways. Material capabilities are a principal source of power, but critical choices must be made about which capabilities to develop and how to use them.[62]

In the post–Cold War era, the United States continues to devote a disproportionate percentage of its wealth to developing and maintaining extraordinary military capabilities. Most countries cut back on military spending in the aftermath of the Cold War but the US outlay increased. Between 2001 and 2010 the US defense budget increased by 128 percent.[63] In 2003, the United States spent $417 billion on defense, 47 percent of the world total.[64] In 2008, it spent 41 percent of its national budget on the military and its two ongoing wars. By 2010 the US defense budget stood at $693 billion and still accounted for over 43 percent of world defense spending.[65] In absolute terms this was twice the total of Japan, Russia, the United Kingdom, Germany, and China combined. By 2012 the US defense budget stood at over $700 billion and climbed to an estimated figure of over $868 billion if the cost of foreign wars, homeland security, and other related expenses are included.[66] Not surprisingly, it is the only state with a global military reach.[67] Democratic and Republican administrations alike have bet that off-the-scale

[62] The Cold War demonstrated the irrelevance of certain raw forms of power. The USSR and United States developed impressive nuclear arsenals and diverse delivery systems for them. These weapons were all but unusable. The principal purpose for which they were designed—all-out superpower war—would have constituted mutual, if not global, suicide. Intended to deter the other side, nuclear weapons and forward deployments of their delivery systems became a principal cause of superpower conflict and greatly extended the Cold War. See Lebow and Stein, *We All Lost the Cold War*, chap. 13.

[63] Stockholm International Peace Research Institute, *SIPRI Yearbook 2011* (Stockholm: Stockholm International Peace Research Institute), 158.

[64] Elisabeth Sköns, Catalina Perdomo, Sam Perlo-Freeman, and Petter Stålenheim, "Military Expenditure," in *SIPRI Yearbook 2004*, Stockholm International Peace Research Institute, http://www.sipri.org/yearbook/2004/files/SIPRIYB0410.pdf, 311–13 (accessed 5 January 2012).

[65] Stockholm International Peace Research Institute, *SIPRI Yearbook 2011*, 9.

[66] Robert Johnson, "The 2012 Defense Budget Is the Highest since World War II," *Business Insider*, 19 July 2011, http://www.businessinsider.com/2012-us-defense-budget-largest-since-world-war-ii-2011-7 (accessed 25 February 2013); Kimberly Amadeo, "FY 2012 US Federal Budget," *About.com*, 11 February 2012, http://useconomy.about.com/od/usfederalbudget/p/US-Government-Federal-Budget-FY2012-Summary.htm (accessed 25 February 2013).

[67] Global Issues, "World Military Spending," 25 February 2007, http://www.globalissues.org/Geopolitics/ArmsTrade/Spending.asp#USMilitarySpending (accessed 23 February 2012); Christopher Hellman, "Highlights of the Fiscal Year 2008 Pentagon Spending Request," 5 February 2007, http://www.armscontrolcenter.org/archives/002239.php (accessed August 2010).

levels of military expenditure will sustain, if not increase, the standing and influence that traditionally comes with military dominance.

Does all this expenditure on the military serve American interests at home and abroad? It clearly encourages military interventions, because Washington has a decisive military superiority over many possible adversaries and a need to use its military arm to maintain support for funding it. The Anglo-American invasion of Iraq offers the most recent evidence that military power does not necessarily confer influence, especially when it is used in inappropriate ways. When intervention is at odds with prevailing norms and practices, it can seriously erode a state's influence.

This phenomenon is an anomaly for most realist and liberal understandings of power, but not for an approach that disaggregates influence from power and directs our attention to its social as well as material basis. Such a shift by no means ignores material capabilities. It nevertheless grounds the study of influence in the shared discourses that make it possible.

We must also consider the counterfactual: the situation the United States would have found itself in if, after the Cold War, it had followed Europe's lead and redirected most of its military spending to more productive uses. Suppose it had dramatically increased funding of education, scientific research, the creation and maintenance of infrastructure, and the beefing up of enforcement of banking, investment, and income tax—radically cut during the administrations of Ronald Reagan and George H. W. Bush? It almost certainly would have had a more robust and innovative economy, avoided the banking crisis, much of the federal deficit and costly loans from China. A stronger and more independent American economy would have made the United States a more powerful arbiter of international economic issues and made others more willing to accept its leadership. So too would have subsequent restraint in dealing with Afghanistan and Iraq.

Liberals tend to be more sanguine about America's leadership, believing that it can be assured through a mixture of traditional institutional power and Nye's "soft power" mentioned earlier, which supposedly derives from the worldwide appeal of American culture and its way of life.[68] Consumption of Coca-Cola, the sporting of blue jeans and interest in American TV and movies are assumed, in unspecified ways, to make foreign publics more receptive and supportive of US foreign policy goals.[69] Nye is quick to concede that soft power, like material

[68] Joseph S. Nye Jr., *Soft Power: The Means to Success in Worlds Politics* (New York: Public Affairs, 2004), 5–11.

[69] See Joseph S. Nye Jr., "The Future of American Power," *Foreign Affairs* 89, no. 6

power, is diffuse, reliant on both local interpreters and a willing audience. Governments accordingly find it difficult to exploit soft power or anticipate its outcomes. Senior American policy makers nevertheless routinely invoke soft power as another mechanism for enhancing US influence.[70]

The concept of soft power is soft in conceptualization and weak in empirics. What is the leap of logic that leads from attraction to American culture or its products to support for American foreign policy? The appeal of Japanese electronics, Chinese clothes and Cuban cigars has not made Americans any more pro-Japanese, Chinese, or Cuban. Quite the reverse may be the case in response to the "invasion" of Chinese products in European and American markets.[71] There has been an equally negative reaction to some American exports, like MacDonald's and fast food chains more generally. They have aroused anti-American feeling in Europe and become the target of attacks and demonstrations. Most consumers seem capable of distinguishing between a country's products and its policies. Every anti-American demonstration in Europe and Asia features protesters clad in jeans. Many other popular American exports—Apple products, for example—neither support nor oppose American foreign policy nor are seen as symbolic in this sense by those who purchase them. Those few American entertainment ventures that are distinctly opposed to any American imperial project, like the widely acclaimed *South Park* and *The Daily Show*, are extremely popular abroad. They may build respect for American democracy and toleration of dissent, but certainly not for the country's foreign policies.

Material capabilities serve as an important basis of power, but even the cursory discussion above reveals that the translation of power into influence is far from automatic. It depends on the development and wise use of certain kinds of capabilities, and these vary as a function of circumstances. During World War II, military power was the most important kind of power, and the United States and USSR wisely invested in it. In the postwar period, its utility declined and its use undermined, rather than enhanced, the power of the two so-called superpowers. The

(2010): 2–14; G. John Ikenberry, *Liberal Order and Imperial Ambition* (Cambridge: Polity, 2006), especially 1–18; G. John Ikenberry, ed., *America Unrivaled: The Future of the Balance of Power* (Ithaca, NY: Cornell University Press, 2002); John M. Owen IV, "Transnational Liberalism and American Primacy: or, Benignity Is in the Eye of the Beholder," in Ikenberry, ed., *America Unrivaled*, 239–59; and Thomas Risse, "US Power in a Liberal Security, in Ikenberry, ed., *America Unrivaled*, 260–83.

[70] Hillary Rodham Clinton, "Leading through Civilian Power: Redefining American Diplomacy and Development," *Foreign Affairs* 89, no. 6 (2010): 13–24.

[71] Globescan/Program on International Policy Attitudes, "Global Views of United States Improves While Other Countries Decline," *BBC Views*, 18 April 2010, 7; "BBC Poll: Germany the Most Popular Country in the World."

overreliance of the USSR on its military power made it incapable of effectively building legitimacy for the communist regimes it imposed in Eastern Europe. We should note that the term *bipolarity* was developed and deployed in the United States in the early 1950s and was part and parcel of the effort to justify the continuing expenditure on military instruments. In today's world, military power is only maintained at the cost of other forms of power that are arguably just as important.

Attempts to translate power directly into influence, even when successful, consume resources—often at a prodigious rate. They succeed only so long as threats are available and effective. The same is true of bribes. The United States provides more than $1.5 billion in military aid to Egypt and $3 billion to Israel every year. It is not at all evident what it gets in return. The regime of Hosni Mubarak, the recipient of this aid until 2012, channeled much of it into the pockets of family members and regime supporters and spent the rest on a largely useless military. Egypt under Mubarak maintained peace with Israel, but his brief successor, Mohamed Morsi, who came to power without any US backing, pledged to do this as well.[72] Israel continually flouts the US administration's wishes, most consistently on the question of settlements on the West Bank. In 2012, its leaders threatened to attack Iran's nuclear facilities in the face of US opposition.[73] Here, too, bribery did not bring compliance.

The most effective form of influence is persuasion. It consists of efforts to convince others that it is their interest to do what you want them to do. When successful, other actors are often willing to contribute resources of their own toward the common goal. Persuasion must build on shared values and advocate policies that involve accepted practices. If a state is asking other political units to accept its leadership, a serious effort must be made to convince their representatives that they will have meaningful input and that the initiatives in question will not go beyond commonly agreed upon goals. Material capabilities can be critical, but so is the wise choice of goals and political skill in the form of coalition building and maintenance. Persuasion is greatly assisted by past successes in cooperation and leadership, which create a degree of trust and propensity to cooperate again. Of equal importance, cooperation helps to build shared, if not common, identities that make cooperation and persuasion more likely in the future. Coalition building and implementation of any

---

[72] Joel Greenberg, "Israel: Egypt's President Mohamed Morsi Pledges New Peace Efforts," *Washington Post*, 31 July 2012, http://articles.washingtonpost.com/2012-07-31/world/35489115_1_netanyahu-and-peres-president-morsi-peace-efforts (accessed 25 February 2013).

[73] Cf. Calev Ben-David, "Israel Plans Iran Strike; Citizens Say Government Serious," 15 August 2012, http://www.bloomberg.com/news/2012-08-14/israel-plans-for-iran-strike-as-citizens-say-government-serious.html (accessed 25 February 2013).

common policies require what is best described as political and moral power, not only material capabilities. Depending on the nature of the initiative, it also benefits from institutional and technical expertise.

Persuasion ultimately rests on the notion of legitimacy; a concept that Ian Hurd maintains successfully rivals coercion and self-interest in explaining the behavior of states in the context of international organizations.[74] Hurd relies on organizational sociologist Mark Suchman's definition of legitimacy as "a generalized perception or assumption that the actions of an entity are desirable, proper, or appropriate within some socially constructed system of norms, values, beliefs, and definitions."[75] Legitimacy "refers to the normative belief by an actor that a rule or institution ought to be obeyed. It is a subjective quality, relational between actor and institution, and defined by the actor's perception of the institution. The actor's perception may come from the substance of the rule or from the procedure or source by which it was constituted."[76]

Legitimacy facilitates authority, according to Hurd: "When an actor believes a rule is legitimate, compliance is no longer motivated by the simple fear of retribution, or by a calculation of self-interest, but instead by a sense of moral obligation."[77] Legitimacy should be considered a long-run, low-cost means of social control as compliance becomes habitual when values are internalized. Where an actor accepts a rule because it is perceived as legitimate, that rule assumes an authoritative quality. The rule is then in some sense hierarchically superior to the actor and helps to shape its behavior. Over time, it contributes to the actor's definition of its interests, even of its identity. An organization that is perceived as a legitimate rule maker has authority vis-à-vis its members. The character of power accordingly changes when it is exercised within a framework of legitimate relations and institutions. The concepts of power and legitimacy might be said to come together in the exercise of "authority."[78]

Hegemonic Functions and Hēgemonia in the Global System

The distinction between power and influence becomes even more evident when we examine hegemony. Many realists and liberals describe

---

[74] Ian Hurd, "Legitimacy and Authority in International Politics," *International Organization* 53, no. 2 (1999): 379–408.

[75] Mark Suchman, quoted in Hurd, "Legitimacy and Authority in International Politics," 387.

[76] Hurd, "Legitimacy and Authority in International Politics," 381.

[77] Ibid., 387.

[78] Ibid., 400–403.

hegemony as a precondition of international order because they believe only a hegemon can provide leadership, and public economic and security goods. The claims rest on the assumptions that power confers influence, and that only hegemons can perform certain functions by virtue of their material capacities. We dispute both foundational claims. In this section we identity three critical functions that must be performed to sustain the current economic and political order: agenda setting, custodianship, and sponsorship. In the chapters that follow we will show that hegemony is not essential to any of them, and that its pursuit by the United States actually stands in their way of efforts by other actors to help perform these functions.

The first function, *agenda setting*, describes the capacity to initiate, legitimize, and advocate policy issues. These issues cut across the spectrum of social, economic, political, and security concerns. They are characteristically associated with "progressive" agendas such as environmentalism, human rights, social or economic justice, or civilian protection. They appeal to broad conceptions of justice, because in today's world this is a precondition for successful adoption. Agenda setting seeks to have these issues debated within regional or global organizations or broadly representative multilateral forums. It relies heavily on persuasion, generally in an institutional context, and arguably constitutes the most important form of leadership, as it does in domestic politics.[79]

Most liberals and—commonly—realists, by contrast, downplay the role of agency in multilateral policy making. In summarizing what is regarded as the authoritative definition of international regimes, for example, Stephen Krasner describes them as "sets of implicit or explicit principles, norms, rules and decision-making procedures around which actors expectations converge," without ever describing how and why expectations converge beyond the leadership a hegemon is expected to provide. That leadership is attributed to the hegemon's material capacities to underwrite the cost of the regime.[80] Yet material capabilities do not ineluctably promote successful leadership. One need only contrast the US and Soviet experience with their respective European partners during the Cold War. NATO worked much more by consensus and the Warsaw Pact by dictation, with profound consequences for the behavior and survival of both alliance systems. The difference was not due to material capabilities—both superpowers towered above their re-

---

[79] John W. Kingdon, *Agendas, Alternatives, and Public Policies* (Boston: Little, Brown, 1984).

[80] Stephen D. Krasner, "Structural Causes and Regime Consequences: Regimes as Intervening Variables," in Stephen D. Krasner, ed., *International Regimes* (Ithaca, NY: Cornell University Press, 1983), 2.

spective partners in this respect—but to their leadership styles and abilities.

To be effective, agenda setting requires the adoption of proposed measures in the context of multilateral venues that are designed for negotiation. Simple advocacy of a policy, even at the negotiating table, is an insufficient litmus test. Persuasion relies as much on the legitimacy of the proposal as on the sticks and carrots of material power. The problem of civilian protection offers a telling example of how agenda setting works. Norway, far from being a great power, nevertheless played an important role in the promotion of the concept of civilian protection. In the 1990s, the Norwegian government awarded funds to the Peace Research Institute of Oslo to think through the concept and what would be required to implement it.[81] In the UN, Norway worked with middle powers like Canada to promote human security. The Norwegians focused much of their efforts on promoting the "responsibility to protect" (R2P) doctrine in collaboration with other states and nongovernmental organizations, including the Brussels-based International Crisis Group. R2P seeks to invert the traditional realist focus on sovereignty and the rights of states by stressing their responsibility to protect civilians or be subject to the prospect of multilateral intervention.[82] By 2001, the R2P initiative had gained significant momentum and won the unstinting support of then UN secretary general Kofi Annan. Annan had earlier expressed the sentiment that, "even national sovereignty can be set aside if it stands in the way of the Security Council's overriding duty to preserve international peace and security."[83]

Members of the Bush administration had other ideas, and Anglo-American intervention in Afghanistan and Iraq slowed the momentum toward UN adoption of R2P. Many members feared that it would be

[81] Steven Radelet, *A Primer on Foreign Aid*, Working Paper no. 92 (Washington, DC: Center for Global Development, 2006), 5.

[82] Simon Reich, "The Evolution of a Doctrine: The Curious Case of Kofi Annan, George Bush and the Doctrines of Preventative and Preemptive Intervention," in William Keller and Gordon Mitchell, eds., *Hitting First: Preventive Force in US Security Strategy* (Pittsburgh: University of Pittsburgh Press, 2006), 45–69.

[83] "Secretary-General Reflects on 'Intervention' in Thirty-Fifth Annual Ditchley Foundation Lecture," UN Press Release, SG/SM/6613, 26 June 1998, http://www.un.org /News/Press/docs/1998/19980626.sgsm6613.html (accessed 3 July 2012); Gareth Evans and Mohamed Sahnoun, *The Responsibility to Protect: A Report by the International Commission of Intervention and State Sovereignty* (Ottawa: International Development Research Center, December 2001), http://www.dfait-maeci.gc.ca/iciss-ciise/pdf/Commission -Report.pdf (accessed 3 July 2012); Simon Reich, "Power, Institutions and Moral Entrepreneurs," ZEF Discussion Papers on Development Policy 65 (Bonn: Center for Development Research [ZEF], 2003), http://www.zef.de/publications.htm (accessed 4 November 2005); Bruce W. Jentleson, Coercive Prevention: Normative, Political and Policy Dilemmas," Peaceworks 35 (Washington, DC: United States Institute of Peace, 2000), 20.

used by major powers as a pretext to intervene in other states. Norway and its allies persevered, noting that American efforts to legitimate their invasion of Iraq had been rejected by the UN. Over the next two years, they worked to widen their basis of support by enlisting key states from the Global South. By 2005, the language of the R2P doctrine was embraced by the UN as consistent with Chapters VI and VIII of the UN Charter. At that time, over 150 world leaders adopted R2P, legitimating the use of force through multilateral intervention initiatives sanctioned by the UN Security Council.[84]

Still, the Norwegians persisted with their efforts at the UN, and R2P was embedded in a civilian protection framework adopted by the UN in 2009.[85] The Obama administration formally adopted R2P's principles as part of US policy in its *National Security Strategy*, issued in 2010.[86] R2P had become operational: it found instantiation in UN resolutions about Kenya's 2008 postelection violence and then in Darfur before being embraced in Libya.[87] We are not suggesting that Norway single-handedly caused the adoption of R2P's principles. Other nations played an important role. Yet the evidence suggests that it is hard to overlook Norway's instrumental political, intellectual, and policy role as a staunch, unwavering supporter even in the years after the US invasion of Iraq when it became politically less popular and its adoption appeared unfeasible.

The second of our three functions is *custodianship*. The liberal variant of hegemony focuses largely on management of the international economy. Charles Kindleberger famously identified the set of economic tasks a hegemon (although not a term he actually used in that context) must perform in this connection in acting as a stabilizer of the global system.[88]

---

[84] UN General Assembly, "2005 World Summit Outcome," Articles 138 and 139, A/60/L.1, 15 September 2005.

[85] Svein Atle Michelsen to the UN Security Council, "SC: Protection of Civilians in Armed Conflict," 7 July 2010, http://www.norway-un.org/Statements/Archived-State ments/Statements-2010/Security-Council/SC-Protection-of-Civilians-in-Armed-Con flict (accessed 5 June 2013).

[86] US National Security Council, *National Security Strategy, 2010*, 48.

[87] UN Security Council, "Security Council Approves 'No-Fly Zone' over Libya, Authorizing 'All Necessary Measures' to Protect Civilians, by Vote of 10 in Favor with 5 Abstentions," 17 March 2011, (accessed 16 May 2011); Evans and Sahnoun, *The Responsibility to Protect*; Mark Leon Goldberg, "A 'Responsibility to Protect' in Libya," http://www.undispatch.com/a-responsibility-to-protect-in-libya (accessed 16 May 2011); Irwin Cotler and Jared Genser, "Libya and the Responsibility to Protect," *New York Times*, 28 February 2011, http://www.nytimes.com/2011/03/01/opinion/01iht-edcotler01.html (accessed 16 May 2011). For an analysis of the American perspective, see Bruce W. Jentleson, "The Obama Administration and R2P: Progress, Problems and Prospects," *Global Responsibility to Protect* 4, no. 4 (2012–13): 399–423.

[88] Charles P. Kindleberger, *The World in Depression, 1929–1939* (Berkeley and Los Angeles: University of California Press, 1973), 305.

Although not systematically examined by leading liberals in the field of international political economy, Kindleberger's work on the Great Depression nonetheless forms the foundation for their thinking. Liberals and some realists insist that only a hegemon can maintain stable patterns of exchange within a preexisting but evolving global economic structure.[89] Because the United States has played this role in the postwar world, liberals assert, the rules of exchange and finance have remained consistent, based on principles of the free exchange of goods and services. The result had been unprecedented and widely distributed economic growth.

This is a questionable claim. The United States has often transgressed the principles liberals describe as essential by adopting protectionist measures in the name of "fair trade." It shook the foundations of the global economic order by unilaterally ending the convertibility of the dollar when it "closed the gold window" in 1973. It exploited its position by borrowing vast sums of money and at times running high rates of inflation that it would not have been possible for any other country to do without encountering sanctions.[90] It engendered the 2008 Great Recession through lax financial regulation. The image of American hegemony as marked by a broader, enlightened conception of self-interest, and of being indispensible to growth and stability, is not only self-serving but inaccurate.

Reliant on Kindleberger, liberals have characterized the United States as a benign actor; during the Great Depression and its aftermath, it was needed as a stabilizer to provide a series of public goods. His account is the foundation upon which liberal accounts of American hegemony have been constructed. Susan Strange offers a markedly different interpretation of the postwar period, one in which purposive American efforts at financial deregulation have undermined its capacity for global economic management.[91] She characterizes American policies as motivated by a long-term, systematic effort to accrue benefits and offload costs. Arguably, the United States has succeeded. In the Vietnam era, it exported its relatively large deficits and enjoined its major trading partners to hold dollar debt through a series of sticks and carrots that included delinking the dollar to gold. In the last decade, the United States

[89] Gilpin, *War and Change in World Politics*, 173–75; Ikenberry, *Liberal Leviathan*, 18–22.

[90] Joanne Gowa, *Closing the Gold Window: Domestic Politics and the End of Bretton Woods* (Ithaca, NY: Cornell University Press, 1983); Fred Block, *The Origins of International Economic Disorder: A Study of United States International Monetary Policy from World War II to the Present* (Berkeley and Los Angeles: University of California Press, 1977), 182–98.

[91] Susan Strange, *Casino Capitalism* (Oxford: Blackwell, 1986); Susan Strange, *Mad Money: When Markets Outgrow Governments* (Ann Arbor: University of Michigan Press, 1998).

generated unprecedented public and private debt, a phenomenon that accelerated in the aftermath of the 2008 global financial crisis until the two forms of debt began moving in opposite directions by 2010 as public bailouts and programs essentially reduced private debt. Both during the Vietnam era and the Great Recession, Washington's exploitation of its position destabilized existing patterns of global finance.[92] Chinese and Japanese investors have—and still do—subsidize American consumers. The US has been a regular exploiter, rather than provider, of public goods.

Washington pumped huge sums of money into the system after World War II to help others rebuild their economies, and to create markets for US good. In later decades, it borrowed money in lieu of balancing its trade deficit or raising taxes, and thus failed to play the role of lender of last resort. The US reliance on Keynesian deficit spending policies, combined with large public debts well before the 2008 crisis, made it massively indebted to countries like Japan and China. They hold large dollar currency reserves as a result of favorable export balances.

American borrowing took the form of the issuance of US Treasury bills. By March 2011, the treasury estimated that China's holding of US Treasury bills had reached $1.16 trillion, making it the largest foreign lender. Japan's holdings amounted to $882.3 billion by the end of 2010. The total foreign holdings of US Treasury debt stood at $4.44 trillion and the entire national debt had reached $14.3 trillion.[93] The pace of borrowing has accelerated in the last few years without much evidence of the funds being put to infrastructure or other forms of investment. By the beginning of 2013, debt levels had grown significantly; foreign holdings of US Treasury debt ballooned to over $5.5 trillion and the national debt reached almost $16.5 trillion.[94] The United States relies on China's willingness to hold on to these Treasury bills and maintain the value of the dollar and, by doing so, to avoid defaulting on payment of its public debt. Only the United States could carry such debt without having to embark on stringent budget cuts imposed by multilateral organizations such as the International Monetary Fund (IMF), other national govern-

---

[92] Block, *The Origins of International Economic Disorder*, 182–98.

[93] Michael Shedlock, "China Holdings of US Treasuries Revised Up 30%; An Unsustainable Model," *Mish's Global Economic Trend Analysis*, 1 March 2011, http://www.safe haven.com/article/20135/china-holdings-of-us-treasuries-revised-up-30-an-unsustain able-model (accessed 13 June 2011).

[94] "Major Foreign Holders of US Treasury Securities," http://www.treasury.gov/re source-center/data-chart-center/tic/Documents/mfh.txt (accessed 27 January 2013); "US National Debt Clock," http://www.brillig.com/debt_clock (accessed 27 January 2013).

ments, or private bankers. American behavior has become increasingly feckless and destabilizing, and far from propping up the financial system as lender of last resort, the United States has emerged as its primary borrower and an increasingly irresponsible one.

The United Kingdom, Germany, and France, America's closest allies, rebuffed US attempts at global economic coordination in the closing year of the Bush administration and the first term of the Obama administration. These three are among the Group of Eight (G8) countries that comprise the world's traditionally largest economies. Today, the United States thus neither leads nor lends. If we assess the US role by the economic management functions thought critical by liberals, it is not a hegemon.

For the time being, the global economic system functions, for better and worse, without a hegemon. Leadership, economic management, and security provisions are no longer interrelated. Key management functions—providing market liquidity, reinforcing open trading patterns, market and currency stability, and reinforcing patterns of economic development—take place without a hegemon. Divorced from the concept of hegemony, these functions are best described as "custodianship."

In the 1980s, following processes of market liberalization inspired by US president Ronald Reagan and UK prime minister Margaret Thatcher, these functions became increasingly reliant on market dynamics and monetary policy in lieu of state regulation. Liberalization made multilateral state-to-state coordination more complex, unwieldy, and ineffective. This complexity was responsible for the failure to coordinate monetary policy that contributed to the stock market crash of 1987.[95] Market-directed custodianship is still possible when facilitated by bilateral or multilateral negotiations and agreements involving state and nonstate actors. But it must be coupled with carefully regulated economic policies that use markets sensibly.[96] In chapter 4, we will examine the feasibility of such efforts.

Two economic developments in the last several decades are particular pertinent to our argument. The first is the growth of the global marketplace and, with it, the decline of national models of capitalism, especially in the West. Deregulation, privatization, and liberalization, inspired by the recipe that became know as the Washington Consensus, made economies more permeable and harder to guide by governments

[95] Jude Wanninski, "Crash of 1987: A Case Study," *Polyconomics*, 3 May 2002, http://www.polyconomics.com/ssu/ssu-020503.htm (accessed 14 June 2011); Mark Thoma, "Fasten Your Seatbelts," *Economists View*, 13 August 2006, http://economistsview.typepad.com/economistsview/2006/08/please_return_t.html (accessed 14 June 2011).

[96] Duncan Snidal, "The Limits of Hegemonic Stability Theory," *International Organization* 39, no. 4 (1985): 579–614; Keohane, *After Hegemony*, 38.

than had been the case between 1945 and the 1980s.[97] The second development is the faltering of older multilateral financial institutions such as the World Bank and IMF as they became less capable of coping with the intensified market gyrations, although this trend was attenuated by European intervention (as will be discussed in chapter 3). Having been the catalyst for both developments, the United States is increasingly unable to guide or control markets. Institutions designed to coordinate policy, such as the Group of Seven (G7), have proved no more effective. The expansion of that "club" to twenty states has made interstate collaboration on a global scale that much more difficult. These developments have increased the risk of moral hazard; banks, corporations, and even countries (e.g., Cyprus, Greece, Ireland, Portugal, and Italy) are regarded as "too big" to allow to fail.[98] The 1997 Asian financial crisis and the 2008 global economic crisis suggest that Susan Strange's fear of "casino capitalism" is increasingly becoming a reality.

These developments offer further evidence that the United States does not act responsibly or performs the economic functions attributed to a hegemon.[99] China, often in partnership with other Asian states, is beginning to assume some of these functions.[100] China's role is not hegemonic but confined to the economy and to sustaining financial liquidity and engendering growth.[101] Beijing has made no attempt to assume economic dominance or create multilateral institutions based on its priorities or values. China's clear strategic goal is to buttress the global economy, which serves its interests and enhances its influence. China's limited role is nonetheless essential to the effective functioning of a stable financial system. We explore its emerging custodianship in chapter 4.

The third element of hegemony is *sponsorship*, which encompasses enforcement of rules, norms, agreements, and decision-making processes as well as the maintenance of security to enhance trade and fi-

---

[97] Robert H. Wade, "US Hegemony and the World Bank," *Review of International Political Economy* 9, no. 2 (2002): 215–43.

[98] Richard Swedberg, "Capitalism and Ethics: How Conflicts of Interest-Legislation Can Be Used to Handle Moral Dilemmas in the Economy," *International Social Science Journal* 57, no. 185 (2005): 481–92; Paul Blustein, *The Chastening: Inside the Crisis that Rocked the Global Financial System and Humbled the IMF* (New York: Public Affairs, 2001); J. Bradford DeLong and Barry Eichengreen, "Between Meltdown and Moral Hazard: The International Monetary and Financial Policies of the Clinton Administration," Working Paper 8443 (Cambridge, MA: National Bureau of Economic Research, 2001).

[99] Carla Norrlof, *America's Global Advantage: US Hegemony and International Cooperation* (Cambridge: Cambridge University Press, 2010): 5–6.

[100] Ibid., 2–8.

[101] Kevin Yao, "China Economy to Underpin Global Demand in 2013—CIC," 26 January 2013, http://uk.reuters.com/article/2013/01/26/uk-china-economy-growth-idUK BRE90P04T20130126 (accessed 28 January 2013).

nance.[102] Liberals and realists consistently maintain that only hegemons can provide such enforcement because of their preponderance of material power. They assume that American hegemony is legitimate in the eyes of other important actors who welcome its leadership and enforcement as beneficial to global stability and their national interests. When empirical support is mustered for these claims, the foreign voices invariably cited are those of conservative politicians in allied states or authoritarian leaders who benefit personally from US backing. During the Cold War, German conservatives welcomed US leadership as a means of offsetting Soviet power and of constraining Social Democratic opponents. Leaders of South Korea, Taiwan, South Vietnam, the Philippines, Iran, Egypt, and various Latin American states were, to varying degrees, dependent on US military and foreign aid and happy to say in public what Washington wanted to hear to keep these dollars flowing. Their opponents regarded US influence as regressive as it supported regimes opposed to democracy and human rights.

There has been a noticeable decline in pleas for US leadership since the end of the Cold War, and as noted earlier, a corresponding increase in opposition to US military and economic initiatives. Since the Iraq War, the United States has undergone a shift in its profile from a status quo to a revisionist power.[103] A BBC World Service poll conducted in early 2007 indicated a significant increase in the standing of countries associated with alternate visions of the international system. When asked what countries exerted a positive influence in the world, Canada and Japan topped the list at 54 percent, followed by France (50 percent), Britain (45 percent), China (42 percent), and India (37 percent).[104] More recent surveys reveal that the United States is not perceived as acting in the interests of the international community. Whatever legitimacy its leadership once had has significantly eroded as publics around the world are particularly worried about the way in which the United States uses its military power.[105] In one 2012 global survey, for example,

---

[102] Simon Reich, *Global Norms, American Sponsorship, and the Emerging Patterns of World Politics* (Basingstoke, England: Palgrave Macmillan, 2010) 62–63.

[103] Reus-Smit, "Unipolarity and Legitimacy."

[104] BBC World Service, "Israel and Iran Share Most Negative Ratings in Global Poll," *BBC News*, 6 March 2007, http://news.bbc.co.uk/2/shared/bsp/hi/pdfs/06_03_07_per ceptions.pdf (accessed 5 February 2013).

[105] Pew Research Global Attitudes Project, "Obama More Popular Abroad Than at Home, Global Image of US Continues to Benefit," 17 June 2011, http://www.pewglobal .org/2010/06/17/obama-more-popular-abroad-than-at-home (accessed 26 September 2011); Pew Research Global Attitudes Project, "Global Opinion of Obama Slips, International Policies Faulted," 13 June 2012, http://www.pewglobal.org/2012/06/13/global -opinion-of-obama-slips-international-policies-faulted (accessed 28 January 2013); "BBC Poll: Germany the Most Popular Country in the World."

majorities (or in the single case of India, a plurality) disapproved of the American use of drones in every country surveyed except for the United States.[106]

Leadership and legitimacy are closely connected, and enforcement clearly depends on the latter. In situations where US efforts at enforcement have been seen as legitimate (e.g., Korea, the First Gulf War, and Libya), international support has been forthcoming, and with it, backing by relevant regional and international organizations—notably the UN Security Council. Key to the legitimacy of enforcement has been a common perception of threat but also a commitment on Washington's part to limit its military action in pursuit of a consensus. It often requires collaborative decisions concerning processes of implementation as well. The administration of President Harry Truman won support for the liberation of South Korea, but not the invasion of North Korea; and the administration of George H. W. Bush for the liberation of Kuwait, but not the overthrow of Saddam Hussein. When George W. Bush insisted on the invasion of Iraq with the goal of removing Saddam, he was unable to gain support from NATO or the UN. When the administration went to war in the absence of international institutional support, it had to cobble together a coalition based largely on bribes and threats. Its subsequent decline in standing was precipitous, and this began before the insurgency in Iraq.

The theoretical and policy lessons of these experiences are straightforward. Material power is a necessary but insufficient condition for enforcement. The latter depends on legitimacy, an important component of influence. In its absence, even successful enforcement—as defined by Washington—will not be perceived as such by other states, and possibly as aggrandizement, as the Iraq invasion was by public opinion in France, Germany, Canada, and Japan. Such perceptions undermine legitimacy and make future enforcement more difficult.

Sponsorship can entail the threat or use of force, and here the United States tries hard to live up to theoretical expectations. It has unparalleled military expertise and capacity and has been involved in more wars, for more years, than any other state since 1946, apart from the United Kingdom and France (largely because they fought so many colonial wars in the immediate postwar period).[107] Liberals tend to downplay or ignore the military element of hegemony, focusing more on economic incentives and soft power. Violence in their writings fades into

---

[106] See Statista, "Public Opinion on US Use of Drone Strikes, by Country 2012," http:// www.statista.com/statistics/233004/global-opinion-on-us-drone-strikes (accessed 30 May 2013).

[107] See Mack, "The Changing Face of Global Violence (Part 1)," especially 28.

the background under a wealth of incentives and rules. Even Ikenberry claims that the United States, while it provides security, nevertheless exercises remarkable self-restraint and refrains from overt aggression.[108] The historical record suggests otherwise.

Enforcement of security is foundational to the concept of sponsorship. It entails a willingness to enforce global security and its rules and norms, or at least underwrite the costs of doing so. It nevertheless also requires the greatest powers to refrain from acting unilaterally and preemptively. Sponsorship strategies must be responsive to collectively perceived needs and implemented with the backing—and preferably the active collaboration—of a wide coalition of other actors. It entails the use of material power in the context of broader decision making and consensus. It requires what former US secretary of state Hillary Rodham Clinton characterized as a willingness "to accept the responsibility of mobilizing action."[109]

Why should any state act as a sponsor? A great power may do so for reasons that have nothing to do with hegemony. It may be a state in decline, hoping to regain status by enforcing generally accepted norms. It may be a powerful state aspiring to enhance its legitimacy or prestige, and with it the willingness of others to accept its leadership on other issues. A great power may do so, or join with others toward this end, because its leaders simply see their state as better off in sustaining the current arrangements. Perhaps they even worry that chaos is otherwise a real possibility. In sum, sponsorship and enforcement can be motivated by self-interest and a commitment to regional or global norms.[110]

Self-interest is one of the more imprecise terms in the political lexicon, and is often invoked by realists to explain any policy ex post facto. Realists have equated it with security and liberals have equated it with wealth, while constructivists attempt to reconstruct the different understandings of actors. We side with constructivists in believing that actor goals vary in their importance, framing, and pursuit. We must accordingly refrain from imposing our formulations on leaders or their states, but rather struggle to understand how they frame and apply the concept of interest. History indicates that there are often wide variations within the same policy-making elite. People are loath to make hard choices from among their goals, and policy makers are no different; they can construct their interests in ways that appear contradictory, even irrational, to outsiders.

[108] Ikenberry, *After Victory*, 248, 257–73.
[109] Clinton, "Leading through Civilian Power."
[110] Gilpin, *War and Change in World Politics*, 96–105; Michael Doyle, "Liberalism and World Politics," *American Political Science Review* 80, no. 4 (1986): 1151–69.

Thucydides, Plato, and Aristotle distinguished between short- and longer-term interests. For the fifth- and fourth-century BCE Greeks, *hēgemonia* was associated with *timē*—the gift of honor.[111] *Timē* was bestowed informally by free consent of the Greek community as reward for achievements, and retained by consent, not by force. Sparta and Athens were so honored because of their contributions during the Persian Wars. Athens also earned timē because its intellectual and artistic accomplishments made it the "school of Hellas." Hēgemonia requires material capabilities, but those capabilities must be used to advance the common interests of the community.

The Greeks used the term *archē* to describe rule based largely on force, or the threat of it. Well-known examples of despotism include the Mongol Empire, the Nazi occupation of Europe and, arguably, the control exercised by Soviet Union in Eastern Europe during the Cold War. When a despot's power declines, or it loses its will to crush any opposition, demise becomes imminent. A hegemon in the Greek sense that makes loyal subjects out of conquered and foreign peoples—the Romans are the best example—can endure long after its power has waned.[112]

Hēgemonia requires a justification that is acceptable to a significant proportion of those who are ruled. Some empires evoked religious myths, as did the Egyptians and Mayans, while others, notably, the Chinese and British, based their rule on their material and cultural achievements—and the timē this conferred. For it to function, allies and subjects must see the hēgemonia they have conferred as continuing to be conducive to their interests. Rome provided guarantees of internal and external security, generally supported the worship of local gods, and offered citizenship and access to its markets to assuage those whom they had subdued by force. The Romans were so successful in legitimizing their rule that they could afford to rely on a relatively small military force, most of it deployed on the periphery of the empire, facing Parthians and Germanic tribes. During the first century of the common era, Rome ruled over a territory that stretched from Britain to Persia with an average of twenty-nine legions, each composed of approximately six thousand men.[113] The British accomplished a similar feat. At the height

---

[111] Russell Meiggs, *The Athenian Empire* (Oxford: Oxford University Press, 1972); Shalom Perlman, "Hegemony and *Arkhe* in Greece: Fourth-Century Views," in Richard Ned Lebow and Barry Strauss eds., *Hegemonic Rivalry: From Thucydides to the Nuclear Age* (Boulder, CO: Westview Press, 1991): 269–88.

[112] Michael Doyle, *Empires* (Ithaca, NY: Cornell University Press, 1986), 37–45; Barry S. Strauss, "The Art of Alliance and the Peloponnesian War," in Charles D. Hamilton and Peter Krentz, eds., *Polis and Polemos: Essays on Politics, War and History in Ancient Greece in Honor of Donald Kagan* (Claremont, CA: Regina, 1997), 127–40.

[113] See Graham Webster, *The Roman Imperial Army of the First and Second Centuries A.D.*

and their legitimacy in the eyes of other actors. They are also affected by domestic and international constraints and opportunities.

Let us now turn to the concrete choices—or debates about choices—of Europe, including the European Union; China; and the United States. They reveal the extent to which these functions are becoming distributed globally, entailing states using different combinations of material and social power, and creating new possibilities of order and disruption. This process is due in the first instance to the failure of the United States to perform in a responsible way, a choice that cannot simply be attributed to loss of power. It also reflects the growing power of other political units and their interest in playing a more important role in world affairs but also their recognition that almost all of their national goals, including well-being, depend on an ordered international system.

Thucydides, Plato, and Aristotle distinguished between short- and longer-term interests. For the fifth- and fourth-century BCE Greeks, *hēgemonia* was associated with *timē*—the gift of honor.[111] *Timē* was bestowed informally by free consent of the Greek community as reward for achievements, and retained by consent, not by force. Sparta and Athens were so honored because of their contributions during the Persian Wars. Athens also earned timē because its intellectual and artistic accomplishments made it the "school of Hellas." Hēgemonia requires material capabilities, but those capabilities must be used to advance the common interests of the community.

The Greeks used the term *archē* to describe rule based largely on force, or the threat of it. Well-known examples of despotism include the Mongol Empire, the Nazi occupation of Europe and, arguably, the control exercised by Soviet Union in Eastern Europe during the Cold War. When a despot's power declines, or it loses its will to crush any opposition, demise becomes imminent. A hegemon in the Greek sense that makes loyal subjects out of conquered and foreign peoples—the Romans are the best example—can endure long after its power has waned.[112]

Hēgemonia requires a justification that is acceptable to a significant proportion of those who are ruled. Some empires evoked religious myths, as did the Egyptians and Mayans, while others, notably, the Chinese and British, based their rule on their material and cultural achievements—and the timē this conferred. For it to function, allies and subjects must see the hēgemonia they have conferred as continuing to be conducive to their interests. Rome provided guarantees of internal and external security, generally supported the worship of local gods, and offered citizenship and access to its markets to assuage those whom they had subdued by force. The Romans were so successful in legitimizing their rule that they could afford to rely on a relatively small military force, most of it deployed on the periphery of the empire, facing Parthians and Germanic tribes. During the first century of the common era, Rome ruled over a territory that stretched from Britain to Persia with an average of twenty-nine legions, each composed of approximately six thousand men.[113] The British accomplished a similar feat. At the height

[111] Russell Meiggs, *The Athenian Empire* (Oxford: Oxford University Press, 1972); Shalom Perlman, "Hegemony and *Arkhe* in Greece: Fourth-Century Views," in Richard Ned Lebow and Barry Strauss eds., *Hegemonic Rivalry: From Thucydides to the Nuclear Age* (Boulder, CO: Westview Press, 1991): 269–88.

[112] Michael Doyle, *Empires* (Ithaca, NY: Cornell University Press, 1986), 37–45; Barry S. Strauss, "The Art of Alliance and the Peloponnesian War," in Charles D. Hamilton and Peter Krentz, eds., *Polis and Polemos: Essays on Politics, War and History in Ancient Greece in Honor of Donald Kagan* (Claremont, CA: Regina, 1997), 127–40.

[113] See Graham Webster, *The Roman Imperial Army of the First and Second Centuries A.D.*

of their empire, at the end of the nineteenth century, they maintained colonies on six continents with an army of 250,000 men supplemented by local forces, mostly Indian.[114]

Thucydides's history of the Peloponnesian War can be read as a homily about the destructive nature of short-term framings of interest. Athens leaves the community that sustains its hēgemonia in pursuit of short-term gains and in the process undermines that community, loses its hēgemonia, and, ultimately, its empire. Plato conceives of wisdom as a form of self-control in which reason educates appetite and spirit alike to forsake short-term gains in terms of longer ones that will bring greater personal fulfillment. Aristotle describes maturity as the ability to pursue more meaningful, longer-term goals, and to achieve them more effectively by cooperative means.

Following the Greeks, we introduce a similar distinction. The question therefore is not whether China, the United States, or any other state is acting out of self-interest or altruism in supporting and defending global order. This is a meaningless binary. Rather, we should ask how leaders of these states have formulated their interests. Do they pursue short-term gains at the expense of their longer-term interests (e.g., extensive American borrowing abroad)? Or, do they act in recognition that their enduring material and security interests are best served through global order and the norms that sustain them? It is this longer-term, more enlightened and mature, understanding of interest that guides our analysis and policy recommendations.

The functions of agenda setting, custodianship, and sponsorship overlap in part. All confer advantages to states that perform them and to the community at large. They require consultation, bargaining, and consensus, but also reflect competition and jockeying for influence among powerful states. We neither suggest there is, nor should be, a division of labor in the global system. Decisions to perform these functions are driven by cultural conceptions, domestic politics, and consideration of national self-interest. Within limits, powerful actors generally attempt to exert what degrees of influence they can. This will depend in part on the nature of their resources but also the priorities they establish

---

(London: Black, 1969); Adrian Keith Goldsworthy, *The Roman Army at War, 100 BC—AD 200* (London: Oxford University Press, 1995); and Edward N. Luttwak, *The Grand Strategy of the Roman Empire: From the First Century A.D. to the Third* (Baltimore: Johns Hopkins University Press, 1976), especially 13–16.

[114] This figure is from 1899, on the eve of the Boer War. In 1880, the British managed with 186,000 men, another 65,000 troops in India, and much smaller forces elsewhere. See Corelli Barnett, *Britain and Her Army, 1509–1970* (New York: Morrow, 1970), especially 272–349; and Byron Farwell, *Mr. Kipling's Army* (New York: Norton, 1981), passim.

Chapter 3

///

Europe and Agenda Setting

Those cultures are dying. People are dying. They're being
overrun from overseas . . . and they have no response. They
have nothing to fight for. They have nothing to live for.
—Rick Santorum, remarks made at the Conservative
Pennsylvania Leadership Conference, 2006

The quote above from former senator and presidential hopeful Rick
Santorum reflects what many Americans think about Europe. Prominent politicians and realists consider the continent a kind of Lilliputian
theme park, run by self-important policy makers whose individual
homelands are weak and who have for decades scrambled for cover
under America's nuclear umbrella. These countries, many Americans
believe, are populated by lazy workers, overrun by impoverished immigrants, struggling to sustain overindulgent welfare, vacation, and
retirement programs, and vulnerable to radical Islamists. They lack the
material resources and willpower that once made some of them leading
powers and indomitable empires.

Many Europeans in turn consider Santorum, the Tea Party, and
Christian evangelicals the epitome of everything they find "a bit odd"
about America. In the words of one British journalist, Santorum is "a
walking, talking incarnation of the gulf between American and European politics" with his emphasis on military power, the stoking of culture wars, and lack of familiarity with, or even interest in, Europe.[1]
American neoconservative Robert Kagan, never one to mince words,
insists,

---

[1] Heather Horn, "Rick Santorum Represents Everything Europeans Find Weird about
America," *Atlantic*, 24 February 2012, http://www.theatlantic.com/international/archive
/2012/02/rick-santorum-represents-everything-europeans-find-weird-about-amer
ica/253553 (accessed 30 March 2012).

It is time to stop pretending that Europeans and Americans share a common view of the world, or even that they occupy the same world. On the all-important question of power—the efficacy of power, the morality of power, the desirability of power—American and European perspectives are diverging. Europe is turning away from power, or to put it a little differently, it is moving beyond power into a self-contained world of laws and rules and transnational negotiation and cooperation. It is entering a post-historical paradise of peace and relative prosperity, the realization of Kant's "Perpetual Peace." The United States, meanwhile, remains mired in history, exercising power in the anarchic Hobbesian world where international laws and rules are unreliable and where true security and the defense and promotion of a liberal order still depend on the possession and use of military might. . . . They agree on little and understand one another less and less. . . . When it comes to setting national priorities, determining threats, defining challenges, and fashioning and implementing foreign and defense policies, the United States and Europe have parted ways.[2]

For Republicans, one of the most annoying things about Europeans is their widespread approval of President Barack Obama. Republicans consider this scandalous and evidence that Obama is more like a European than an American.[3] During the 2012 presidential campaign, Republican John Sununu, former New Hampshire governor and White House chief of staff, caused a stir when he told the press, "I wish this president [Obama] would learn how to be an American."[4]

Some international relations scholars and lawyers make equally denigrating statements about Europeans.[5] It is a widespread certainty among realists within the academy and government that Europeans would behave just like Americans if they had the coercive capacity to do so. Europeans, in their view, must accept a hierarchical relationship in the absence of any capacity to form counterbalancing coalitions.[6] John Mearsheimer famously claimed that European countries were so

---

[2] Robert Kagan, "Power and Weakness," *Policy Review* 113 (2002), http://www.newamericancentury.org/kagan-20020520.htm (accessed 16 February 2011).

[3] Mitt Romney, quoted in E. J Dionne, "Obama Moving to Europe," *Real Clear Politics*, 16 January 2012, http://www.realclearpolitics.com/articles/2012/01/16/moving_obama_to_europe__112765.html (accessed 25 May 2012).

[4] Trip Gabiel and Peter Baker, "Romney and Obama Resume Economic Attacks, Despite a Few Diversions," *New York Times*, 17 July 2012, http://www.nytimes.com/2012/07/18/us/politics/romney-and-obama-resume-economic-attacks.html?_r=1 (accessed 17 July 2012).

[5] Philippe Sands, *Lawless World: America and the Making and Breaking of Global Rules from FDR's Atlantic Charter to George W. Bush's Illegal War* (New York: Viking, 2005).

[6] See William C. Wohlforth, "The Stability of a Unipolar World," *International Security* 24, no. 1 (1999): 5–41, especially 7–8.

weak in the aftermath of the Cold War that some of those countries without nuclear weapons should work to acquire them.[7]

Liberals tend to be less moralistic and more benign, and describe Europe as a pillar of "The West." G. John Ikenberry nevertheless concludes that they have, by necessity, ceded power and with it authority over agenda setting to their American counterparts. The United States sets the agenda, makes the rules, and even transgresses them, and Europe must live with the consequences.[8] Realists and liberals concur that, without power, Europeans are compelled to rely on American goodwill and its self-interest in protecting them.[9] They must seek standing in other ways and propagate discourses that justify these second-best choices.

American policy makers tend to see European weakness and dependence as more of a deliberate choice. The countries of the European Union (EU) channel resources to welfare, social problems, and environmental protection at the expense of their armed forces. US Republican and Democratic administrations have chided Europeans to increase, not cut, defense spending, and to take burden sharing more seriously.[10] European military expenditures fell by 2.8 percent in 2010; Europe was the only one of the world's regions in which there was a decline, and this was essentially unchanged in 2011.[11] The most muscular of European forces are the British, who are slowly integrating their military capacities with the French. When combined, Anglo-French expenditures represent less than 20 percent of the US defense outlay, and their armed forces are less technologically sophisticated and have little global power projection capability. If we combine the United Kingdom, France, Germany, and Italy, European defense spending is still less than a quarter of that of the United States. In every European country except Britain, the percentage of gross domestic product spent on defense has

[7] John J. Mearsheimer, "Back to the Future: Instability in Europe after the Cold War," *International Security* 15, no. 1 (1990): 5–56.

[8] Kagan, "Power and Weakness." For a liberal variant, see G. John Ikenberry, *Liberal Leviathan: The Origins, Crisis, and Transformation of the American World Order* (Princeton, NJ: Princeton University Press, 2011), and G. John Ikenberry, "America's Imperial Ambition," *Foreign Affairs* 81, no. 5 (2002): 44–60, especially 46, 49, 53.

[9] Doug Bandow, "The Continent without a Military," Cato Institute, 25 February 2013, http://www.cato.org/publications/commentary/continent-without-military (accessed 3 March 2013).

[10] US expenditure for 2010 was $698.281 billion. For 2011 it increased to $711.421 billion. "The SIPRI Military Expenditure Database," http://milexdata.sipri.org/result.php4 (accessed 2 February 2013).

[11] Stockholm International Peace Research Institute, "Appendix 4A: Military Expenditure Data, 2001–10," *SIPRI Yearbook*, http://www.sipriyearbook.org/view/9780199695522/sipri-9780199695522-div1-44.xml; http://www.sipri.org/yearbook/2012/04 (accessed 2 February 2013).

fallen since 2001. In the United States it had increased by over 50 percent according to that measure, and over 120 percent in absolute terms.[12]

Critics of Europe seize on this data to accuse Europeans of free riding.[13] European leaders and journalists respond that their level of spending is adequate to their level of perceived threat. Different levels of defense spending clearly encode different visions of the world and conceptions of self-interest. Off-scale American defense spending also reflects the political influence of American defense contractors. Not only neoconservatives and neorealists but also realists more generally assume there is a correct, objective approach to foreign and security policy—the national interest—and that it is a function of material capability and physical location.

In practice, conceptions of national interest inevitably reflect culture and history and the lessons they generate. Characterizations of the past and lessons based on them are sufficiently diverse to give rise to competing visions of a national interest and foreign policies based on it. In the United States, Hamiltonian and Jeffersonian visions of America's role in the world continue to have their partisans, who frequently come down on different sides of important foreign policy questions.[14] The kind of analysis offered by realists is rooted in one of many possible understandings of America's role in the world. It is based on a particular—and in our judgment, questionable—reading of American history and international relations.[15] To suppose it is appropriate to other states is not only parochial but involves a fundamental contradiction. Most realists, and many liberals, consider America and its role in the world to be unique. They attribute its enormous power to its political and economic system, which in turn reflects its values, traditional openness to immigrants, and new ideas and practices. Realism and liberalism both claim to be universally applicable paradigms but are rooted in particularistic understandings of the United States.

Critics of Europe err as well in clustering all European states together. Earlier we argued that it is inappropriate to treat countries like the United States and China as unitary actors. Their policies are neither

---

[12] Ibid.

[13] Ted Galen Carpenter and Marian L. Tupy, "US Defense Spending Subsidizes European Free-Riding Welfare States," *Daily Caller*, 12 July 2010, http://www.cato.org/publications/commentary/us-defense-spending-subsidizes-european-freeriding-welfare-states (accessed 2 February 2013); "Gates Assails NATO over Willingness to Share Costs," *International Herald Tribune*, 11–12 June 2011; Stephen M. Walt, "Why Bob Gates Needs a Course in IR Theory," *Economist*, 25 February 2010, http://walt.foreignpolicy.com/posts/2010/02/25/can_you_say_free_rider_problem (accessed 2 February 2010).

[14] Hans J. Morgenthau, *The Purpose of American Politics* (New York: Knopf, 1960).

[15] John J. Mearsheimer, *The Tragedy of Great Power Politics* (New York: Norton, 2001).

consistent nor coherent because they are the product of input from constituencies with diverse interests and goals. Changes in foreign policy often reflect changes in the balance of power among these actors and in their positions. To complicate matters further, central governments and foreign policy bureaucracies can pursue conflicting policies. We nevertheless argued with regard to the United States—and will do so in chapter 4 with China—that foreign policy elites in countries adhere to a range of nationally specific visions of their country's role in the world and how it should be achieved or maintained. These visions are reflected in academic and journalistic discourses, and there is usually some interplay between them and policy, recognizing that there are often intense controversies about how they apply to particular problems or cases.

China and the United States are individual countries with a central government charged with making foreign policies. Europe, by contrast, is a region that has close to fifty independent states and several would-be states. Twenty-eight of these political units belong to the European Union, which also attempts to have a foreign policy, albeit one that rests on a consensus among its members. There are other European groupings, most notably Scandinavia, whose countries share many features of a distinct and older foreign policy vision. The leading countries of the EU—among them Germany, France, and Italy—have their own foreign policy traditions, as has the somewhat more peripheral United Kingdom. We cannot speak of Europe, or a single European conception of European self-interest.

This national diversity generates diverse policy preferences. Eurobarometer public opinion surveys consistently reveal that public opinion within the EU is generally more likely to vary with country of residence, as opposed to other sociological or demographic factors. Different countries have different public priorities and policy preferences toward them. In 2010, two years into the global economic crisis, majorities in the EU's poorer countries were more concerned about inflation, a deteriorating economic situation, and unemployment. They were deeply pessimistic about the future. In several other, generally richer, countries the biggest priority was health care. Majorities in some countries worry more about public debt, others about terrorism.[16]

There is a burgeoning literature that characterizes the European Union, and thus Europe itself, as somehow more ethical than other regions, a claim given credence by the awarding of the Nobel Peace Prize to the EU in 2012. We evaluate this literature toward the end of this chapter, but are skeptical of such claims. Evidence that neither Europe-

---

[16] "Public Opinion in the European Union," *Eurobarometer* 74 (2011): 15.

ans nor the EU itself are more ethical than others is offered by the considerable variation in attitudes toward immigrants, as we discuss later in this chapter.[17] Nationalism remains evident across Europe, and right-wing parties have grown in strength as a result of the global financial crisis that devastated many European economies. These parties have performed at historic levels in France and Greece and brought down the government in the Netherlands. In Hungary, far-right groups have been powerful enough to assume power and institute antidemocratic reforms. Dissatisfaction in general remains high in Europe, and by May 2011, voters had turned eleven European governments out of office. Thus, notions of a "gentler, kinder Europe," or of a uniform one, can easily be exaggerated and at times seem downright misplaced. There are contending visions of what Europe is and should become that dictate different approaches to neighboring countries and the rest of the world.

Europe's Foreign Policy Consensus

Yet despite the remarkable national and cultural diversity of Europe, there is a dominant foreign policy perspective when it comes to Europe's role in the world and the means by which the EU or its members gain and exercise influence. Arguably, there is more of a consensus on these issues than there is in the United States. If American visions of the world generally rest on competing understandings of what made America, the European consensus is a response to two wars that came close to destroying the continent's culture and wealth and killed large numbers of its people.

The rejection of American-style realism is nearly universal from Portugal to the Russian border. The principal exception is the right wing of the British Conservative Party.[18] Europeans have developed an alternate approach to foreign policy that emphasizes deliberation, compromise, consensus, and diplomacy over the threat or use of force. This orientation should not be regarded as a second-best alternative dictated by a relative lack of material wealth. Nor is it altruistic. It is a considered response to the experience and seeming lessons of two world wars. European states started both conflicts, and Europe, not North America,

---

[17] Ariane Chebel d'Appollonia, *Frontiers of Fear* (Ithaca, NY: Cornell University Press, 2012), 28, table 1.

[18] Some realists concur. See Stephen Van Evera, "Primed for Peace: Europe after the Cold War," *International Security* 15, no. 3 (1990–91): 7–57, especially 18–29.

was their principal battleground. Some forty million European combatants and civilians died in these wars.

European approaches to foreign policy start from the assumption that the use of force is generally counterproductive and is therefore an instrument of the last resort. It can only be used effectively for humanitarian purposes, and then only with the backing of appropriate regional and international organizations. European policy makers recognize the importance of power, but also the self-restraints that must be put on its use if national and common interests are to be served. More than their American counterparts, they see the interests of their countries intimately connected to those of the wider European, if not global, communities while not assuming, unlike their US counterparts, that they have a right to lead.

Europeans understand the links between material power and political influence differently from their American counterparts. Many Europeans see an inverse relationship between power politics and influence. To them, this is evident in their rise in influence that accompanied Western Europe's rejection of power politics.[19] These countries have gained respect and legitimacy, regionally and globally. European approaches to foreign policy can be understood in terms of our distinction between *archē* and *hēgemonia*. Many in the United States are fixated on archē, which frames goals unilaterally and relies more on coercion than persuasion to achieve them. Such an approach, we have argued, has become increasingly costly and ineffective. European policy makers, by contrast, seek ends that are widely understood to be in the general interest of the region, if not of the international community. The EU rarely resorts to bribes or threats, but seeks consensus by means of a process of compromise and persuasion that bemuses many Americans.[20] Success brings with it a disposition to follow Europe's lead even over disputable issues.

No country better illustrates the benefits of this strategy than Germany. It was historically feared by its neighbors for its hegemonic aspirations and use of coercion and brute force toward this end. The king-

[19] Andrei S. Markovits and Simon Reich, *The German Predicament: Memory and Power in the New Europe* (Ithaca, NY: Cornell University Press, 1997).

[20] Ian Manners, "The Normative Ethics of the European Union," *International Affairs* 84, no. 1 (2008): 45–60; Richard G. Whitman, "Norms, Power and Europe: A New Agenda for the Study of the EU and International Relations," in Richard Whitman, ed., *Normative Power Europe: Empirical and Theoretical Perspectives* (Basingstoke, England: Palgrave, 2011), 1–24. For a realist critique, see Adrian Hyde-Price, " 'Normative' Power Europe: A Realist Critique," *Journal of European Public Policy* 13, no. 2 (2006): 217–34; and Adrian Hyde-Price, "A 'Tragic Actor'? A Realist Perspective on Ethical Power Europe," *International Affairs* 84, no. 1 (2008): 29–44.

dom of Prussia and the German Empire and the Nazi regime engendered fear and enmity in Europe and beyond. The Federal Republic of Germany (FRG) is almost universally regarded as nonthreatening and legitimate, a view repeatedly reflected in global public surveys.[21] The FRG represents a sharp break with the German past; it has demonstrated a sustained commitment to democracy, civil liberties, and regulated liberal capitalism at home, and to the European project in its foreign policy. It steadfastly adheres to its principles of limited military engagement, the promotion of human rights, and a foreign policy conducted through political and cultural diplomacy and economic investment and assistance. It has refused to participate in military missions, such as in Libya, led by its European neighbors and allies. Its commitment to work through regional and multilateral institutions has made Germany more influential today than at any time in its past. It is widely regarded as a viable model for other countries, and a 2013 poll proclaimed it to be the most popular country in the world.[22]

The German strategy has made others more receptive to its policy preferences. Cypriots, Greeks, Irish, and Portuguese have been subject to the strictures of German-advocated financial austerity even as they were widely disliked by large portions of the population in each country, largely because they were pursued through regional mechanisms. These policies are the product of persuasion, negotiation, and bargaining rather than being imposed unilaterally. While swathes of local populations disliked both the policies and the Germans in particular for their role, they did not criticize the deliberative process of decision making itself.

Germany is not alone. Other European states, and the EU, have become more insistent on their values and norms as they have become more successful and influential. Chief among these norms is the refusal to use force for anything other than humanitarian purposes, and generally only when it is authorized by relevant regional or international organizations. This norm reflects one understanding of the "just war" doctrine. The European consensus also finds expression, although by no means exclusively, in a preference for agenda setting. Agenda setting is a complex process. It requires an effective capacity to frame debates about policy issues in terms of the values at stake, determines who participates in deliberations and the nature of the deliberative process, and influences the range of options considered legitimate.

---

[21] "Europe Less, China More Popular in global BBC poll," 11 May 2012, http://www .bbc.co.uk/news/world-18038304 (accessed 25 May 2012); European Commission, "Public Opinion," http://ec.europa.eu/public_opinion/index_en.htm (accessed 23 July 2012).

[22] Andrei S. Markovits and Simon Reich, *The German Predicament*; "BBC Poll: Germany the Most Popular Country in the World," 23 May 2013, http://www.bbc.co.uk/news /world-europe-22624104 (accessed 29 May 2013).

Constructivists and many other students of politics understand that "biggest" or "most powerful" does not necessarily mean "dominant."[23] Constructivists are not alone in recognizing agenda setting as a competitive process in which legitimacy helps actors frame an issue and get it on the agenda. Successful actors push issues of interest to others as well as themselves, and advocate policies consistent with shared values to build a consensus. Agenda setting benefits from institutionalization. This can take the form of protocols, codes, laws, or—in its most powerful manifestation—formal organizations.[24]

A substantial literature has developed on agenda setting in Europe. It analyzes efforts by nongovernmental organizations (NGOs), corporations, individual states, and the EU to pursue consensual policy agreements through multilateral and regional forums.[25] The substantive focus of this research has been on what realists would regard as "soft" issues such as human rights, regulatory standards, and the environment.[26] Over time, however, European efforts at agenda setting have come to encompass broader and important economic and security issues. These include problems of civilian protection, humanitarian intervention, and postwar state building.

As we mentioned in chapter 2, among the most ardent supporters of the formal adoption of the "responsibility to protect" doctrine by the UN have been European governments. The doctrine's most noted campaign advocate, former Australian foreign minister Gareth Evans, was head of the Brussels-based International Crisis Group when he spearheaded the UN campaign to get its precepts adopted as UN policy.[27]

---

[23] See Richard Ned Lebow, *A Cultural Theory of International Relations* (Cambridge: Cambridge University Press, 2008), chap. 9.

[24] See Simon Reich, *Global Norms, American Sponsorship and the Emerging Pattern of World Politics* (Basingstoke: Palgrave, 2010), 50–62.

[25] Ian Manners, "Normative Power Europe: A Contradiction in Terms?" *JCMS: Journal of Common Market Studies* 40, no. 2 (2002): 235–58; Manners, "The Normative Ethics of the European Union"; Whitman, "Norms, Power and Europe."

[26] Arlo Poletti and Daniela Sicurelli, "The EU as Promoter of Environmental Norms in the Doha Round," *West European Politics* 35, no. 4 (2012): 911–32; Richard Youngs, "Normative Dynamics and Strategic Interests in the EU's External Identity," *JCMS: Journal of Common Market Studies* 42, no. 2 (2004): 415–35; Charles Parker, and Christer Karlsson, "Climate Change and the European Union's Leadership Moment: An Inconvenient Truth?" *JCMS: Journal of Common Market Studies* 48, no. 4 (2010): 923–43; Richard Black, "US Criticized on 2C Climate 'Flexibility' Call," 7 August 2012, http://www.bbc.co.uk/news/science-environment-19161799 (accessed 17 August 2012). Karen E. Smith, "The Limits of Proactive Cosmopolitanism: The EU and Burma, Cuba and Zimbabwe," in Ole Elgström and Michael Smith, eds., *The European Union's Roles in International Politics: Concepts and Analysis* (Abingdon, England: Routledge, 2006), 155–71; Karen E. Smith, "Speaking with One Voice? European Union Co-ordination on Human Rights Issues at the United Nations," *JCMS: Journal of Common Market Studies* 44, no. 1 (2006): 113–37.

[27] Gareth Evans and Mohamed Sahnoun, *The Responsibility to Protect: A Report by the*

R2P, as the doctrine became known, justifies multilateral military intervention when states fail to guarantee the physical safety and human rights of their citizens. Although never formally enshrined as UN policy, R2P has been much debated and endorsed there and, albeit informally, was the justification for multilateral intervention in Libya. We discuss this intervention in chapter 5. While not the only advocates of R2P, the Europeans nevertheless played an invaluable role in its promotion.

Other examples of European agenda setting include evolving labor and environmental standards for corporations, anticorruption in government contracts, and campaigns for the preservation of rare wildlife.[28] These several initiatives and R2P balance military and market-based considerations with social, environmental, or human rights commitments. In this section, we examine two cases. The first is the institutionalization of globalization. It challenges the core liberal claim that the United States has engineered a global capitalist system, and that Europeans have ceded power to the Americans. We show how Europeans were able to subvert the American project of bilateral, market-driven, and ad-hoc globalization and replace it with a more formalized, multilateral, and rule-driven structure.

Our second case, the global prohibition of landmines, looks at how Europeans limited the use of one of the most widely used twentieth-century armaments. The overwhelming majority of states signed and do adhere to this treaty. These states voluntarily gave up their right to use a cheap and useful military instrument in the knowledge that some other states might not make a comparable commitment and so they might find themselves at a military disadvantage. The treaty has been effective in another sense; it influenced the behavior of some countries that did not sign it, notably the United States. Treaty advocates have rightly hailed it as a great success and harbinger of future limitations on weapons. The unilateral decision by many states to abandon the use of a cheap and plentiful armament poses a challenge to realist theory.

GLOBALIZATION

American academics have portrayed globalization as a process shaped by the United States to serve its interests. Many journalists and writers

International Commission of Intervention and State Sovereignty (Ottawa: International Development Research Center, 2001). http://www.dfait-maeci.gc.ca/iciss-ciise/pdf/Commission-Report.pdf (accessed 3 July 2012).

[28] Simon Reich, "When Firms Behave 'Responsibly,' Are the Roots National or Global?" *International Social Science Journal* 57, no. 3 (2005): 289–308.

have equated globalization with Americanization. The reality is different and more complex. Globalization has taken two distinct paths. The first is structured by an American vision of market liberalization. It is corporate driven with a few key bilateral agreements, limited planning, and an underlying premise that economic "might makes right." The second track is the European approach that finds expression in multilateral agreements and more institutionalized forms of globalization. It gives a key role to international organizations, and is more sensitive to the social as well as economics consequences of globalization. In contrast to the American neoliberal theories that profits are ultimately good for everyone because prosperity will trickle down, the European approach is rooted in a more egalitarian theory of justice.[29]

This latter form of managed globalization, articulated and driven by European actors, eventually prevailed. Its success sharply contradicts liberal claims that American ideas and power, both hard and soft, shaped globalization. Liberals describe the world as dominated by a market-driven, laissez-faire—and thus largely unregulated—structure set in motion by Americans for mutual benefit.[30] They deny that there is, or needs to be, any authoritative "hand" managing the global economy.[31] It is what Ikenberry refers to as "an open and loosely rule-based system."[32]

In this narrative, liberal principles were encapsulated in the Bretton Woods system. They were later consolidated by the policies of the administrations of US president Ronald Reagan and UK prime minister Margaret Thatcher; the collapse of the Soviet Union; and the opening up of Russian and East European markets through "shock therapy" and Asia through the economic crisis of 1997. Liberals insist on emphasizing the importance and beneficial effects of American rule building through institutions. But the initial effect was often the converse: institutions, to the extent that they served US interests, really just reinforced the fluid-

[29] Rawi Abdelal and Sophie Meunier, "Managed Globalization: Doctrine, Practice and Promise," *Journal of European Public Policy* 17, no. 3 (2010): 350–67.

[30] John Williamson, ed., *Latin American Adjustment: How Much Has Happened?* (Washington DC: Institute for International Economics, 1990); Douglas C. North, *Structure and Change in Economic History* (New York: Norton, 1981); Douglas C. North and Robert Thomas, *The Rise of the Western World: A New Economic History* (New York: Cambridge University Press, 1973); Robert O. Keohane, *After Hegemony: Cooperation and Discord in the Modern World* (Princeton, NJ: Princeton University Press, 1984).

[31] Stephen D. Krasner, "Structural Causes and Regime Consequences: Regimes as Intervening Variables," in Stephen D. Krasner, ed., *International Regimes* (Ithaca, NY: Cornell University Press, 1983).

[32] G. John Ikenberry, "A World of Our Making," *Democracy: A Journal of Ideas* 21 (2011), http://www.democracyjournal.org/21/a-world-of-our-making-1.php?page=all (accessed 9 July 2012).

ity of markets and lack of rules. It is akin to when US presidents appoint heads of departments with the intent of them doing nothing or dismantling authoritative regulatory structures, as Ronald Reagan did with the Department of the Interior and George W. Bush did with the Food and Drug Administration. As Rawi Abdelal and Sophie Meunier note,

> According to conventional wisdom, globalization occurred because the United States and United Kingdom embraced ad hoc globalization during the early 1960s. Markets for goods and capital became international again, the first era of internationalization having ended during the interwar years. At various moments, American and British policy-makers adopted unilateral action, bilateral pressure, and even multilateral negotiations to foster this liberalization. Major corporations took advantage of this new-found liberalization by exporting and outsourcing, and in so doing rein-forced the process of globalization. Thanks to economic and technological changes, globalization is seen as an ineluctable tidal wave crushing borders without which national policy initiatives became impotent.[33]

The United States, according to the liberal version of the story, was thus able to effectively endorse its benign version of hegemony, one that promoted free market capitalism and liberal democracy as a bulwark against communism.[34] One set of critics of the liberal position, such as former French foreign minister Hubert Védrine, who famously characterized the United States as a "hyperpower," focused on the US capacity to bully other states in order to create large-scale ad-hoc deals.[35] A second group has focused more on the US capacity to create global institutions, such as the International Monetary Fund and the World Bank, that serve America's interests. American-trained economists mostly run these institutions,[36] with the remaining minority being sympathetic to US preferences.[37] Still, what these critics share with liberals is a belief

---

[33] Ibid.

[34] "To Paris, US Looks Like a 'Hyperpower,' " *New York Times*, 5 February 1999, http://www.nytimes.com/1999/02/05/news/05iht-france.t_0.html (accessed 9 July 2012).

[35] Hubert Védrine, *France in an Age of Globalization* (Washington DC: Brookings Institution Press, 2001); Fred Block, *The Origins of International Economic Disorder: A Study of United States International Monetary Policy from World War II to the Present* (Berkeley and Los Angeles: University of California Press, 1977); Fred Block, "Controlling Global Finance," *World Policy Journal* 13, no. 3 (1996): 24–34; Susan Strange, *Mad Money: When Markets Outgrow Governments* (Ann Arbor: University of Michigan Press, 1998).

[36] See Catherine Weaver, "The World's Bank and the Bank's World: Towards a Gross Anatomy of the World Bank," paper presented at the Annual Conference of the International Studies Association, 24 March 2006, San Diego, 11–12.

[37] Robert H. Wade, "US Hegemony and the World Bank: The Fight over People and Ideas," *Review of International Political Economy* 9, no. 2 (2002): 215–43; Robert H. Wade, "The US Role in the Long Asian Crisis of 1990–2000," in Arvid Lukauskis and Francisco L. Batista-Rivera, eds., *The Political Economy of the East Asian Crisis and its Aftermath: Tigers in Distress* (Cheltenham, England: Edward Elgar, 2001), 195–226; Ngaire Woods, "The

that, for better or worse, the United States has dominated a market-driven process.

Yet a very different narrative challenges this broad characterization of a conventional, unregulated, and only loosely managed postwar system. In this alternative, Europeans have played a guiding role as agenda setters in the formation of a managed global economy. This managed system has two thrusts: first, a *top-down* component largely imposed by political and bureaucratic elites at the global level through authoritative international organizations. Second, a *bottom-up* initiative delineating corporate acceptable behavior driven by NGOs and socially conscious firms.

Abdelal and Meunier focus on the top-down aspect, specifically on the successful efforts of European policy makers to arrest the process of American-style ad-hoc globalization away from the United States. They diverted it, they suggest, into a process of European-driven (particularly French-driven) "managed globalization."[38] Ad-hoc globalization was characterized by a tendency to ignore "the need to legitimate the processes of cross-border market integration."[39] The American version "brought liberalization without organizing, or even supervising, markets."[40] It produces a kind of Thrasymachean justice, the will of the stronger without recourse to elements of legitimacy.

Managed globalization shares ad-hoc globalization's goal of liberalization but has significantly different philosophical foundations, forms of authority, and social and economic implications. In this version, globalization is steered by managers, politicians, and bureaucrats creating codified rules and enforced by empowered institutions, not by deregulation and the elimination of institutional constraints.[41] There is little room for bilateral deals in which American interests predominate. Exemplified by the way the EU functions, the rule of law is paramount, constraining the behavior of even the most powerful actors, and decisions are negotiated, the product of deliberation that is more likely to yield socially acceptable outcomes.[42]

But how were Europeans able to refine its character away from the US version? Not surprisingly, the process was incremental. Dating from

---

United States and the International Financial Institutions: Power and Influence Within the World Bank and the IMF," in Rosemary Foot, Neil MacFarlane, and Michael Mastanduno, eds., *US Hegemony and International Organizations* (New York: Oxford University Press, 2003), 92–114; Ngaire Woods, *The Globalizers: the IMF, the World Bank and Their Borrowers* (Ithaca, NY: Cornell University Press, 2006); Joseph Stiglitz, *Globalization and Its Discontents* (New York: Norton, 2001).

[38] Abdelal and Meunier, "Managed Globalization."
[39] Ibid., 350.
[40] Ibid., 351.
[41] Ibid., 352.
[42] Ibid., 352–53.

the 1980s, a series of appointments of (largely) French bureaucrats—most of whom had served or were linked to the administration of François Mitterrand—to senior positions in international organizations proved critical according to Abdelal and Meunier. Pascal Lamy became the head of the World Trade Organization (WTO), Michael Camdessus became the managing director of the International Monetary Fund (IMF), and Henri Chavranski chaired the influential Committee on Capital Movements and Invisible Transactions of the Organisation for Economic Co-operation and Development (OECD).

All favored the liberalization of the global economy. Yet they also vocally advocated the development of global rules for a global economy, cognizant of the importance of the antiglobalization protests dating from the late 1980s onward. As a first stage, these men advocated strengthening a rule-based system, and its capacities for enforcement, within the European Commission. They harnessed and managed neoliberalism for the purposes of market-based integration to make it compatible with a more just social democratic model of society.[43] Yet the doctrine of managed globalization grew far beyond its French roots to create a European consensus position. The Europeans embraced supranational rules and jurisdictions that gave bureaucracies supervisory and regulatory responsibilities for the long-term sustainability of market practices.[44]

In practice, this meant creating strong institutions built on the basic supposition that global markets needed to be authoritatively managed by global institutions enforcing multilateral agreements. The WTO, set in up 1995, provides a good example of how this process evolved in practice. There the EU "strongly supported clear rules for settling trade-related disputes." And this meant "codifying rules for reporting violations, adjudicating disputes, and implementing resolutions to facilitate trade liberalization."[45] These rules would be equitably applied to both the strong and the weak. Strategically, the Europeans recognized that building a successful coalition in favor of this agenda entailed broadening the WTO's membership and thus diluting US influence. So, despite American misgivings about its potential loss of sovereignty and about the admission of a variety of countries, including both China and Russia, the authority of the organization has grown as its numbers have consistently expanded to the level of 158 members by 2013.

The European strategy has worked: there has been a shift toward a greater centralized, institutionalized, and thus a rule-driven system of

[43] Ibid., 355.
[44] Ibid., 355–56.
[45] Ibid., 357.

trade. The WTO is the one international agency that oversees the rules of international trade, policing free trade agreements, and settling trade disputes between governments and organizes trade negotiations. Its decisions are absolute and every member must abide by them; trade sanctions are imposed against countries that breach the rules.[46] Invariably, this new form of globalization suffers from a series of problems. A labored negotiation process has led to paralysis, epitomized by the failure of the Doha Round—to the consternation of many Americans. But there is plentiful evidence that the rules of trade have evolved and markets for trade have become increasingly regulated.

The equitable and effective application of the WTO's rules, illustrating the capacity of global institutions to manage even the most powerful states, is epitomized by its treatment of the United States itself. While the United States won its first two cases under the organization's dispute-settlement mechanism, it then lost some high-profile ones. Among the most significant was the case of the steel tariff dispute under the George W. Bush administration in 2002–3.

Bush, unlike several of his predecessors, was an avowed critic of multilateral institutions. This hostility intensified in the aftermath of the UN's rebuff of his administration's request for the organization's approval for the invasion of Iraq. So it was no major surprise when, in March 2002, the Bush administration snubbed the WTO and unilaterally replaced a 1 percent tariff on imported steel with tariffs of between 8 and 30 percent. These new tariffs were designed to remain in effect for three years; they were justified by the United States, citing a purported surge in subsidized foreign steel imports, but were in fact designed to gain political support for the administration in a number of key electoral states. North American Free Trade Agreement members and several other strategic partners were exempted from these tariffs, making the impact all the more pointed for Brazilian, Chinese, Japanese, Korean, Taiwanese, and major European producers. The EU responded that it would impose retaliatory tariffs, thus risking a trade war, and a claim was filed against the United States with the Dispute Settlement Body of the WTO supported by steel producers from all these countries.

The WTO ruled against the US tariffs in November 2003, challenging the US claim of an import surge. Contrary figures in fact verified that steel imports had actually declined. The WTO's Dispute Board authorized the largest ever penalty to be imposed against a WTO member state to date, over $2 billion, and the EU threatened to expand its tariffs against US products in support of the WTO ruling. In the face of mount-

[46] "Profile: World Trade Organization," 15 February 2012, http://news.bbc.co.uk/2/hi/europe/country_profiles/2429503.stm (accessed 8 August 2012).

ing pressure, the Bush administration withdrew the tariff, signaling a victory for the WTO against a hitherto vociferous and powerful opponent with key interests at stake. The victory of the WTO over the United States signaled an important milestone in European efforts to ensure that global rules would drive trade practices.

Trade, however, is not the only sector in which international organizations attempted such reforms. The US may have sponsored the creation of international financial institutions like the International Monetary Fund and The World Bank in the postwar period. But in their formation it ensured itself a position within both that allowed it to dictate market-driven solutions in the first five decades of their existence.[47] This was what was commonly dubbed the Washington Consensus—an elixir of neoliberal tax, exchange rate, liberalization, and privatization policies that its critics suggested served the interests of the US Treasury Department.[48]

After the appointment of James Wolfensohn as the World Bank's president in 1995, however, the organization began reconstituting itself to be more rule-driven and equitable in addressing the needs of both the powerful and the powerless in its aid policies.[49] Similarly, the IMF attempted to shake off the mantle of being exclusively driven by neoliberal policies. Finally, a new series of corporate initiatives have attempted to create authority and order out of market chaos—all in the name of promoting "the human face of capitalism."

Reflecting this trend has been the advances made in the broad set of bottom-up activities clustered under the umbrella of "corporate social responsibility" (CSR), an area in which European corporations, often in collaboration with NGOs, have been very active. Not surprisingly, they would rather steer clear of laws and regulations that limit their own behavior. They prefer voluntary agreements based on principles and norms. Such agreements are best reflected in a corporation's code of conduct—a firm's formal statement of principles and practices. Interestingly, these codes operate in an area in which firms, states, shareholders, NGOs, and international organizations intersect around a variety of noneconomic issues with significant economic and social implications,

[47] Robert H. Wade, "The Invisible Hand of the American Empire," *Ethics and International Affairs* 17, no. 2 (2003): 77–88.

[48] The term *Washington Consensus* is commonly first attributed to John Williamson in his 1989 report "What Washington Means by Policy Reform," in John Williamson, ed., *Latin American Readjustment: How Much Has Happened?* (Washington DC: Peterson Institute for International Economics, 1990), http://www.iie.com/publications/papers/paper.cfm?researchid=486 (accessed 5 June 2013).

[49] James D. Wolfensohn, "Foreword," in *World Development Report 2000–2001: Attacking Poverty* (New York, Oxford University Press, 2000), v–vii.

including environmental, labor, and employment equality standards. In examining CSR's growth and pattern of development, however, what becomes clear is that it is not only European politicians and bureaucrats who prefer managed globalization in contrast to their American counterparts. European corporations clearly do as well.

Dating from the 1970s, codes are not legally binding. But they nevertheless conform to the general notion of managed globalization: codes create rules, albeit informal ones, about how to manage the relationship between market competition and noneconomic factors. Furthermore, strictures and penalties do exist for their abrogation; once published, codes provide a benchmark against which various stakeholders—governments, NGOs, and intergovernmental organizations as well as the social media—can assess a firm's behavior. Transgression has its costs: to claim to be a 'green corporation' and then to be characterized as a major polluter, for example, can be extremely damaging in terms of both publicity and sales (which can translate into the price of a firm's shares).

So while codes are voluntary, new communication technologies that can inform consumers about corporate behavior enhance the power of those employing naming and shaming strategies. CSR, and codes in particular, are therefore another way to manage globalization, a socially constructed counterpart to the formal rules and procedures imposed from above by global organizations. When powerful, these self-imposed norms can help manage the behavior of firms, the same way formal organizations can manage the behavior of states.

In the last two decades, European corporations, aided, abetted, and cajoled by the EU, national governments, and NGOs, have been at the forefront of instituting wide-ranging norms to which firms abide. Beyond simple trade issues, European corporations have worked to extend the codes, and their CSR activities more generally, into issues relating to environment sustainability, cultural protection, workplace employment, and trading conditions.[50] They and the EU have been major agenda setters in promoting socially and environmentally conscious corporate behavior. This is not purely altruistic: firms have come under significant pressure to demonstrate their credentials as 'good citizens'—a result of a variety of tactics employed largely by European NGOs and states, often discussed in venues provided by intergovernmental organizations. These practices have been exported, reflected in the evolving content of corporate codes of conduct.

The net overall effect has been that many of the world's largest firms have palpably converged toward the European position on CSR. In

---

[50] Abdelal and Meunier, "Managed Globalization."

2002, for example, there were distinct differences among American, European, and Asian corporate views about the importance, structure, substance, and application of corporate codes. Codes were then largely distinguished by region rather than, for example, by economic sector. European corporate codes were the most expansive and progressive. They referenced global norms and emphasized the importance of global protocols and conventions such as the Universal Declaration of Human Rights, the International Labor Organization (ILO) Convention, OECD Guidelines, and the UN Global Compact. European codes were most wide-ranging in their definition of the 'stakeholder,' recognizing the needs of shareholders, clients, employees, suppliers, and the general community. Substantively, Europeans were most concerned with institutions that uphold the rule of law. Their firms also consistently ranked higher on a series of issues regarding environmental sustainability than American or Asian firms.

In contrast, American corporate codes at that time were largely long, legalistic documents. They overwhelmingly focused on two issues, shareholder rights and protection from discrimination, because they are enshrined in domestic legislation. Most US firms, for example, had a code of ethics because it was mandated by the Sarbanes-Oxley Act of 2002.[51] Equal opportunity legislation was also a driver of the content of codes, most codes mentioning elements of race, gender, religion, national origin, age, or disability. Few US codes cited any non-American guidelines, and none then cited the UN's Universal Declaration or the OECD Guidelines. Not surprisingly, American corporations were marginally more likely to discuss anticorruption measures than were their European counterparts—given the primacy the issue was accorded in Sarbanes-Oxley. Conversely, American corporations were less likely then European firms to address concerns about the importance of the rule of law, or of abiding by local laws where they had investments overseas—because these elements were not emphasized in the same legislation.

Asian corporations (then overwhelmingly Japanese and Korean firms) generally substantially differed in all categories in 2002. They were less likely to have codes than corporations in the other two regions; if they had codes, they were succinct and thus less detailed. They had few references to global agreements or stakeholders. They avoided discussing the rule of law; the issues of corruption, labor rights, and nondiscrimination; and the importance of abiding by domestic legislation in foreign countries. The one area that they did emphasize more

---

[51] "Final Rule: Disclosure Required by Sections 406 and 407 of the Sarbanes-Oxley Act of 2002," http://www.sec.gov/rules/final/33-8177.htm (accessed 10 July 2012).

than their counterparts was environmental resources and energy—not surprising given that Japan and Korea suffer from a deficit of both.[52] In sum, there was little evidence that the principles associated with corporate social responsibility had made any inroads in Asia at all.

Despite a plethora of claims about the adaptive abilities and supposed cosmopolitan cultures of global corporations, there was no evidence of the emergence of a best-practice model in managing their social and environmental conduct. Things, however, looked very different a decade later when *not* having expansive, progressive codes and *not* ascribing to the language of global protocols has become more the exception than the convention for corporations originating from OECD states.

In short, codes from firms across the OECD today look more like those of European firms a decade ago. The EU has played a central role in this development as an agenda setter, dating from its visionary Green Paper of 2001 that laid out its CSR agenda and strategy. It is worth quoting at length:

> By stating their social responsibility and voluntarily taking on commitments which go beyond common regulatory and conventional requirements, which they would have to respect in any case, companies endeavor to raise the standards of social development, environmental protection and respect of fundamental rights and embrace an open governance, reconciling interests of various stakeholders in and overall approach of quality and sustainability . . . This action leads to the development of new partnerships and new spheres for existing relationships within the company regarding social dialogue, skills acquisition, equal opportunities, anticipation and management of change, at the local or national level with reference to the reinforcement of economic and social cohesion and health protection, and more generally on a global level, concerning environmental protection and respect of fundamental rights.[53]

The EU's expressed goal was to develop a strategy to promote these concepts at the European and global levels, and a policy framework in which business would take a proactive role. It sought to engender innovative practices, enhance transparency, and increase the reliability of evaluation and validation in ways consistent with international initiatives such as the UN Global Compact (2000), the ILO's Tripartite Declaration of Principles concerning Multinational Enterprises and Social

[52] Reich, "When Firms Behave 'Responsibly,' Are the Roots National or Global?"

[53] Commission of the European Communities, "Promoting a European Framework for Corporate Social Responsibility," 18 July 2001, COM (2001) 366 final, http://eur-lex.europa.eu/LexUriServ/site/en/com/2001/com2001_0366en01.pdf (accessed 11 July 2012).

Policy (1977/2000), and the OECD Guidelines for Multinational Enterprises (2000).[54]

So began the EU's very public global campaign seeking corporate support for these protocols. By 2006, the commission published a new policy position paper strongly supporting a business-led initiative, the European Alliance for CSR. It identified eight priority areas for EU action, including the development of regional and global support for these principles.

The EU's strategy of persuading, imploring, and cajoling its own firms, ably assisted by NGOs in Brussels, proved a remarkable success. The number of EU enterprises that signed up to the ten CSR principles of the UN Global Compact, for example, rose to over 1,900 by 2011. But there were other benchmarks of its influence: The number of organizations with sites registered under the Environmental Management and Audit Scheme, for example, increased from 3,300 to over 4,600 between 2006 and 2011. The number of EU companies signing transnational company agreements with global or European workers' organizations, covering issues such as labor standards, increased from 79 to 140 in the same period. Finally, the number of European enterprises publishing sustainability reports rose from 270 to over 850 in these five years, according to the guidelines of the Global Reporting Initiative. The influence of the EU's strategy is just as evident at the national level. By 2011, fifteen European countries had developed domestic policy frameworks designed to promote CSR.

The 2001 Green Paper also tangibly influenced the agenda of global organizations. By 2011, the updated OECD Guidelines for Multinational Enterprises, the ten principles of the United Nations Global Compact, the ISO 26000 Guidance Standard on Social Responsibility, the ILO Tripartite Declaration of Principles concerning Multinational Enterprises and Social Policy, and the UN Guiding Principles on Business and Human Rights *all* included the values and key points espoused in the original paper.

This process of convergence is also reflected in the nationality of the signatures to the UN Global Compact. It is the most comprehensive and important statement about how firms can best manage the effects of globalization, with its focus on social justice, environmental sustainability, fair labor practices, and corporate transparency. By 2012, it listed over eight thousand participants from 135 countries among its members.[55] Four hundred sixty-nine American organizations had formally

---

[54] Ibid.
[55] United Nations Global Compact, "UN Global Compact Participants," http://www.unglobalcompact.org/ParticipantsAndStakeholders/index.html (accessed 10 July 2012).

ascribed, among them some of its foremost firms, drawn from every sector of manufacturing production—not simply "clean" industries.[56] Asia also has significant representation: China had 270 participants, Japan 378, and South Korea 219. Among the remaining members of the five-nation coalition known as BRICs (Brazil, Russia, India, China, and South Africa), Brazil had 465 participants, India had 280, and Russia had 57. In effect, the Global Compact—reflective of values first articulated comprehensively by Europeans—has become a universal statement that is widely embraced around the globe.

The US has no comparable national government framework. Individual American states, notably California, have attempted to develop environmental initiatives and the Obama administration has promoted piecemeal aspects of the CRS agenda, such as the development of new environmental technologies. American corporations, business associations, NGOs, and academic institutions, however, have proven less reticent than their government to follow the European lead. In addition to signatures to the Global Compact, many have made aspects of the European agenda a cornerstone of their corporate practices. From Starbucks' focus on fair trade in coffee to American clothing retailers like Patagonia who demand fair labor practices by their suppliers, and even to oil companies who support the development of renewable energy ventures, the notion of corporate social responsibility has made great strides in the last decade.

The narrative of unfettered markets in a loosely integrated global system, reinforced by global institutions and guided by the United States to everyone's benefit, is therefore clearly a product of a liberal's view of the world. But this purportedly benign view is contradicted by an alternative perspective in which globalization is managed in varied formal and informal ways—thus mitigating, if not always guiding, the effects of global markets.

LANDMINES

The prohibition and removal of landmines represents another important example of agenda setting, one squarely in the domain of security. For over a century, states have regarded landmines as a central military tool in national defense. Their prohibition runs counter to traditional

---

[56] United Nations Global Compact, "Participants Search," http://www.unglobalcom pact.org/participants/search?business_type=all&commit=Search&cop_status=all &country[]=209&joined_after=&joined_before=&keyword=&listing_status_id=all &organization_type_id=&page=1&per_page=250&sector_id=all (accessed 11 July 2012).

defensive strategies and practices, and was initially opposed by most armed forces. Advocates mobilized a wide range of other actors and interests including governments, NGOs, intergovernmental organizations and prominent individuals like Princess Diana of Wales, who functioned as a "celebratory entrepreneur" prior to her death. Holdouts remain against the protocols and treaty, some of them powerful states like the United States. Yet there is compelling evidence that even their behavior, in key cases, has been influenced in important ways by the emergent antilandmine regime.

Our case study of globalization challenged a key tenet of liberalism. The landmine case poses an equally powerful conundrum for realists. Through the collective and coordinated efforts of NGOs and governments, Europeans effectively contributed to putting landmines on the international security agenda. Conversely, the United States was effectively thwarted by a coalition of less powerful states. Europeans and their allies, in effect, overcame direct opposition from Washington, which opposed a global ban and sought, unsuccessfully, to create an alternative global forum where the issue could be negotiated more to its liking. Landmine prohibition was not a security issue in which the United States was indifferent or passive. American leaders had a keen interest in the outcome, attempted to set a different agenda, but lost the leadership battle and initially refused to support the outcome. Ultimately, however, Washington reversed many of its practices and became the agreement's biggest sponsor.

The modern landmine eradication initiative began in the 1970s with the efforts of the Swiss-based International Committee of the Red Cross (ICRC), which met with some success, influencing Protocol II of the Convention on Conventional Weapons in 1980. It included both prohibitive and restrictive elements in a broad-ranging agreement on the use of landmines, booby traps, and similar devices.[57] It formed the backdrop for the events of the 1990s that witnessed parallel efforts by Europeans to produce a treaty banning landmines and the Americans' fight to prevent it.

The European campaign was spearheaded by NGOs that supported the ICRC's efforts to promote mine eradication. The most important European NGOs were Handicap International (France), Medico International (Germany), and the Mines Advisory Group (United Kingdom).[58]

---

[57] International Committee of the Red Cross, "Protocol (II) on Prohibitions or Restrictions on the Use of Mines, Booby-Traps and Other Devices. Geneva, 10 October 1980," http://www.icrc.org/ihl.nsf/FULL/510?OpenDocument (accessed 12 June 2012).

[58] Three American organizations—Human Rights Watch, Physicians for Human Rights, and the Vietnam Veterans of America Foundation—comprised the remaining founder members.

In 1992, they joined with American NGOs and the ICRC to create the International Campaign to Ban Landmines (ICBL); that year the EU passed a resolution requesting a five-year moratorium on the export of antipersonnel mines.

Europe and Canada set the agenda. In 1993, Handicap International convinced the Mitterrand government to declare that France would voluntarily abstain from the export of landmines.[59] Other NGOs found political traction with European governments in the course of the next three years. In 1994, the Canadian government tabled the issue of an antilandmine initiative at the Group of Seven (G7) meeting in Naples.[60] That same year, the Swedish government, responding to an initiative by Rädda Barnen, an NGO also known as the Swedish Save the Children, declared that "an international total ban against antipersonnel mines is the only real solution to the humanitarian problem the use of mines causes."[61]

In 1995, Belgium became the first country to ban the production, use, trading, or stockpiling of landmines and was followed by Norway and Switzerland. Non-European powers then joined the bandwagon. Philippines president Ferdinand Ramos, fighting insurgents who used landmines against his forces, offered strong support for the ban.[62] Public opinion around the world responded favorably to what was now a high-publicity campaign for a landmine treaty.[63] Isabelle Daoust, a humanitarian law adviser for the Canadian Red Cross, later observed that global popular support for a landmine ban is why the agreement is sometimes referred to as the "people's treaty."[64]

In 1996, Sweden established the Swedish Explosive Ordnance Disposal and Demining Center, subsequently helping to remove mines in Afghanistan, the Balkans, Cambodia, Eritrea, and Sri Lanka. Menschen gegen Minen (MgM), a German NGO, began similar operations in Angola, Mozambique, and Namibia. It set up the MgM Network, an Internet forum in which demining experts, relief workers, and researchers

[59] Maxwell A. Cameron, Robert J. Lawson, and Brian W. Tomlin, "To Walk without Fear," in Maxwell A. Cameron, Robert J. Lawson and Brian W. Tomlin, eds., *To Walk without Fear: The Global Movement to Ban Landmines* (Oxford: Oxford University Press, 1998), 1–28.

[60] John English, "The Ottawa Process: Paths Followed, Paths Ahead," *Australian Journal of International Affairs* 52, no. 2 (1998): 121–32.

[61] Cameron, Lawson, and Tomlin, "To Walk without Fear."

[62] English, "Ottawa Process."

[63] Cameron, Lawson, and Tomlin, "To Walk without Fear."

[64] Isabelle Daoust, *Canada's Role in the Ottawa Process* (Ottawa: Canadian Council on International Law, 2007); Swiss Campaign to Ban Landmines, *Engaging in Non-State Actors in a Landmine Ban: A Pioneering Conference (Full Conference Proceedings)* (Geneva: Swiss Campaign to Ban Landmines, 2000), 41.

could exchange information. The following year, the British military established the Mine Information and Training Center, an initiative aimed at facilitating the flow of information and training military and civilian organizations about demining.

These initiatives contributed to an assertive and increasingly coherent campaign. In 1996, the UN Review Conference for the Convention on Certain Conventional Weapons, called at France's request, adopted the Amended Mines Protocol. It amended the original Protocol II of 1980 by making it applicable to civil wars as well as interstate ones and placing tighter controls on the use and transfer of antipersonnel mines.[65] In the opinion of the ICBL, this protocol was insufficient and only reinforced its members' belief that a total prohibition on landmine use was necessary.[66] The ICBL's efforts received useful publicity when Princess Diana visited Angola in early 1997, and later war-torn Bosnia and Mozambique, and she voiced support for a comprehensive landmine ban.[67] One reason advocates were able to get such widespread support was that they were able to reframe the issue from one of military utility to societal impact.

A European coalition developed as more states joined the campaign. Pro–landmine ban governments were elected in Britain and France in 1997, and Spain and Italy also voiced their support.[68] In May, a joint statement issued by the German, French, and British foreign ministers helped to push other EU states toward support of a landmine ban.[69] Public vocal advocacy by successive EU Presidents from the Netherlands, Ireland, and Luxembourg led to an ever wider European consensus promoting a prohibition.[70]

[65] United Nations Office at Geneva, "Disarmament," http://www.unog.ch/80256EE6 00585943/%28httpPages%29/4F0DEF093B4860B4C1257180004B1B30?OpenDocument (accessed 9 August 2012). See also Stuart Casey-Maslen, "The Context of the Adoption of the Convention on the Prohibition of the Use, Stockpiling, Production and Transfer of Anti-Personnel Mines and Their Destruction (Anti-Personnel Mine Ban Convention)," Audiovisual Library of International Law, 18 September 1997, http://untreaty.un.org /cod/avl/ha/cpusptam/cpusptam.html (accessed 9 August 2012).

[66] English, "Ottawa Process"; International Campaign to Ban Landmines, "Ban History," http://www.icbl.org/index.php/icbl/Treaty/MBT/Ban-History (accessed 17 June 2012); International Committee of the Red Cross, "Protocol on Prohibitions or Restrictions on the Use of Mines, Booby-Traps and Other Devices as amended on 3 May 1996 (Protocol II to the 1980 CCW Convention as amended on 3 May, 1996)," http://www.icrc .org/ihl.nsf/FULL/575?OpenDocument (accessed 17 June 2012).

[67] English, "Ottawa Process."

[68] David Long, "The European Union and the Ottawa Process to Ban Landmines," *Journal of European Public Policy* 9, no. 3 (2002): 429–46.

[69] Ibid; see also *Ann Peters, "International Partnerships on the Road to Ban Anti-Personnel Landmines* (Washington, DC: Open Society Institute), 15.

[70] The European exceptions were Finland and Greece, who believed that the prohibi-

These efforts gained traction in global organizations. The creation of the United Nations Mine Action Service in October 1997 proved a watershed, serving as the UN focal point for antilandmine action.[71] It is responsible for coordinating mine action within the UN and for providing mine action assistance during humanitarian emergencies and peacekeeping operations at the field level. The campaign for a global ban came to fruition in 1997.

The Ottawa Process, as it became known, involved prominent individuals, NGOs, and representatives of fifty governments who came together at the invitation of Canadian foreign minister Lloyd Axworthy. His aim was to "fast-track" diplomatic initiatives to ban landmines. Both the original and revised drafts that formed the foundation for discussions were submitted by Austria.[72] The EU also contributed by offering a binding joint action on the eve of the signing of the Ottawa Convention that prohibited the transfer and production of antipersonnel mines.[73]

Canada's intervention at this stage was undoubtedly important; one analyst of the process offers the counterfactual that "had Canada not sponsored a new diplomatic initiative, it would have taken months, if not years, for activists to get the issue back on the global agenda."[74] Yet the European role remained prominent, if not decisive; all but the first and last meetings were hosted by Germany, Belgium, and Norway. One hundred twenty-two states signed the Convention on the Prohibition of the Use, Stockpiling, Production and Transfer of Anti-Personnel Mines and on Their Destruction during the time that it was open for signature (December 1997 through 1999). It entered into force on 1 March 2009, after the requisite number of forty ratifications or accessions.[75]

tion ran contrary to their national security interests. See Long, "European Union and the Ottawa Process to Ban Landmines"; Peters, "International Partnerships on the Road to Ban Anti-Personnel Landmines"; Cameron, Lawson, and Tomlin, "To Walk without Fear"; and Lesley Wexler, "The International Deployment of Shame, Second-Best Response, and Norm Entrepreneurship: The Campaign to Ban Landmines and the Landmine Ban Treaty," *Arizona Journal of International and Comparative Law* 20 (2003): 586–89.

[71] Websites of the United Kingdom Mines Information and Training Centre, http://www.army.mod.uk/15462.aspx, and the Electronic Mine Information Network, http://www.mineaction.org (both accessed 27 May 2013).

[72] Long, "The European Union and the Ottawa Process to Ban Landmines," 434; Casey-Maslen, "The Context of the Adoption of the Convention on the Prohibition of the Use, Stockpiling, Production and Transfer of Anti-Personnel Mines."

[73] Long, "The European Union and the Ottawa Process to Ban Landmines."

[74] Julian Davis, *The Campaign to Ban Landmines: Public Diplomacy, Middle Power Leadership and an Unconventional Negotiating Process* (Toronto: Canadian Institute of International Affairs, 2004), 2.

[75] Casey-Maslen, "The Context of the Adoption of the Convention on the Prohibition of the Use, Stockpiling, Production and Transfer of Anti-Personnel Mines."

The provisions of the convention were sweeping and uncompromising. Landmines were broadly defined to include so-called "smart" (self-deactivating) as well as "dumb" (nondeactivating) weapons. States were required to destroy all antipersonnel mine stockpiles under their jurisdiction or control in no more than four years. In addition, each signatory had to clear all antipersonnel mines in areas it controlled within ten years.[76] The universal and unremitting tone of the key provisions is remarkable.

The Europeans and their allies were able to get agreement on a ban in the face of incessant American opposition to a blanket prohibition. Dating from the administration of President Bill Clinton, Washington had tried unsuccessfully to control the negotiations. Unable to reconcile its demands with the terms of the agreement within the contours of those favored by the Europeans and their allies, the United States sought to create another venue for negotiation where it could affect its desired outcome. US efforts were handicapped by its insistence that it be given a blanket exemption for the use of smart mines in Korea's demilitarized zone. To critics, this nonnegotiable American demand was one more instance in which Washington sought privileged exemptions to universal agreements, as it did with the International Criminal Court, where it sought a blanket exemption from prosecution for American military personnel. The paradox is that the United States was both among the greatest opponents of the Ottawa Convention and yet its greatest sponsor. While maintaining its use of landmines in Korea, the United States embarked on the largest, most extensive and ambitious demining program in history—effectively, materially sponsoring the very agreement that it refused to ratify.

The United States had played a central role in limiting the form and scale of mines through both domestic legislation and international agreements for four decades. It had supported landmine clearance and victim support programs.[77] Pressured by the Vietnam Veterans of America, the Clinton administration clearly made efforts to assume a leading role; it declared a moratorium on the export of mines and created a humanitarian demining program.[78] Afghanistan, Cambodia, Kuwait, northern Iraq, Somalia, El Salvador, and Mozambique all received demining assistance from the United States. President Clinton, in attempting to seize the initiative on the issue, went before the UN General Assembly in 1994 and called for the elimination of all forms of landmines.

[76] Ibid.

[77] US Department of Defense, Bureau of Political-Military Affairs, "History of Anti-Landmine Efforts," 29 July 2003, http://www.policyalmanac.org/world/archive/land mines.shtml (accessed 25 June 2012).

[78] It was renamed the US Humanitarian Mine Action Program in December 2002.

By 1996 Clinton announced that he would seek a global ban, with the critical caveat being an exemption for the United States.[79] A series of American initiatives followed. Yet Europeans, their allies, and the increasingly influential NGO community demanded an unconditional global prohibition be instituted without exception and without the negotiations being confined to a few big producers.

The incredulous American response was an attempt to develop a different venue for discussion, the Conference on Disarmament (CD).[80] Seeking to derail the Ottawa process by drawing in the major producers, exporters, and users of landmines to an alternative forum, Clinton stated that the CD would pursue a ban in incremental stages through US leadership.[81] But, while sympathetic to the efforts in Ottawa, the United States would not pursue a policy entailing unacceptable risks to its armed forces.[82] Yet neither Clinton's proposal nor his claims for US leadership found much support among an increasingly impatient set of nonproducer states or the clamoring NGO community, and the major producer states were uninterested in participating in the CD.[83] So, undeterred, the Ottawa Convention went ahead and a treaty was signed.[84] The position of the Europeans and Canadians, augmented at this point by other middle powers, had resoundingly usurped American efforts at leadership.

The CD initiative, predictably, failed. Yet despite this fact, and overt US opposition to the universal prohibition, the United States has nonetheless effectively continued to sponsor a treaty that it opposed.[85] This process included American support for the setting up of the Geneva International Center for Humanitarian Demining in collaboration with the major proponents of the Ottawa Convention as well as providing critical matching funds for the International Trust Fund for Demining and Victims Assistance, enabling other countries to double the impact of their funding.

---

[79] "Landmine Policy," Transcript, *PBS Newshour*, 16 May 1996, http://www.pbs.org/newshour/bb/military/land_mines_5-16.html (accessed 10 August 2012).

[80] Cameron, Lawson, and Tomlin, "To Walk without Fear," 27.

[81] "Transcript: Clinton Remarks on Landmines," 17 September 1997, http://www.usembassy-israel.org.il/publish/press/whouse/archive/1997/september/wh4918.htm (accessed 10 August 1997).

[82] Ibid.

[83] Cameron, Lawson, and Tomlin, "To Walk without Fear," 27.

[84] For the text of the Treaty, see International Campaign to Ban Landmines, "Convention on the Prohibition of the Use, Stockpiling, Production and Transfer of Anti-Personnel Mines and on Their Destruction," http://www.icbl.org/treaty/text/english (accessed 27 May 2013).

[85] Julian Davis, "The Campaign to Ban Landmines: Public Diplomacy, Middle Power Leadership and an Unconventional Negotiating Process," *Journal of Humanitarian Assistance* 15 May 2004, http://sites.tufts.edu/jha/archives/836 (accessed 4 February 20013).

TABLE 3.1.
US Humanitarian Mine Action Budget, 1999–2010
(US$ millions)

Year	Contribution
1999	$81.3
2000	$100.6
2001	$81.8
2002	$76.9
2003	$93.0
2004	$109.3
2005	$95.9
2006	$94.5
2007	$69.8
2008	$85.0
2009	$118.7
2010	$129.6

Source: US Department of State, "U.S. Humanitarian Mine Action Budget," 30 November 2009, http://www.state.gov/t/pm/wra/c12023.htm (accessed 24 June 2012).

The aggregate figures in the decade that followed demonstrate a clear continuation of that pattern. American assistance in support of the global landmine prohibition program grew from just under $200 million to almost $500 million by 2010.[86] In addition, the American domestic Mine Action Assistance budget grew by over 150 percent between 1999 and 2010, to $129.6 million (see table 3.1), representing as much as one quarter of all global expenditures.[87] In total, between 1993 and 2010, the United States committed over $1 billion to its landmine eradication effort.

The United States has used its demining initiative as a way of deflecting widespread criticism of its refusal to sign on the Ottawa Process.[88] Its efforts reach every part of the world, providing assistance to more

[86] International Campaign to Ban Landmines, *Landmine Monitor 2011* (Geneva: International Campaign to Ban Landmines, 2011), 52.

[87] For the International Campaign to Ban Landmines' *Landmine Monitor* reports for 2002, 2003, 2006, and 2011, see http://www.the-monitor.org/. See also US Department of State, "The United States Is a World Leader in Humanitarian Mine Action," 30 November 2009, http://www.state.gov/r/pa/prs/ps/2009/nov/132591.htm (accessed 14 June 2012).

[88] Wexler, "The International Deployment of Shame"; Stacy Bernard Davis and Donald F. Pat Patierno, "Tackling the Global Landmine Problem: The United States Perspective," in Cameron, Lawson, and Tomlin, eds., *To Walk without Fear*, 125–34.

then eighty countries.[89] It initiated more than sixty major public and private partnerships.[90] Indeed, since the ban was enacted, the US role has grown in prominence. In addition to increasing its bilateral aid to countries in every region of the world, it has issued authoritative reports and statistical data; created training programs and information centers at universities and think tanks as well as in the government and military branches; produced documentaries and awareness campaigns; and sponsored educational curricula, workshops, and conferences. Demonstrating the bipartisan nature of the US effort, the Bush administration announced its new landmine policy in February 2004, which included the elimination of all persistent landmines from the US arsenal; pursuing a ban on the sale or export of "dumb mines" in addition to banning their use by US forces as of 2010; and ensuring a baseline level of $70 million annually for landmine eradication efforts.[91]

Like the prior case on globalization, the landmines case presents a challenge to proponents of mainstream hegemonic formulations and thus the importance of the United States in agenda setting. Realist theory cannot account for the success of the Europeans and their allies, and conversely the failure of the United States, to achieve explicit goals in a key international security area.[92] Nor can it account for why so many states made a unilateral decision to give up a low-cost defensive weapon of war.[93] In the decade following the signing of the convention, eighty-six countries destroyed their stockpiles while only sixty-three said they had none to destroy.[94] Despite this diplomatic failure, the United States did sponsor the numerous aspects of the eventual agreement with which it concurred. While rules and norms constrained its behavior, as critics claimed, it nonetheless found ways to complement

[89] US Department of State, "To Walk the Earth in Safety: Humanitarian Mine Action Funding," 1 July 2011, http://www.state.gov/t/pm/rls/rpt/walkearth/2011/176627.htm (accessed 18 June 2012).

[90] US Department of State, "Landmines: Major Public-Private Partnerships," 22 June 2012, http://www.state.gov/t/pm/rls/othr/misc/52830.htm (accessed 27 June 2012).

[91] US Department of State, "US Landmine Policy," 27 February 2004. http://www.state.gov/t/pm/wra/c11735.htm (accessed 20 June 2012).

[92] Nicola Short, "The Role of NGOs in the Ottawa Process to Ban Landmines," *International Negotiation* no. 4 (1999): 481–500; Wexler, "The International Deployment of Shame," 571. On middle powers, see Don Hubert, *The Landmine Ban: A Case Study in Humanitarian Advocacy* (Providence, RI: Brown University, 2000).

[93] See Richard Price, "Compliance with International Norms and the Mines Taboo," in Cameron, Lawson, and Tomlin, eds., *To Walk Without Fear*, 340–63, especially 344; and Kenneth R. Rutherford, "The Evolving Arms Control Agenda: Implication of the Role of NGOs in Banning Antipersonnel Landmines," *World Politics* 53 (2000): 74–114, especially 106.

[94] International Campaign to Ban Landmines, *Landmine Monitor 2009* (Geneva: International Campaign to Ban Landmines): 16–17.

them with its own interests—an issue that we explore at greater length in chapter 5.[95]

Europe in Comparative Perspective

European success illustrates the validity of our claims that power and influence are by no means the same thing and that the latter often requires legitimacy. Agenda setting in particular depends on consensus and institutionalized processes of decision making. It can be frustratingly slow, even torturous, especially to Americans brought up to believe that foreign policy should be emphatic, dynamic, and lacking in ambivalence. From our perspective, neither markets nor a desire to emulate America's economic or political models drives the global system. European viewpoints and agenda setting are, we suggest, more influential than Americans recognize.

This does not mean that European leaders are particularly ethical or less guided by considerations of national interest than others. As the next two chapters on the US and China document, there are always some academics ready to provide an unqualified narrative of their country as virtuous, progressive, and prudent. European international relations scholars are no different. In the last several decades, they have fostered the image of a benign, cosmopolitan EU that they explicitly contrast to the continued centrality of realist thought in the United States.[96] This campaign recently a big boost from noted German philosopher Jürgen Habermas in 2011 when he proclaimed that the EU and its constitutional evolution serve as a template for the rest of the world.[97]

One does not have to look far to find domains in which European policy is far from ethical. On issues of terrorism and immigration, and the relationship between them, the European record is as deplorable as the American one. Here, as in the United States, the two issues have often become intertwined, as the identity of one has often gelled with the other in the eyes of European policy makers and publics. The EU's treatment of asylum seekers and illegal migrants, and its aiding and abetting in the transportation of possible terrorist prisoners to "black hole" prisons, has been severely criticized. The EU's response to unregulated immigration and asylum flows was to deport many of those caught and send them to detention camps in Libya prior to the fall of

---

[95] Wexler, "The International Deployment of Shame," 605.

[96] Manners, "The Normative Ethics of the European Union," 66.

[97] Jürgen Habermas, *Zur Verfassung Europas* [On Europe's Constitution] (Frankfurt: Suhrkamp, 2011).

Muammar Gaddafi. Libya was specifically chosen because it is not a signatory to several UN agreements protecting the human rights of those detained—notably the UN Convention on Human Rights.

EU members also cooperated extensively with the United States in the practice of extralegal rendition, leading to the torture of many people so imprisoned, often in Poland and Romania.[98] A Council of Europe report in 2006 suggested that detainees were subject to inhumane and degrading treatment there, including torture.[99] Britain and twenty-four other countries, most of them European, may now face legal sanctions.[100] It might be tempting to assume that many of these provisions originated in the United States in the aftermath of 9/11 and that European governments and the EU were unwilling or unwitting accomplices. But this was not the case, as many aspects of these policies originated within Europe and the EU itself; policy convergence occurred when the United States moved closer to European policies. Immigration policy was used to deter terrorists and terrorism policy was used to deport immigrants.[101] These are important cases where EU behavior advanced an unethical agenda.

Comparably, we understand that agenda setting doesn't always work. The need for legitimacy, usually evident in a willingness to make sacrifices, and thus a capacity to build a consensus, ensures that European efforts fail under the wrong circumstances. Arab-Israeli negotiations are a case in point. For historical reasons to do with colonialism and the Holocaust, coupled with the European reliance on Middle Eastern oil, neither the Israelis nor their varied Arab counterparts have much faith in any European initiative. They tend to see them as self-serving, partisan, and unreliable interlopers.

Nonetheless, our key conclusion is that European efforts at agenda setting have worked more often than is recognized by American scholars, in cases that cannot simply be dismissed as insignificant. The same is true for Chinese efforts at buttressing the global economic system, a claim we will address in chapter 4.

---

[98] Amnesty International, *Report 2005: The State of the World's Human Rights* (2005), http://www.amnesty.org/en/library/info/POL10/001/2005, 35 (accessed 27 May 2013).

[99] Referenced in Council of Europe, *Secret Detentions and Illegal Transfers of Detainees Involving Council of Europe Member States: Second Report*, 11 June 2007, http://assembly .coe.int/Documents/WorkingDocs/2007/edoc11302.htm (accessed 1 July 2013).

[100] Ian Cobain, "CIA Rendition Report Author Believes UK Could Face Human Rights Court," *Guardian*, 7 February 2013, http://www.guardian.co.uk/world/2013/feb/05 /cia-rendition-report-uk-court?INTCMP=SRCH (accessed 27 May 2013).

[101] Chebel d'Appollonia, *Frontiers of Fear*.

Chapter 4

//

China and Custodial Economic Management

> Part of the world's economic problem today is that the United
> States has resigned (or been discharged) as leader of the world
> economy, and there is no candidate willing and acceptable to
> take its place.
>
> —Charles P. Kindleberger, "Dominance and
> Leadership in the International Economy"

The resurgence of China has become a matter of growing concern for
American policy makers and academics. Policy memos, newspaper
articles, and academic journals describe China as an emerging behemoth. Analysts sharply disagree about its consequences. Realists generally portray China as a revolutionary power intent on dominating Asia
and changing the rules of the global economy to its own benefit at others' expense. Liberals depict Chinese leaders as focused primarily on
economic development and increasingly tamed and constrained by virtue of their country's growing dependence on foreign markets and investment. Both interpretations are structural and all but ignore Chinese
culture and history and how they might influence the state's thinking
about security and economic policy. They also use evidence selectively.
Some of the most widely quoted newspaper columnists, and alas, the
occasional scholar, offer quotes and figures that can be interpreted to
support their position and ignore those that cannot.

Fortunately, there is impressive work on Chinese politics and foreign
policy by knowledgeable Western scholars who are fairer in their use of
evidence and more cautious in their judgments. We are not China experts, but international relations (IR) scholars, and draw heavily on
their analyses. We bring to the table familiarity with international relations theory and its applications to security and international political
economy. Our analysis makes use of our theoretical knowledge and a
more specific literature on China. Our goal is to say something about

Chinese approaches to foreign policy, but also to use the China case to say something about hegemony and its alternatives.

Making sense of China is somewhat easier than trying to understand the Cold War–era Soviet Union. That country was characterized by extreme secrecy, official publications that rarely, if ever, deviated from the party line, and analysts and scholars for the most part unwilling to express their own views. China is a relatively open society. Its newspapers are responsive to its leadership, but publish a surprising range of opinions, as do various Chinese ministries, organizations, and businesses. As all scholars who deal with their Chinese counterparts know, they can be quite outspoken at scholarly gatherings, and more so in private. The Chinese make far more data about their economy available than did the Soviets. This provides Western analysts with useful information about such matters as the frequency of violent protests in rural China, the Chinese military budget, and debates over force structures, Chinese energy shortages, and—of particular interest to us—the views of Chinese analysts about American foreign policy goals. While these should not be viewed naively, they do provide us with more insight than is often admitted by American IR scholars who commonly ignore them.

This information does not allow us to resolve the question of what China wants. One reason for this is the diversity of views on these subjects within the country. Consider the problem in reverse: Chinese analysts attempting to fathom America's goals. Their answers would depend on which segment of American opinion they listened to, and even then, any smart observer would know that American foreign policy reflects not only presidential goals and congressional pressures and constraints, but also unpredictable compromises with relevant bureaucracies. While China is not a pluralist country in the same sense as the United States, its policies do reflect input from diverse internal sources and different understandings of international constraints and opportunities. So the best that analysts in either country can do is identify trends and construct narrative forecasts they believe more likely than others—but in full recognition that events at home or abroad can bring about significant and unanticipated shifts in policy. The events of 9/11 had this effect for United States, as have other political and economic shocks for both countries. Certainty is out of the question, and for this reason so is prediction. Cautious judgments and forecasting—in the expectation of updating and revision—are the best we can provide.

With these caveats in mind, we offer a critique of the realist and liberal positions on China. Any argument advanced with near certainty, as is so often the case with these analyses, can be regarded as hyperbole. Even more serious accounts by area specialists run into difficulty when they interpret Chinese goals and policies in terms of paradigms of largely Ameri-

can origin. Realist and liberal scholars assume that their respective paradigms are based on universal principles that apply with equal force to all
regions of the world. The only analyses we should take seriously are those
based on careful empirical work that uses Chinese sources and interprets
data in terms of Chinese understandings of the issues in question.

We advance arguments as hypotheses, not as dogma. We believe our
arguments to be consistent with Chinese culture and policies, but recognize that other readings are possible and that new evidence could call
this and any reading into question. We are also aware that there are
multiple Chinese perspectives and that the country's policies could
change as a result of shifts in power within the elite favoring those with
different policy preferences.

We have three starting points that we think critical to any serious
analysis. The first is the need to understand Chinese foreign policy
goals and means with reference to Chinese culture and history.[1] The
relevant history includes the last sixty years of the People's Republic,
but also imperial history, as contemporary understandings of the successes, failures, and traditions of communist and imperial China are the
crucible in which contemporary policies are forged. Just like their
American counterparts, Chinese analysts and leaders regularly think in
terms of historical analogies and use them to formulate and mobilize
support for policies. Different Chinese narratives about the past encourage different framings of security and economic issues, and framings at
odds with those nested in the realist or liberal paradigms.

Another starting point is the need to factor in the different perspectives that exist within the Chinese elite. One example will suffice. There
are three distinct points of view among Chinese analysts and leaders
about US policies toward Taiwan. The dominant perspective characterizes the United States as a "nervous hegemon" that supports Taiwan as
a means of constraining an increasingly powerful China. A minority but
well-represented view is the "entangled ally" thesis. It stresses the difficulty Washington would face in giving up a long-standing ally and its
fear of losing credibility if it does. A smaller number of analysts adhere
to the "democratic missionary" interpretation that sees the United
States as committed to upholding Taiwanese democracy and using it to
foster political change in China.[2] These perspectives prompt their advo-

---

[1] Peter Hays Gries, *China's New Nationalism: Pride, Politics, and Diplomacy* (Berkeley
and Los Angeles: University of California Press, 2004); Peter Hays Gries, "Identity and
Conflict in Sino-American Relations," in Alastair Iain Johnston and Robert S. Ross, eds.,
New Directions in the Study of China's Foreign Policy (Stanford: Stanford University Press,
2006), 309–39.

[2] Andrew Bingham Kennedy, "China's Perceptions of US Intentions toward Taiwan,"
Asian Survey 47, no. 2 (2007): 268–87.

cates to endorse different policies toward Taiwan and the United States. They encourage them, in a mirror image of their American counterparts, to interpret most of what the United States does in terms of their preferred perspective.

The final starting point concerns data, both Chinese and foreign. Mostly, we rely on economic data and Chinese commentary on it, as China's role in the international economy is the primary focus of this chapter. We also draw on respected interpretations of Chinese history that Chinese analysts and officials use to interpret information from home and abroad. As our book is about hegemony and its alternatives, with particular reference to the global economy, we will make the case for Beijing's economic policies reflecting its emerging custodial role. We address other aspects of foreign policy *en passant*. It is admittedly artificial to focus on one domain of policy to the near-exclusion of others, but this is the only feasible strategy in a single book chapter. Any attempt to address foreign and security policy in more detail would take space away from efforts to document our principal contentions about China's custodial functions.

We reject the notion that Chinese leaders have formulated any elaborate "game plan" about how to use their growing power to reconstitute the global political or economic system.[3] Their goals are built on a conception of national long-term self-interest that is embedded in a historical and cultural context. These objectives are consistent with efforts at buttressing the global system, often at a short-term cost—according to the evidence. While inferring motive from behavior is always problematic, we contend that there are general understandings within the Chinese leadership about foreign goals and the means most conducive to achieving them. In November 2002, President Jiang Zemin told the Sixteenth Party Congress,

> The first two decades of the twenty-first century are a period of important strategic opportunities, which we must seize tightly and which offer bright prospects. . . . We need to concentrate on building a well-off society . . . in this period. The two decades of development will serve as an inevitable connecting link for attaining the third-step strategic objectives for our modernization drive. . . . A new world war is unlikely in the foreseeable future. It is realistic to bring about a fairly long period of peace in the world and a favorable climate in areas around China.[4]

[3] David M. Lampton, *The Three Faces of Chinese Power: Might, Money, and Minds* (Berkeley and Los Angeles: University of California Press, 2008), 25–27.

[4] "Full Text of Jiang Zemin's 'Report' at 16th Party Congress," Section 9, "On the International Situation and Our External Work," Sixteenth National Congress of the Communist Party of China, Beijing, 8 November 2002, http://english.people.com.cn/200211 /18/eng20021118_106985.shtml (accessed 4 June 2013).

We suggest that this speech, and many others like it since, provide an accurate account of China's medium-term goals: to develop economically, protect the country's sovereignty, maintain peaceful relations with neighbors and the world more generally, and facilitate the reunification of Taiwan by peaceful means. The Chinese often refer to their "core interests," defined as the "state system and national security," "sovereignty and territorial integrity," and "the continued stable development of China's economy and society." Many cautious realists accept these assertions.[5] They are concerned with what happens next. Is China using the language of peaceful development to lull its neighbors and the West into letting down their guard until it develops sufficient economic and military strength to challenge them?[6] Such a strategy cannot be ruled out, but we see it as inconsistent with much of China's current behavior and how imperial China sought to exercise influence in eras when it engaged actively with its neighbors.

In chapter two, we described the ancient Greek concept of *hēgemonia* and distinguished it from the modern idea of hegemony. Hēgemonia describes an honorific status conferred on a leading power because of the services it has provided to the community. It confers a right to lead, based on the expectation that this leadership will continue to benefit the community as a whole. Hēgemonia represents a clientalist approach to politics: the powerful gain honor in return for providing practical benefits to the weak. The latter willingly accept their inferior status in return for economic and security benefits and the constraints such an arrangement imposes on the powerful.

Imperial China structured relations with most of its neighbors along the lines of hēgemonia—theorized, naturally, in different language. We contend that it is has emerged as a template for many contemporary Chinese leaders, officials, and intellectuals. It differs from both hegemony and a balance of power in fundamental ways. China, in our view, seeks to consolidate an effective regional security posture based on clientalism even as it assumes (albeit at this stage, as we document, in a limited fashion) many of the custodial global economic management functions as its resources expand. The Chinese elite has little interest in global hegemony—or even regional hegemony—defined as effective and economic political control over other political units. China is nevertheless assuming some of the key functions of international economic management, albeit at a relatively immature level

---

[5] Lampton, *The Three Faces of Chinese Power*, 27–32; Tang Shiping, "From Offensive to Defensive Realism: A Social Evolutionary Interpretation of China's Security Strategy," in Robert S. Ross and Zhu Feng, eds., *China's Ascent: Power, Security and the Future of International Politics* (Ithaca, NY: Cornell University Press, 2008), 141–62.

[6] Lampton, *The Three Faces of Chinese Power*, 25–35, 252–74.

compared to the brief period of American dominance in the late 1940s and into the 1950s.

Chinese history and culture, and contemporary economic and political realities, position it as a growing but conservative power. Chinese leaders appear intent on preserving a global economic system from which their country is currently the greatest beneficiary. Alistair Iain Johnson not unreasonably characterizes China as a "status quo power."[7] It may be dissatisfied with the current global system. But any changes it advocates are marginal, not revolutionary. At home and abroad, China's primary goal is economic, political, and social stability as it consolidates its export of goods, services, cash, and people and increases its import of money, natural resources, technology, and other forms of knowledge. Above all, its leaders seek to avoid more acute ethnic conflict, any regression into poverty and political chaos, and to resist what they perceive as challenges to their country's sovereignty.[8]

China is willing to provide some economic public goods such as overseas development aid, foreign direct investment, and funds for the purchase of foreign bonds because its leaders consider them beneficial to national interest. They are not willing to invest heavily in multilateral organizations for fear that doing so will infringe on their country's sovereignty and involve them in missions that are strategically unimportant or even counterproductive to their interests. There is a wide consensus among Chinese leaders—in sharp contrast to their American counterparts—that influence is not achieved and maintained through multilateral leadership and the blunt use of power. They prefer subtler combination of bilateral and regional diplomatic negotiations and market mechanisms.

This chapter consists of five sections. We begin with a critique of realist and liberal understandings of China. We then outline the key historical and cultural factors that we believe influence China's security and economic priorities and the means considered appropriate to advancing them. The third section examines China's security policy, and the fourth its nascent role in global economic management in terms of culturally embedded understandings of self-interest. Our analysis points to the conclusion—starkly at odds with realist and liberal understandings—that China is playing an increasingly important custodial role in global economic management. We conclude by revisiting the question of China's goals in light of our analysis.

---

[7] Alastair Iain Johnston, "Is China a Status Quo Power?" *International Security* 27, no. 4 (2003): 5–56.

[8] Joshua Cooper Ramo, *The Beijing Consensus: Notes on the New Physics of Chinese Power* (London: Foreign Policy Centre, 2004), 12–14.

AMERICAN ANALYSTS AND CHINESE POWER

Many prominent American realists write with certainty about China's ambitions. They depict China as the inheritor of the Japanese mantle: a threatening, rising challenger to American hegemony, with the difference that its economy will soon overtake that of the United States.[9] Realists and many liberals interpret current Chinese policies as narrowly self-interested, inconsistent with any broader global interest in stability. China, they assert, not only fails to provide public goods, unlike the United States, but is the source of many economic problems given its unwavering focus on exports and growth and its largely unconvertible currency that is unfairly pegged to the US dollar.[10]

The most anguished realists are "offensive realists," led by John Mearsheimer, Aaron Friedberg, and Christopher Layne. Drawing on power transition theory, they argue that a rising China will assert itself—by war, if necessary—and demand a change in the rules of the system.[11] Offensive realists ignore any countervailing evidence by insisting that the past is no guide to future behavior because calculations and goals will shift once the opportunity for hegemony presents itself.[12] Journalists and politicians who aim to influence a wider audience propagate offensive realism, in its most alarmist form.[13] Power transition has become more or less the conventional wisdom in the policy community, where it is the dominant frame of reference for assessing the possible

[9] Robert Kaplan, "Don't Panic about China," *Atlantic*, 28 January 2010, http://www.theatlantic.com/magazine/archive/2005/10/dont-panic-about-china/307926 (accessed 5 June 2013); "China Military 'Closing Key Gaps,' "25 August 2011, http://www.bbc.co.uk/news/mobile/world-asia-pacific-14661027 (accessed 25 August 2011).

[10] Kaplan, "Don't Panic about China"; John Lee, "China Won't be a Responsible Stakeholder," *Wall Street Journal*, 1 February 2010, http://online.wsj.com/article/SB100014240 52748704722304575037931817880328.html (accessed 5 March 2013); Elizabeth C. Economy, "The Game Changer: Coping with China's Foreign Policy Revolution," *Foreign Affairs* 89, no. 9 (2010): 142–54.

[11] John J. Mearsheimer, *The Tragedy of Great Power Politics* (New York: Norton, 2001), 400; John J. Mearsheimer, "China's Unpeaceful Rise," *Current History* 105 (2006): 160–162; John J. Mearsheimer, "Trouble Brewing in the 'Hood," *Sydney Morning Herald*, 3 August 2011; Aaron L. Freidberg, "The Future of US-China Relations: Is Conflict Inevitable?" *International Security* 30, no. 2 (2005): 7–45; Aaron L. Freidberg, *A Contest for Supremacy: China, America and the Struggle for Mastery in Asia* (New York: Norton, 2011); Christopher Layne, "The Waning of US Hegemony—Myth or Reality?" *International Security* 34, no. 1 (2009): 147–72.

[12] Mearsheimer, *The Tragedy of the Great Powers*, 402.

[13] Steven W. Mosher, *Hegemon: China's Plan to Dominate Asia and the World* (San Francisco: Encounter, 2000); Stefan Halper, *The Beijing Consensus: How China's Authoritarian Model Will Dominate the Twenty-First Century* (New York: Basic Books, 2010).

consequences of China's rapid rise to great power status.[14] It is an article of faith among neoconservatives like former deputy secretary of defense Paul Wolfowitz, who insists, "In the case of China . . . the obvious and disturbing analogy is the position of Germany, a country that felt it had been denied its 'place in the sun,' that believed it had been mistreated by other powers, and that was determined to regain its rightful place by nationalistic assertiveness."[15] It is also embraced by moderates like former deputy assistant secretary of state Susan Shirk, who asserts, as if it were fact, "History teaches us that rising powers are likely to provoke war."[16]

The two most prominent formulations of power transition theory see war as the most likely outcome, but disagree about who initiates it. Kenneth Organski and Jacek Kugler contend the dominant nation and its supporters are generally unwilling to grant rising powers more than a small part of the advantages they derive from the status quo. Rising powers accordingly become increasingly dissatisfied and go to war against dominant powers to impose orders more favorable to them. War is most likely of longest duration and greatest magnitude when a dissatisfied challenger enters into approximate parity with the dominant state. Order is most secure when all the great powers are satisfied with the structure of the system.[17]

Robert Gilpin focuses on the decline of dominant powers.[18] In ordering and defending the system, dominant states inevitably make cumulative commitments that come to exceed their capabilities. Imperial overstretch "creates challenges for the dominant states and opportunities for the rising states of the system." The latter aspire to remake "the rules governing the international system, the spheres of influence, and most important of all, the international distribution of territory."[19] Dominant states see preventive war as the most attractive means of eliminating this threat. It is not the only strategy available. They can reduce their commitments or possibly reduce their costs through further expansion. Dominant powers can also ally with states who have an interest in defending the status quo, seek rapprochements with less threatening states, or appease challengers by making concessions to them.[20]

---

[14] For a cautious treatment, see Robert S. Ross and Zhe Feng, eds., *China's Ascent: Power, Security, and the Future of International Politics* (Ithaca, NY: Cornell University Press, 2008).

[15] Paul Wolfowitz, "Remembering the Future," *National Interest* 59 (2000): 42.

[16] Susan Shirk, *China: Fragile Superpower* (New York: Oxford University Press, 2007), 4.

[17] A.F.K. Organski, *World Politics* (New York: Knopf, 1958); A. F. K. Organski and Jacek Kugler, *The War Ledger* (Chicago: University of Chicago Press, 1980).

[18] Robert Gilpin, *War and Change in World Politics* (Cambridge: Cambridge University Press, 1981).

[19] Ibid., 186–87.

[20] Ibid., 191–93.

Benjamin Valentino and Richard Ned Lebow demonstrate that there is no historical evidence to support power transition theory.[21] They constructed a data set of great power wars from 1648 to the present that reveals that rising powers hardly ever attack great powers, or vice versa. Historically, rising powers are accommodated and rewarded, and power transitions are the result of wars, not the causes of them. Power transition also errs in thinking that there is a hegemonic power capable of imposing its preferences regionally or globally. Since 1648, no power has been in a position to impose its preferences on a regional—let alone, international—system and dictate the rules of war and peace. Power transitions involving leading powers are rare and are not the result of gradual differences in economic growth rates, as power transition theories expect. The only examples of such transitions are Russia overtaking France and the United States overtaking Russia in the late nineteenth century, neither of which involved war.

Leading states often aspire to the status of a dominant power. They are not content with their position and advantages, and attempt to gain more power through further conquests. By means of their augmented power, they impose their preferences on others. Habsburg Spain, France under Louis XIV and Napoleon, Wilhelmine and Nazi Germany, and, arguably, the United States in the post–Cold War era are cases in point. None of these states was seriously threatened by rising powers or coalitions of great powers. They went to war because they thought they were powerful enough to become more powerful still. Perceptions of strength, not of weakness and threat, are the precondition and incentive for many, if not most, superpower wars.

Lebow uses an expanded data set to offer a more general analysis of interstate war in *Why Nations Fight*.[22] His evidence indicates a pattern of conflict that is the reverse of that predicted by power transition theories. Great power wars arise in the absence of hegemony, not because of it. These wars lead to power transitions and peace settlements that often impose new orders by virtue of a consensus among the leading powers. These orders are never dictated by a single power but by a coalition of them, and endure as long as a consensus holds among the major powers responsible for upholding them.

With two notable exceptions, leading powers have avoided the intentional challenges of other great powers or rising powers. They generally prefer to make war against smaller third parties and once great

[21] Richard Ned Lebow and Benjamin Valentino, "Lost in Transition: A Critique of Power Transition Theories," *International Relations* 23, no. 3 (September 2009): 389–410; Jack S. Levy, "Power Transition Theory and the Rise of China," in Ross and Feng, eds., *China's Ascent*, 11–33, for another critical assessment.

[22] Richard Ned Lebow, *Why Nations Fight* (Cambridge: Cambridge University Press, 2011).

but now seriously declining great powers, although they have frequently been drawn into war with other great powers when these smaller wars escalate. Rising powers devote a high proportion of their income to their armed forces and wage frequent wars of expansion. In the period under discussion, Prussia, Russia, Germany, and Japan generally avoided attacking leading powers, their preference being once again for warring against smaller third parties and once great but declining powers. As a rising power, the United States also conformed to this pattern, attacking Mexico and Spain.[23]

Equally striking, and in sharp contrast to power transition theories, is the general failure of leaders and the media to distinguish the general power balance from the military one. There has been much discussion among US policy makers and in the media about the rising power of China and concern that it could challenge the United States at some point in the not too distant future. In its 2011 annual report, the US Department of Defense warned that the People's Liberation Army is developing key power projection capabilities that include submarines; advanced air and defense systems, containing ballistic and cruise missiles; and broad navy capabilities that include aircraft carriers.[24] As in the Cold War, the defense department has strong budget incentives to inflate greatly a would-be adversary's military capabilities and intentions.

Independent analysts contend that China's military power does not reflect its latent power, and that this is largely a matter of choice. China's defense expenditures, while rising rapidly in the last several years, have remained well below those of the United States in absolute terms and less than half the percentage of its gross domestic product (GDP). China's material capabilities have not given it the power to restructure the international system in its favor, let alone challenge a great power like the United States. The evidence is plentiful. Telling testimony comes from Tai Ming Cheung, director of a US Department of Defense–sponsored project on Chinese military technology carried out at the University of California–San Diego. In a 2013 lecture in Paris, Cheung suggested that Chinese efforts to develop key "disruptive" and "component" military technologies had generally been unsuccessful. China is in no position to challenge the United States globally and will probably have to buy military technology from Russia to shore up its position in the short to medium term. This, Cheung suggested, is evidence of failure given the decline of Russia's capacities in military technologi-

---

[23] See Lebow, *Why Nations Fight*, chap. 4.

[24] US Department of Defense, *11th Annual Report to Congress on Military and Security Developments Involving the People's Republic of China* (Washington, DC: US Department of Defense, 2011).

cal innovation. China's leaders are pinning their hopes on developing their capacities in the long term, although there remain evident and significant barriers to them doing so.[25]

Should war come between the United States and China, it will not be a result of a power transition. The greater risk is that conflict will arise from the misperception that such a transition is imminent. Power transition theory could be made self-fulfilling and generate its own corroboration where history has hitherto failed to oblige. Power transition is not unique in this potential. Realism, more generally, may have become to some degree self-fulfilling. Security discourses in China and elsewhere in Asia—much more so than in Europe—tend to take realism's fundamental propositions as verities. It would be ironic if US-China relations deteriorated because each power based its expectations on how the other would behave on theories that lack any empirical support. One Chinese scholar warns that his country "has spent a lot of time learning from rising powers like Russia, Japan, and Germany, so as to avoid the mistakes of past rising powers. The United States should spend time learning how previous dominant powers dealt with rising powers [peacefully]."[26]

More moderate defensive realists like Charles Glaser suggest that the prospects for hegemonic war may be reduced by mutual defensive postures that have the goal of forestalling exaggerated threat perception and overreaction by one or both countries. Glaser nevertheless employs a questionable historical comparison: between the US-China relationship and the Cold War one between the United States and the Soviet Union. On the basis of this comparison he argues that China's rise can be peaceful, but that this outcome is far from guaranteed. Contrary to offensive realists, he does not believe that basic pressures generated by the international system will force the United States and China into conflict. Nuclear weapons, separation by the Pacific Ocean, and reasonably good political relations should enable both countries to maintain high levels of security and avoid military policies that severely strain their relationship. Washington's political need to protect its allies in Northeast Asia complicates matters somewhat, but there are strong grounds, he insists, for believing that the United States can continue to maintain

[25] Tai Ming Cheung, "How China Innovates in Defense Science and Technology," lecture at Centre d'Etude des Relations Internationales, Sciences Po, Paris, 31 January 2013. For further discussion see Tai Ming Cheung, "The Chinese Defense Economy's Long March from Imitation to Innovation," *Journal of Strategic Studies* 34, no. 3 (June 2011): 325–54; and Tai Ming Cheung, *Fortifying China: The Struggle to Build a Modern Defense Economy* (Ithaca, NY: Cornell University Press, 2009), 2.

[26] International Conference on East Asia Cooperation and Sino-US Relations, Beijing, 3–4 November 2005, quoted in Lampton, *The Three Faces of Chinese Power*, 34.

its nuclear umbrella over Japan and South Korea without unduly provoking China.[27]

Liberals, not surprisingly, respond favorably to Glaser's underlying optimism, although they often disagree with his argument. Geoffrey Garret objects to Glaser's historical comparison on the grounds that close economic relations and interdependence between the United States and China make any comparison with the Soviet Union deeply problematic.[28] Liberal expectations of good relations rest on several reinforcing assumptions. Economic development will further enlarge the rapidly growing Chinese middle class, which, sooner or later, will insist on political inclusion through democratic reforms. In keeping with the democratic peace thesis, a democratic China will be a peaceful China.[29] Liberals contend that even in the absence of democratic reforms, economic interdependence will blunt any Chinese propensity toward aggression.[30]

Liberals characterize the existing international order as one of economic and political openness that can peacefully accommodate China's rise. The United States and other leading powers are expected to incorporate China into this order in a manner that facilitates its economic development. Rational Chinese leaders will prefer accommodation to the risks inherent in any struggle to overturn the system and establish an order more to its own liking.[31] Neither liberals nor realists base their predictions on an analysis of Chinese history.

THE VIEW FROM BEIJING

Chinese analysts, scholars, and journalists consistently challenge realist and liberal interpretations. Zheng Bijian, a prominent Chinese spokes-

---

[27] Charles Glaser, "Will China's Rise Lead to War? Why Realism Does Not Mean Pessimism," *Foreign Affairs* 90 (2011), http://www.foreignaffairs.com/articles/67479/charles-glaser/will-chinas-rise-lead-to-war (accessed 24 May 2011).

[28] Geoffrey Garrett, "Chinese–US Economic Relations after the Global Financial Crisis," in Jane Golley and Ligang Song, eds., *Rising China: Global Challenges and Opportunities* (Canberra: ANU Press, 2011), 149–72.

[29] Michael Santoro, "Global Capitalism and the Road to Chinese Democracy," *Current History* 99, no. 638 (2000): 263–67.

[30] See Joshua Cooper Ramo, *The Beijing Consensus: Notes on the New Physics of Chinese Power* (London: Foreign Policy Center, 2004), 36; Thomas Lum and Dick K. Nanto, *China's Trade with the United States and the World* (Washington DC: Congressional Research Service, 2007), especially 3; Garrett, 'Chinese–US Economic Relations after the Global Financial Crisis."

[31] Glaser, "Will China's Rise Lead to War?"

man, insists that China can "peacefully rise to great power status" through what he calls "the developmental path." He maintains that China will not follow the path of Germany in the decades before World War I, or those of Germany and Japan leading up to World War II, when these countries violently plundered resources and sought world or regional hegemony. Neither will China follow the superpowers vying for domination during the Cold War; instead it will transcend ideological differences to strive for peace, development, and cooperation globally.[32] The Chinese can therefore be dissatisfied with the status quo, and advocate change, without seeking to destabilize the system.

Shi Yinhong, a professor of international relations at Beijing's Renmin University, made a similar point in a *People's Daily* online forum at the end of 2007: China need not dance to the West's tune, but risks alienating other countries, including those in the developing world, if it refuses to become a "responsible stakeholder."[33] This view has become dominant in Beijing, judging from official statements. The trick is to engage on China's terms. In his March 2008 address to the National People's Congress, Foreign Minister Yang Jiechi argued that China should take on more international responsibility, but in an à la carte way that serves its own interests.[34] While we must be careful to take such statements at face value, they do indicate that China can be a dissatisfied yet responsible stakeholder.

Western conceptions of hegemony and balance of power are largely alien to China. Present-day Chinese officials and scholars understand them only because they are familiar with relevant Western literature. In order to fathom China's motives, priorities, goals, and indeed its behavior, we need to apply concepts indigenous to the Chinese political vocabulary.

At the heart of Chinese thinking is the distinction between the notion of power and influence. Imperial China established a clientalist relationship, or tributary system, with its developed neighbors. In its relations with its Confucian neighbors, Korea, Vietnam, Japan, and the Ryukyus—and farther afield in the short-lived era of trade and exploration—China sought honor in the form recognition of its cultural supremacy and centrality. In return, it provided practical security and economic rewards. Lesser states often referred to China as the "cultural

---

[32] Zheng Bijian, "China's Peaceful Rise to Great-Power Status," *Foreign Affairs* 84, no. 5 (2005), 18–24.

[33] Shi Yinhong, quoted in Minxen Pei, "Playing Ball," *South China Morning Post*, 29 December 2008.

[34] "Out into the World: China is Ready to Become a Good Citizen—But on Its Own Terms," *Newsweek*, 31 December 2008, http://www.thedailybeast.com/newsweek/2008/12/31/out-into-the-world.html (accessed 14 February 2013).

efflorescence" or the "domain of manifest civility" based on its closer approximation of Confucian ideals. The tributary system found institutional representation in *investiture*, a diplomatic protocol by which a state sent envoys to China to accept explicitly their subordinate status. Subsequent embassies were required to reaffirm the relationship, exchange information, and arrange for trade and cultural exchanges. Tributary states had to adopt the Chinese calendar in all communications with the emperor.[35] These forms of obeisance were acknowledgments of Chinese cultural superiority, not political overlordship.[36]

China had no desire to impose its vision on the world, but was interested in stable and productive relations with its neighbors. Such a system—surprisingly similar to the ancient Greek understanding of *hēgemonia*—worked to the advantage of both parties: the strong gained honor while the weak gained protection and trade advantages. Of equal importance, this arrangement encouraged China in accord with its self-image and honorific status.[37] Here, too, the ancient Greek and Chinese systems were similar as honor brought with it a set of rules that imposed self-constraint.

David Kang argues that this clientalist arrangement accounts for the glaring discrepancy in the frequency of war between the European and East Asian regional systems. From 1368 to 1841—from the onset of the tributary system up to the Sino-British Opium War, there were only two wars involving China, Korea, and Japan. These episodes aside, the three countries maintained peaceful and even friendly relations, which became more stable as they became more powerful. The key to peace was the unquestioned dominance of China, in cultural as well and economic and military domains, and its reluctance to expand territorially at the expense of its "civilized" neighbors. Other states accepted China's primacy and sought to benefit from it culturally and economically. Korean, Vietnamese, and Japanese elites copied Chinese institutional, linguistic, and cultural practices, which in turn facilitated closer and more productive relations with China.[38]

[35] Frederick M. Nelson, *Korea and the Old Orders in Asia* (Baton Rouge: Louisiana State University Press, 1945), 11–20; James L. Hevia, *Men from Afar: Qing Guest Ritual and the Macartney Embassy of 1793* (Durham, NC: Duke University Press, 2005): 124–33; David C. Kang, *China Rising: Peace, Power, and Order in East Asia* (New York: Columbia University Press, 2007), 56.

[36] Gregory Smits, *Visions of Rykyu: Identity and Ideology in Early Modern Thought and Politics* (Honolulu: University of Hawaii Press, 1999), 36; Kang, *China Rising*, 57.

[37] Donald N. Clark, "Sino-Korean Relations under the Ming," in *The Cambridge History of China*, vol. 8, Denis Twitchett and Frederick W. Mote, eds., *The Ming Dynasty, 1368–1694, Part 2*, 272–98. (Cambridge: Cambridge University Press, 1998): 272–99; Kang, *China Rising*; David C. Kang, *East Asia before the West: Five Centuries of Trade and Tribute Asia* (New York: Columbia University Press, 2010).

[38] Kang, *China Rising*, 82–106. For a contrary view stressing internal conflicts, see War-

Present-day Chinese leaders and many of their domestic critics appear to envisage a similar role for their country. Evidence can be adduced from how Beijing has sought to structure its relationship with both Koreas and Thailand. If China seeks regional hēgemonia of this kind, its foreign policy goals and American economic and security interests appear fully compatible as it was, albeit for different reasons, between the United States and Britain in the nineteenth century.

In imperial times there were two neighbors that could not be integrated into a clientalist relationship: the nomads of inner Asia and Japan. The nomads were unprepared to accept such a relationship, and the Chinese tried to manage them through a combination of carrots and sticks. They were to some degree dependent on the nomads, as they supplied the army with horses, while nomads depended on China for various finished goods. Both sides used violence to coerce the other into making trade concessions, but the nomads also periodically conducted raids to get goods and women for free. Historically the balance of power swung back and forth between the two groups, with China succumbing on two occasions to conquest by nomadic peoples.[39]

Japan posed a different problem. It rejected a clientalist relationship because it wanted to supplant China as the center of the universe. Elsewhere, Lebow has argued that Japan's deeply ambivalent relationship with China—characterized by equal doses of admiration and resentment—reveals the insecurity of the late cultural developer.[40] Such countries are keen to excel and copy much of the culture and technology of leading powers while proclaiming their superiority. This is another way in which Japan was like Germany. Over the centuries, Japanese leaders struggled to make the minimum accommodations to China that would allow a profitable trade. In the late nineteenth century, in which it was military strong, it sought to supplant China as the leading regional power by force.[41]

---

ren I. Cohen, "China's Rise in Historical Perspective," in Guoli Liu and Quansheng Zhao, eds., Managing the Chinese Challenge: Global Perspectives (London: Routledge, 2008), 23–40; Andrew J. Nathan and Andrew Scobell, *China's Search for Security* (New York: Columbia University Press, 2012); and Andrew Scobell, *China's Use of Military Force: Beyond the Great Wall and the Long March* (Columbia University Press, 2003).

[39] Morris Rossabi, "The Ming and Inner Asia," in Twitchett and Mote, eds., *The Cambridge History of China*, vol. 8, 221–71; John Mears, *Analyzing the Phenomenon of Borderlands from the Comparative and Cross-Cultural Perspectives* (unpublished manuscript, 2001), http://webdoc.sub.gwdg.de/ebook/p/2005/history_cooperative/www.historycooperative.org/proceedings/interactions/mears.html; Peter Perdue, *China Marches West: The Qing Conquest of Central Eurasia* (Cambridge, MA: Harvard University Press, 2005).

[40] Richard Ned Lebow, *A Cultural Theory of International Relations* (Cambridge: Cambridge University Press, 2008), cha8.

[41] Kawazoe Shoji, "Japan and East Asia," in *The Cambridge History of Japan*, vol. 3, Kozo Yamamura, ed., *Medieval Japan* (Cambridge: Cambridge University Press, 1990), chap. 9;

The last two decades of Chinese foreign policy offer evidence for our supposition. Beijing has sought accommodations with all of its neighbors. They in turn have sought accommodation with China. Despite the phenomenal growth of Chinese power there has been no effort to balance against it by China's neighbors, with the exception of Taiwan.[42]

In almost every case where it shares a frontier with another country, it has been a contested one. This abiding problem is the inheritance of colonialism, where lines were drawn on maps by administrators and never really demarcated. Beginning with India in the 1960s, Chinese leaders sought to overcome these conflicts through a policy of concession. In return for territorial settlements that invariably favored the other country, China demanded recognition, any halt to the support or de facto sanctuary of armed opponents of its government and the right of hot pursuit if they launched attacks across the Chinese border. This approach has led to the settlement of seventeen of China's twenty-three territorial disputes, with China usually receiving less than 50 percent of the contested land. For various reasons, but primarily due to bad intelligence and nationalist outbidding in the parliament, the Indians spurned all offers of compromise and provoked a disastrous war with China in 1962. After decisively defeating the Indian army on two fronts, Chinese forces withdrew for the most part to their prewar positions.

Beijing has adhered scrupulously to its border treaties and relations with all of its neighbors—even India—have improved. A possible exception has been the dispute with Japan, prompted by the Japanese government's move in 2012 to purchase the Diaoyu/Senkaku Islands. Japan's attempt to consolidate its claims of sovereignty over them, fully supported by the country's prime minister Shinzo Abe, who assumed office in December 2012, is in abrogation of the postwar Cairo Declaration of 1943 and the Potsdam Agreement of 1945, and thus of international law. In China, nationalist opinion and local authorities fanned the issue; for the latter it became a vehicle in a regional power struggle.[43] So far there has been more oratory than actual confrontation. It is nevertheless a troubling situation because of Japan's nationalist government and the prospect of China's more moderate government nevertheless feeling compelled to respond for domestic political reasons.

Ronald P. Toby, *State and Diplomacy in Early Modern Japan: Asia in the Development of the Tokugawa Bakufu* (Stanford, CA: Stanford University Press, 1991), 170–72.

[42] Lampton, *The Three Faces of Chinese Power*, 175; Kang, *China Rising*, 193.

[43] Stephanie Kleine Ahlbrandt, "Dangerous Waters," *Foreign Policy*, 17 September 2012, http://www.foreignpolicy.com/articles/2012/09/17/dangerous_waters (accessed 5 March 2013); Martine Bulard, "China: As You Were," *Le Monde Diplomatique*, 6 December 2012, http://mondediplo.com/2012/12/06china (accessed 5 March 2013).

Two major flash points remain: Tibet and Taiwan. The vast majority of Chinese consider both territories part of China and therefore a domestic question. There is widespread resentment against India and the West for what is seen as interference in Chinese affairs and infringement upon Chinese sovereignty. From the Western perspective, China has run roughshod over the civil and cultural rights of Tibetans and other minorities in western China and Mongolia. Its policy of populating these areas with Chinese settlers, reminiscent of Joseph Stalin's policies in the Baltics, Karelia, the Crimea, and parts of the Caucasus, is deeply offensive to indigenous residents. It is increasingly evident that while these policies provoke internal unrest they will not seriously damage or threaten relations with the West.

Sino-American rapprochement and the end of the Cold War have partially defused the Taiwanese conflict. China remains committed to national unification as a matter of principle and has pledged to go to war if Taiwan should ever declare its independence. China's political elite believes that Taiwanese independence would disrupt China's social stability, national unity, and great power aspirations. Once again, there are grounds for cautious optimism. The Taiwanese independence movement seems to be waning rather than growing and the economic integration of the two states is increasing rapidly. In 2005, 70 percent of Taiwan's direct foreign investment was in China, and 40 percent of its exports went across the Taiwan Strait. Tourist exchanges have increased, and over one million Taiwanese business people and their families have homes on the mainland. Time is on Beijing's side, and its government appears content to let matters run their natural course. If China suffers an economic decline, or if Taiwan declares its independence, a clash could occur in the strait, one that could draw in the United States and put the two most powerful states in the world on a collision course.[44]

China's foreign policy since 1949, and even more so in the last two decades, has been marked by caution designed to enhance regime stability, sustain self-determination, and avoid hegemonic interference. Its few resorts to force—in Korea in 1950, Tibet in 1950, and along the Indian frontier in 1962—were arguably defensive in nature or associated with national unification. Only the war with Vietnam in 1979 lends itself to another narrative.[45] Following the Chinese communist takeover

[44] Steve Chan, *China, the US, and the Power-Transition Theory: A Critique* (New York: Routledge, 2008), 92; Peter Hans Gries, *China's New Nationalism*, 11; Yong Deng, *China's Struggle for Status: The Realignment of International Relations* (New York: Cambridge University Press, 2008): 257–58.

[45] Neville Maxwell, *India's China War* (New York: Random House, 1970); John W. Garver, "China's Decision for War with India in 1962," in Alastair Iain Johnston and Robert S. Ross, eds., *New Directions in the Study of China's Foreign Policy* (Stanford: Stanford

in 1949, the United States was seen as the linear descendant of Japan; a predatory power encouraged by China's division and relative weakness to encroach military on its territory. This understanding was clear in internal Chinese descriptions of the United States on the eve of the Korean War, and an important reason the communists felt compelled to intervene.[46] The United States is no longer regarded this way by most influential Chinese, nor is present-day Japan. However, neither country fits the traditional Chinese understanding of how clients should behave. They do not expect this kind of conformity from the United States, and really have no category into which to fit powerful and sophisticated barbarian states. The arrival of European powers in China in the nineteenth century created a similar problem. Meaningful accommodation accordingly requires changes in the understanding elites have of one other and the working out of some mutually acceptable framework for their relations.

Another useful metric for assessing Chinese intentions is its adherence to global norms. Rosemary Foot and Andrew Walter conducted an exhaustive comparative evaluation of China and the United States in this regard. They considered norms regarding the use of force, macroeconomic policy, nuclear nonproliferation, climate change, and financial regulation.[47] In recent decades, they find, China has moved from a position of generally low behavioral consistency toward gradually higher levels in all categories.[48] In no domain, however, is its adherence comparable to the highest levels of compliance by some states. A case in point is Beijing's failure to value denuclearization of North Korea and Iran over its parochial interests regarding both states, although its signals regarding the former suggest that its view may be changing under its new leadership.[49] Where Chinese compliance is high, as with respect

---

University Press, 2006), 86–130; Ramo, *Beijing Consensus*, 12; Thomas J. Christensen, "Windows and War: Trend Analysis and Beijing's Use of Force," in Johnston and Ross, eds., *New Directions in the Study of China's Foreign Policy*, 50–85.

[46] Alan Whiting, *China Crosses the Yalu: The Decision to Enter the Korean War* (New York: Macmillan, 1960); Christensen, "Windows and War."

[47] Rosemary Foot and Andrew Walter, *China, The United States and the Global Order* (Cambridge: Cambridge University Press, 2011).

[48] For similar arguments, see Allen Carlson, "More Than Just Saying No: China's Evolving Approach to Sovereignty and Intervention Since Tiananmen," in Johnston and Ross, eds., *New Directions in the Study of China's Foreign Policy*, 217–41; Samuel S. Kim, "Chinese Foreign Policy Faces Globalization Challenges," in Johnston and Ross, eds., *New Directions in the Study of China's Foreign Policy*, 276–308.

[49] Kim Young-jin, "Chinese Leader backs NK Denuclearization," *Korean Times*, 28 January 2013, http://www.koreatimes.co.kr/www/news/nation/2013/02/120_129608.html (accessed 8 February 2013).

to the Kyoto Protocol, it often involves low costs. There are some instances of Chinese compliance involving high costs.[50] The principal exception, Foot and Walter argue, is in the area of macroeconomic policy surveillance, where compliance with norms has declined from previously moderate levels as domestic constraints have increased. In other economic areas, compliance has risen as domestic reformers used norm compliance as a strategic means of modernizing China's own financial system.[51]

The Chinese case looks more interesting still when compared with the United States. Washington remains a principal center of norm innovation, but its record of compliance is quite mixed. It has repeatedly chosen to use force unilaterally, overlooks proliferation by friendly states, and spurns International Monetary Fund (IMF) pleas to reduce its deficits. In recent years it has withdrawn commitments to implement financial and climate agreements that it helped to shape. The US position on compliance overall has been characterized by selectivity and inconsistency; support for the Montreal Protocol and the stonewalling of the Kyoto Protocol are cases in point. In both countries, compliance falters when it encounters strong domestic opposition for economic or ideological reasons. Overall, however, Chinese compliance has been rising, in contrast to the United States.[52]

This overview drives home the inadequacy of analyzing foreign policy in terms of power and relative power, no matter how they are conceived and measured. It highlights the importance of the goals political elites seek and the ends they consider appropriate to them. These determine how states acquire and use power, rooted in historical and cultural lessons. Even so, they do not dictate policy. Foreign policy consists of initiatives, responses, and adjustments made in regard to the initiatives, responses, and adjustments of others and the perceived consequences of one's own behavior. Beijing's evolving policy must be analyzed in this broader interactive context.

Considerations of power are never more than an enabling condition and instrumentality. This is not to dismiss their importance; absent its clearly extraordinary economic development, China could not hope to play a key role on the world stage. Nor could this development have occurred without a centrally controlled military that unified and pro-

---

[50] Martin Dimitrov, *Piracy and the State: The Politics of Intellectual Property Rights in China* (New York: Cambridge University Press, 2009).

[51] Foot and Walter, *China, The United States and the Global Order*, 275; Margaret M. Pearson, "China in Geneva: Lessons from China's Early Years in the World Trade Organization," in Johnston and Ross, eds., *New Directions in the Study of China's Foreign Policy*, 242–75.

[52] Foot and Walter, *China, The United States and the Global Order*.

tected the country and its regime. Sophisticated realists like Hans Morgenthau and John Herz understood that power is a means to an end, not an end in itself. Modern-day realists who start with power and infer foreign policy goals from it conduct their analysis the wrong way round.

Foreign policy goals may not determine power, but as power is to some degree fungible, they help determine where resources are invested. Here, too, realist analyses that focus on China's threatening military miss the mark. Without going into details about the order of battle and the trajectory of military spending, certain facts seem incontestable. China has used some of its wealth to upgrade its military forces, but primarily to provide the capability to deal with Taiwan.[53] This includes the usual conventional weaponry and naval armada capable of crossing the Taiwan Strait. There has been no effort to develop serious power projection capabilities, nor high-tech information-based ground and air forces similar to ours. The Chinese navy may have the longer-term goals of developing a denial capability in the South China Sea, but this too is consistent with its regional goals.

China's strategic programs are also minimal. Little has been done in recent years to upgrade nuclear forces. China has perhaps eighteen missiles capable of reaching the United States, all of them armed with only single warheads. These are "city buster" weapons of 4,500 kilotons in comparison to our 450 kiloton warheads on highly accurate multiple independently targetable reentry vehicle missiles. The United States has undertaken significant strategic upgrading since the end of the Cold War. Trident I missiles were replaced with Trident IIIs with GPS navigation systems and larger warheads. Greater accuracy and larger warheads makes them far more deadly if they are used to attack Chinese missile silos. Three warheads targeted on each Chinese silo have a 99 percent chance of destroying all of them while killing fewer than six thousand Chinese, and with hardly any fallout.[54]

Chinese defense spending has grown at double-digit annual rates since 1989, and the pace of modernization has accelerated. Foreign estimates of Chinese defense spending in 2006 ranged from $31 to $90 billion, with $44 billion probably the most accurate figure. By comparison, the United States spent $518 billion in 2004, Russia spent $63 billion, and the United Kingdom $38 billion in 2003. By 2010, these figures stood at $698 billion for the United States, $119 billion for China, $58.7 billion for Russia, and $59.6 billion for the United Kingdom.[55] China

---

[53] Lampton, *The Three Faces of Chinese Power*, 37–76.

[54] Arms Control Association, "US Nuclear Modernization Programs," August 2012, http://www.armscontrol.org/factsheets/USNuclearModernization (accessed 16 February 2013).

[55] Stockholm International Peace Research Institute, "The Top 10 Military Spenders,"

spends a higher proportion of its gross domestic product on the military than many developed countries, at an average of 2 percent between 2008 and 2012. Yet this is a mere fraction of the 4.7 percent spent by the United States in the same period.[56] Its new aircraft carrier is a remodeled older Soviet model, lacking the requisite slingshot technology to launch technologically advanced fighter planes. Its ground forces, while in the process of being modernized, are still primarily configured for domestic use and border protection. Some accounts of Chinese military spending suggest a slowdown in its growth. All of these figures are debatable, as are Chinese military capabilities more generally. What is indisputable, however, is the fallacy of trying to reason from capabilities to intentions. If any more evidence for this truth is required, one need only look back on attempts to do this with regard to the Soviet Union.

China's Custodial Role

In the summer of 2011, as the prospect of a historically unprecedented US government debt default loomed, Chinese foreign ministry spokesman Hong Lei called upon the US government to "adopt responsible measures and policies" toward foreign investors. His comments came a day after Moody's Investor Services advised that it might cut its ratings for US government debt, and Federal Reserve Chairman Ben Bernanke's warning that a default would amount to "a huge financial calamity."[57] Both Standard & Poor's and China's Dagong Global Credit Rating had already downgraded the US credit rating, primarily because of the economy's slow growth and the government's rising debt.[58] The symbolic importance of China berating the United States was unmistakable. The globe's self-appointed economic leader was behaving in a way that undermined its claims of economic centrality and prudence. China, America's chief foreign creditor and formerly a nation committed to autarchy, was expressing concern about irresponsible American

SIPRI Yearbook 2011 (Stockholm: Stockholm International Peace Research Institute, 2011), 9.

[56] World Bank, "Military Expenditure (% of GDP)," http://data.worldbank.org/indicator/MS.MIL.XPND.GD.ZS (accessed 8 February 2013).

[57] Carl Hulse, "Tensions Escalate as Stakes Grow in Fiscal Clash," *New York Times*, 13 July 2011, http://www.nytimes.com/2011/07/14/us/politics/14fiscal.html?pagewanted=all (accessed 30 August 2011).

[58] Bettina Wassener and Matthew Saltmarsh, "China Urges US to Protect Creditors by Raising Debt," *New York Times*, 15 July 2011, http://mobile.nytimes.com/article;jsessionid=AA7D9B8FA19A8361669507ED7AAC4F30.w5?a=816295&f=111 (accessed 15 July 2011).

behavior that again threatened global instability. The previous instance was the subprime mortgage crisis four years earlier.

Yet there has been plethora of American academic, governmental, and popular articles and reports that accuse China of expanding its economic power at a cost of other states through trade, foreign direct investment (FDI), overseas development aid, and a total disregard of macroeconomic imbalances. Chinese FDI is often characterized as a predatory means of enhancing outward trade and the inward procurement of much-needed raw materials.[59] The purchase of US Treasury bills and European government bonds are depicted as investments intended to exert political leverage in a variety of domains, including the formal recognition of China as a 'full market economy' within the World Trade Organization (WTO), a status it craves.[60]

Chinese behavior is undeniably interest-based. China is the primary beneficiary of the existing international economic order. Taylor Fravel argues, in contrast to realist expectations, that "China has pursued foreign policies consistent with status quo and not revisionist intentions."[61] In keeping with this orientation, we maintain that it is assuming a more expansive—if still underdeveloped—custodial role through the combined use of markets and diplomacy in a way that expands its influence while avoiding conflict. A recent example is Beijing's purchase of European government bonds to help avert a Greek default on its debt.[62] This is merely one instance of efforts by China to buttress the global economic system in ways that are currently unmatched by any other state. In the remainder of this chapter we will examine these efforts in the context of the need to address global imbalances, stabilize currencies, reinforce liberal rules in trade and finance, and to act as the lender of

[59] Nargiza Salidjanova, *Going Out: An Overview of China's Outward Foreign Direct Investment* (Washington, DC: US-China Economic and Security Review Commission, 2011), 6–9; Ben White, "Chinese Drops Bid to Buy US Oil Firm," *Washington Post*, 3 August 2005, (accessed 30 June 2011); Andrew Ross Sorkin and Jad Mouawad, "Bid by Chevron in Big Oil Deal Thwarts China," *New York Times*, 20 July 2005, http://www.nytimes.com/2005/07/20/international/asia/20unocal.html (accessed 28 June 2011).

[60] Smita Purushottam, "China Woos Europe: Next Moves on the Eurasian Chessboard," *Global Policy Journal*, 14 February 2011, http://www.globalpolicyjournal.com/blog/14/02/2011/china-woos-europe-next-moves-eurasian-chessboard (accessed 30 June 2011).

[61] M. Taylor Fravel, "International Relations Theory and China's Rise: Assessing China's Potential for Territorial Expansion," *International Studies Review* 12, no. 4 (2010): 506. See also Alastair Iain Johnston, "Is China a Status Quo Power?" *International Security* 27, no. 4 (2003): 5–56; and Kang, *China Rising*.

[62] See comments by Wen Jiabao on a visit to Berlin, in "China and Germany Ink $15bn Trade Deals as Leaders Meet," 29 June 2011, http://www.bbc.co.uk/news/business-13954148 (accessed 29 June 2011).

last resort through both developmental aid and the financing of public debt. These are the functions of global economic management identified as critical by liberal theorists.

Addressing Global Imbalances

Stability and prosperity, as every economic textbook declares, are contingent on maintaining a relative macroeconomic balance in the global economic system. For that system to function smoothly, capital flows must facilitate global trade and finance. A healthy global economy requires high levels of financial integration, at least among the largest economies; relatively equitable current account balances, which are heavily reliant on balanced trade; and globally compatible public and private savings and investment rates.[63] When a reasonable balance is not possible, it is imperative to have a lender of last resort to maintain liquidity flows in an effort to offset or correct imbalances. This is one reason why the United States invested so heavily in rebuilding Europe's industrial capacity in the aftermath of World War II.

Until the end of the 1960s, when the dollar was the world's undisputed reserve currency, the US current account balance ran at zero or a small surplus. That position dramatically eroded in the 1980s, and the US current account deficit peaked at 6 percent in 2006, just before the financial crisis.[64] The critical US shift was symptomatic of a far larger problem. On aggregate, average global imbalances grew by 1 percent between 1970 and 1990. Between 1990 and 2007, they accelerated by a yearly average of 11 percent.[65] More troubling still, account imbalances became concentrated in specific regions. After 1994, the imbalance became more pronounced in the United States, East Asia and in what subsequently became the eurozone. The average regional imbalance as a share of regional GDP increased about 2.6 percent in the United States and East Asia, and by 1.7 percent in the eurozone, but only by about 1.1 percent in the rest of the world. This growing difference between balances among China, Europe and the United States on the one hand and

[63] For a more general discussion see Foot and Walter, *China, The United States and the Global Order*, 1–30.

[64] Joshua Aizenman, "On the Causes of Global Imbalances and Their Persistence: Myths, Facts and Conjectures," in Stijn Claessens, Simon Evenett, and Bernard Hoekman, eds., *Rebalancing the Global Economy: A Primer for Policymaking* (London: Centre for Economic Policy Research, 2010), 23–30.

[65] Caroline Freund, "Adjustment in Global Imbalances and the Future of Trade Growth," in Claessens, Evenett, and Hoekman, eds., *Rebalancing the Global Economy*, 11–22.

those involving the rest of the world on the other explains why policy discussion often focuses on these few countries with the largest negative or positive balances—notably, China and the United States.[66]

In many ways, these imbalances were the product of deliberate American efforts to foster greater financial integration among advanced industrial economies in the 1980s. Subsequently, they were associated with efforts to integrate emerging markets, such as China. This took place at a time when there was a consistent decline in net US public and private savings.[67] American policies accordingly had the effect of making the US government and consumers increasingly reliant on foreign capital to finance their expenditures. Overexpenditure by individual Americans and their government—reflected in low personal savings rates coupled with increased government deficits—became important causes of global imbalances.[68]

The growth in American personal debt has been unmistakable: from a peak of 14.6 percent in 1975, and an average of around 9 percent in the 1980s, the American net savings rate declined to around zero by the turn of the century. It reached a low of -0.5 percent in 2005.[69] Prior to 2005, negative savings rates had not been recorded in the United States since 1933, at the height of the Great Depression. As savings plummeted, debt increased. By 2005, total US household debt, including mortgage loans and consumer debt, stood at $11.4 trillion.[70]

This growth in personal debt finds a parallel in the US federal budget deficit. Since the end of the President Bill Clinton's second term, the annual deficit of US government has increased in size every year. It went from $186.2 billion inflation-adjusted dollars in 2002 to over an estimated $1,500 billion by 2011.[71] As a result, total public debt ballooned to $14.43 trillion by June 2011.[72] Comedian and social commentator Jon

[66] Bank for International Settlements, *81st Annual Report, 1 April 2010–31 March 2011* (Basel, Switzerland: Bank for International Settlements, 2011) 35.

[67] Aizenman, "On the Causes of Global Imbalances," 24.

[68] The personal savings rate is calculated by taking the difference between disposable personal income and personal consumption expenditures, then dividing this quantity by disposable personal income.

[69] Massimo Guidolin and Elizabeth A. La Jeunesse, "The Decline in the US Personal Saving Rate: Is It Real and Is It a Puzzle?" *Federal Reserve Bank of St. Louis Review* 89, no. 6 (2007), 491–514.

[70] Board of Governors of the Federal Reserve System, 9 March 2006, 8, 102, http://www.federalreserve.gov/releases/Z1/20060309/data.htm (accessed 29 January 2011).

[71] Lori Montgomery, "CBO Projects US Budget Deficit to Reach $1.5 trillion in 2011, Highest Ever," *Washington Post*, 26 January 2011, http://www.washingtonpost.com/business/cbo-projects-us-budget-deficit-to-reach-15-trillion-in-2011-highest-ever/2011/01/26/ABKue3Q_story.html (accessed 28 June2011).

[72] Treasurydirect, http://www.treasurydirect.gov/NP/BPDLogin?application=np (accessed 28 June 2011).

TABLE 4.1.
Balance of Payments, 2000–2012 (US$ millions)

Year	Balance
2000	−376,749.0
2001	−361,771.0
2002	−417,432.0
2003	−490,984.0
2004	−605,357.0
2005	−708,624.0
2006	−753,288.0
2007	−696,728.0
2008	−698,338.0
2009	−379,154.0
2010	−492,737.0
2011	−559,880.0
2012	−540,362.0

Source: US Census Bureau, Foreign Trade Division, "U.S. Trade in Goods and Services," 9 June 2011, http://www.census.gov/foreign-trade/statistics/historical/gands.txt (accessed 28 May 2013).

Stewart put this problem into perspective by noting that the $44,500 of public debt owed per American was approximately the same sum owed by Greeks, whose country was in the throes of a budget default.[73] The National Debt Clock calculated a figure: $46,166.89 per resident. By 2013, that figure had reached an average of nearly $52,500.[74]

Figures for the US trade deficit, a third indicator, are just as illuminating. According to the US Census Bureau, the United States has run a trade deficit in goods and services every year since 1969, with the exception of 1973 and 1975. Comparable to the budget deficit, these figures have worsened over time and have ballooned since the turn of the century, again peaking in 2006 on the eve of the financial crisis (see table 4.1).

The US trade deficit with China has become the largest component of the aggregate deficit, increasing for every year except two since 1985. Again, this deficit has accelerated since 2001 (see table 4.2), and reached the point were it has become a politically sensitive issue among American policy makers and politicians.

The growing aggregate trade imbalance between China and the United States has been exacerbated by US policy and the lack of regulatory mechanisms. These include significant tax cuts introduced by the

[73] Jon Stewart, *Daily Show*, Comedy Central, 23 June 2011.
[74] "The US National Debt Clock," http://www.brillig.com/debt_clock (accessed 1 July 2011 and 12 February 2013).

TABLE 4.2.
US Trade Deficit with China, 2000–2012 (US$ millions)

Year	Trade Balance
2000	−83,833.0
2001	−83,096.1
2002	−103,064.9
2003	−124,068.2
2004	−162,254.3
2005	−202,278.1
2006	−234,101.3
2007	−258,506.0
2008	−268,039.8
2009	−226,877.2
2010	−273,063.2
2011	−495,422.5
2012	−315,053.5

Source: US Census, "Trade Goods with China," http://www.census.gov/foreign-trade/balance/c5700.html (accessed 14 February 2013).

administration of President George W. Bush, liberal policies designed to attract foreign funds, low savings rates, and, worst of all, unregulated credit markets that then made personal credit easier to obtain and led to a housing bubble. According to Joshua Aizenman,

> The inflows of capital to the US prolonged the period of low saving in the US, and magnified the duration of the real estate appreciation, deepening the global crisis induced down the road by the growing weaknesses in the US housing market in 2007. Financial distortions in the US were manifested by the growing laxity of borrowing standards, exemplified by the proliferation of mortgages with zero (even negative) down payments. The rise of bundling and securitisation of mortgages reduced the "skin in the game" of mortgage suppliers, changing the business model of mortgage originating banks from risk assessors providing enduring financial intermediation to a commission-based business. In this new environment, profits were determined by the volume of mortgages initiated, and not by its quality (i.e., the successful service of these mortgages). These developments intensified the moral hazard and the exposure to vulnerabilities associated with lower quality of financial intermediation in the US.[75]

Rather than looking at their own responsibility for these burgeoning deficits, American policy makers have repeatedly portrayed China as

[75] Joshua Aizenman, "On the Causes of Global Imbalances," 28.

the source of the problem. They characterize the Chinese as inflexible and opportunistic free riders, assisted by a fixed and inflated exchange rate and competitiveness made possible in part by stolen intellectual property. In contrast to the United States, China's economic growth has been nothing short of meteoric. In 1990, its share of world merchandise trade (the sum of exports and imports) was 2 percent. By 2000, it had doubled to 4 percent, and by 2010, had reached 10 percent.[76] The 2008 recession presaged a decline in global imbalances, providing a potential turning point even as Western economies contracted and China's strengthened. European and American consumers finally cut back on their consumption binge. Real trade declined 12.2 percent in 2009, a figure not reached since the Great Depression. As a result of this deflated demand, global trade imbalances fell by 26 percent.[77] Rebalancing between the United States and China was brought about in the first instance by reduced US demand, but secondarily, by increases in Chinese imports, which was in response to fiscal stimulus policies and rising wages and prices within China.[78] Confronted with a global crisis, China aggressively promoted rebalancing, although this process, according to World Bank officials, clearly posed a threat to China's thriving export market.[79]

This process of rebalancing has been assisted by a new Chinese focus on raising private and corporate consumption rates in China. The decades-old US pattern of personal debt contrasts starkly with historically high Asian personal savings rates. High Asian savings rates have been the result of several reinforcing conditions that promote what is known as precautionary savings: the high cost of housing, the lack of a social safety to assist the ill and elderly, low fertility rates, and the high cost of education. This pattern began to change in response to unprecedented growth in Chinese exports that made extra cash available and to traditionally low rates of personal consumption in China, where the virtues of "deferred gratification" are deeply ingrained.[80] Chinese private consumption rates as a proportion of GDP declined from 50.6 percent to 36.4 percent between 1990 and 2007.

What sets China apart historically, according to Guonan Ma and Wang Yi, is not just this high household savings rate, as many Western commentators suggest, but the combination of high household, corporate, and

[76] Martin Wolf, "Manufacturing at Risk from Global Shift to Asia," 20 May 2011, http://www.ft.com/cms/s/0/cba8a136-829a-11e0-8c49-00144feabdc0.html (accessed 20 May 2011).

[77] Freund, "Adjustment in Global Imbalances and the Future of Trade Growth," 12.

[78] Ibid., 11.

[79] Ibid., 12, table 1, and 17.

[80] Linda Y. C. Lim, "Rebalancing in East Asia," in Claessens, Evenett and Hoekman, eds., *Rebalancing the Global Economy*, 31–38.

government savings rates.[81] Chinese personal saving rates are among the highest ever recorded.[82] The Chinese household savings rate exceeded 53 percent in 2008, far above such countries in the Organisation for Economic Co-operation and Development (OECD) as Germany, known for prudent savings (but at 26 percent, still less than half the rate of China).[83] Chinese corporate consumption rates, as measured as a ratio of GDP, are also estimated to be below 40 percent. This compares to an average of 55 percent for the rest of Asia, which is a very low figure in comparison to the rest of the world.[84] China is thus awash in private and corporate money.[85] Ben Bernanke, chairman of the US Federal Reserve, identified this "global savings glut" as the major cause of global macroeconomic imbalances.[86]

China has moved to address this problem. At the March 2011 annual meeting of the Peoples Congress, the then Communist Party leadership announced that raising China's exceptionally low consumption rate was its top economic priority.[87] Given demographic and structural impediments, changing consumption patterns is no easy task. Recycling corporate and government money through loans, aid, and investments is easier. It is perhaps ironic that prodding Chinese consumers to spend more has become harder than moving in the direction of becoming the global "lender of last resort." Ligang Song has proposed a novel solution that seems to be gaining traction: legal urbanization of China's millions of unauthorized domestic migrant workers. These rural transplants have historically had no access to social welfare resources because of their illicit status. Granting them legal residence would make precautionary savings less vital because it would trigger considerably greater government expenditures on social services. This in turn would increase migrant consumption levels.[88]

[81] Guonan Ma and Wang Yi , "China's High Saving Rate: Myth and Reality," BIS Working Papers 312, June 2010, http://www.bis.org/publ/work312.htm (accessed 5 June 2013).
[82] Michael Pettis, "Rising Chinese Consumption Won't Lead to US Rates Jump," *Financial Times*, 18 April 2011, http://www.ft.com/cms/s/0/cf36cf7c-69b2–11e0-826b-00144feab49a.html#axzz1QlfW5UzD (accessed 28 June 2011).
[83] Ma and Yi, "China's High Saving Rate."
[84] Lim, "Rebalancing in East Asia."
[85] Ryan Clarke, "Expert Analysis on Sino-US Trade and Currency Issues in the United States: Policy Impacts and Future Directions," *China: An International Journal*, 1 March 2011, http://www.thefreelibrary.com/Expert+analysis+on+Sino-US+trade+and+currency+issues+in+the+United . . . -a0252192365 (accessed 17 July 2011).
[86] Ben Bernanke, quoted in Lim, "Rebalancing in East Asia," 32.
[87] Michael Pettis, "Rising Chinese Consumption Won't Lead to US Rates Jump," *Financial Times*, 18 April 2011, http://www.ft.com/cms/s/0/cf36cf7c-69b2–11e0-826b-00144feab49a.html#axzz1QlfW5UzD (accessed 28 June 2011).
[88] Ligang Song, "China's Rapid Growth and Development: An Historical and International Context," paper presented at the 2010 PAFTAD conference at Peking University,

A March 2013 OECD economic survey of China suggests that the Chinese government has recently enjoyed success in addressing these issues. It notes that social spending has increased sharply from under 6 to over 8 percent of GDP as "[n]ational government expenditure on health, social security, employment and other social services rose by over 24% per year on average between 2008 and 2012." Furthermore, "In the four years to 2011, the share of health spending covered by households fell from 40% to 35%, while the coverage of the rural medical insurance system rose to over 97%. As far as rural pensions are concerned, 60% of counties had implemented a scheme by 2011. . . . A 19% increase of such outlays is planned for 2013."[89]

In February 2013 the State Council issued guidelines designed to increase household consumption and social spending and significantly reduce health care costs (arguably among the great sources of precautionary savings). It also announced, consistent with Song's suggestion, that the government will introduce a national residency card based on where someone actually lives, providing urban migrants with access to social services.[90] With consumption still at such low levels among migrants, the OECD report states that their sheer numbers "represents an enormous potential for consumption expansion."[91]

A combination of social reforms and a greater focus on imports means that "[r]ebalancing has made headway: externally, the current account surplus has fallen sharply, from over 10% of GDP in 2007 to under 3%; domestically, growth has lately been pulled more by consumption than by investment."[92] The gross numbers and policy reforms therefore both project a trend consistent with the post-2007 rhetoric.

Chinese corporations, which we identified as another source of the problem, have begun to reduce their huge cash reserves through foreign equity purchases. We treat this development at greater length below.

The growth in Chinese exports to the United States is mirrored by its inroads into the European Union. European imports from China grew at an annual average of 16.5 percent per between 2004 and 2008. Although they declined precipitously in 2009 due to the economic crisis,

---

Beijing, 6–9 December 2010; Ligang Song, personal conversations with Simon Reich, Canberra, Australia, 15 July 2011.

[89] Organisation for Economic Co-operation and Development, *OECD Economic Surveys of China 2013*, http://www.keepeek.com/Digital-Asset-Management/oecd/economics/oecd-economic-surveys-china-2013_eco_surveys-chn-2013-en, 18 (accessed 14 June 2013).

[90] Ibid., 21.

[91] Ibid., 99.

[92] Ibid., 10.

China still recorded a €128 billion surplus and has become Europe's largest supplier of manufactured goods.[93] Awash with dollar and euro foreign exchange reserves estimated at over $3 trillion, the Chinese government has sought to recycle its burgeoning funds and by doing so provide extensive liquidity to the global system. In terms of financial flows, these efforts have heavily focused on the Chinese purchase of American and European government bonds—effectively, sovereign debt. As of December 2010, China held $1.145 trillion dollars, or 26.1 percent of foreign holdings of US federal debt.[94] This figure represented an increase of over 300 percent from five years earlier. In the same period, Japan increased its dollar denominated holdings of US federal debt, from $670 billion to $882.3 billion, but its percentage of the overall share of the debt it holds decreased from 32.9 percent to 19.9 percent as a result of China's massive purchases.[95] Together, Asia's two largest economies were collectively responsible for 46 percent of all foreign holdings of US federal debt by 2011. When unofficial holdings through third parties are included—reputedly, a common practice by China—that country's holdings climb to over 50 percent.[96]

As other major holders of US Treasuries, such as Britain, began to sell their holdings in the first half of 2011, China increased its purchases, much of it through third parties to avoid scrutiny and criticism.[97] Their purchases were surpassed only by those of the US government itself, under its extensive 'quantitative easing' programs.[98] In the aftermath of the 2008 financial crisis, the Chinese government was the largest foreign lender to the US government.

The Chinese also sought to assist European governments in addressing their mounting financial crisis, precipitated by the threatened debt defaults of Greece, Ireland, Portugal, and Spain. By 2010, the European Union (EU) was China's biggest trading partner, together constituting

---

[93] European Trade Commission, "Countries and Regions: China," http://ec.europa.eu/trade/creating-opportunities/bilateral-relations/countries/china (accessed 1 July 2011).

[94] Justin Murray and Marc Labonte, *Foreign Holdings of Federal Debt* (Washington DC: Congressional Research Service, 2011), 2, table 2.

[95] Ibid.

[96] US Treasury, "Major Foreign Holdings of Treasury Securities (in Billions of Dollars)," 16 January 2013, http://www.treasury.gov/resource-center/data-chart-center/tic/Documents/mfh.txt (accessed 14 February 2013).

[97] Josh Noble, "Is China Picking Euro Debt over US Treasuries?" 20 June 2011, http://blogs.ft.com/beyond-brics/2011/06/20/is-china-picking-euro-debt-over-us-treasuries/#axzz2KtZlrMxS (accessed 14 February 2013).

[98] Daniel Kruger, "Chinese Holdings of Treasuries Climbed in April as Fed Purchases Near End," 15 June 2011, http://www.bloomberg.com/news/2011-06-15/chinese-holdings-of-treasuries-climbed-in-april-as-fed-purchases-near-end.html (accessed 1 July 2011).

the world's largest bilateral trade relationship, with commerce totaling $522 billion compared to the $456.8 billion total for US-China trade that year. Like the Americans before them, the Chinese recognized that a collapse of Europe's economy threatened their interests. From 2010 onward, senior Chinese officials routinely visited Europe and made public their commitment to support the eurozone through diplomatic initiatives and the purchase of a variety of debt instruments.

According to Song Zhe, the Chinese ambassador to the EU, his country worried about a decline in the value of the euro and the prospect of further trade protectionism on the part of the EU. China's expressed goal was to "to diversify our portfolio, prevent risk and protect value in foreign exchange." He promised that the Chinese government would purchase bonds issued by Greece and Spain with the expressed intention of stabilizing European financial markets. This statement came in the aftermath of then Spanish prime minister Rodríguez Zapatero's visit to China and meeting with Chinese prime minister Wen Jiabao.[99] During a visit to Brussels in October 2010, Jiabao announced that China had acted as a "real friend" to the eurozone through its recent purchases of a "large quantity" of bonds. He pledged to "maintain the debt stability in the euro zone."[100] The following June, Jiabao reiterated China's long term support for the eurozone economies and the euro itself. "When some European countries were hit by the sovereign debt crisis," he explained, "China has actually increased the purchase of government bonds of some European countries and we have not cut back on our euro holdings. I think these show our confidence in the economies of the European countries and the Eurozone."[101]

The debt crisis that began in April 2009 in Greece threatened to spread to Portugal, Ireland, and Spain given the state of their economies, and the amount of their debt held by banks, private lenders, and the governments in France and Germany. Faced with the mushrooming debt crisis, the EU was desperately looking for external governments and private investors to purchase the bonds to be issued by the new European Financial Stabilisation Mechanism (EFSM) in the hope of preventing budget defaults by multiple governments.[102] The Chinese proved

---

[99] John W. Miller, "China Hopes Its Bond Buys Will Help Shore Up Europe," *Wall Street Journal*, 22 April 2011, http://online.wsj.com/article/SB10001424052748704889404576276911077729544.html (accessed 27 May 2013).

[100] "Asia Buys 20% of EU bond," *Irish Times*, 6 January 2011, http://www.irishtimes.com/newspaper/breaking/2011/0106/breaking50.html (accessed 2 July 2011).

[101] Robert Peston, "Chinese Premier Backing the Euro and the UK," http://www.bbc.co.uk/news/mobile/business-13921701 (accessed 3 July 2011).

[102] "Eurozone Agrees Bail-Out Fund of 500bn Euros," 14 February 2011, http://www.bbc.co.uk/news/business-12460527 (accessed 3 July 2011).

good to their word, becoming a major purchaser of AAA-rated bonds issued by the European Financial Stability Facility (EFSF). China bought an estimated 10–15 percent of the EFSF issuance in May 2011 and a similar amount at the first EFSF sale. These combined investments totaled €1.5 billion. China's EFSM purchases in the prior months of 2011 probably amounted to a further €1 billion, or 4–6 percent of total issuance. Additional purchases quickly followed, and China purchased about US$3.6 billion of debt at the height of the crisis.[103] China led Asian governments in purchasing Irish, Spanish, and Greek government-backed bonds in primary and secondary financial markets.[104] Accurate aggregate figures for Chinese investment in European issued bonds are hard to calculate. But according to one estimate, between the government's China Investment Corporation and the State Administration of Foreign Exchange, investments in the eurozone totaled between $150 and $200 billion between late 2010 and the end of the spring of 2011. This did not include additional investments in pound sterling–denominated assets.[105] Not surprisingly, the psychological effects on financial investors of China's announcements, its signaling of a long-term commitment, and subsequent purchases were probably as important as the actual injection of capital itself.[106]

In what ways does Chinese benefit from these purchases? They were intended to sustain the value of China's European portfolio as its intervention helped to support the value of the euro during the financial crisis. The average value of the euro actually rose against the dollar in the first half of 2011, from $1.33 per euro to $1.44, and oscillated in that range into early 2013. Beijing used the opportunity provided by numerous senior officials' visits to Europe to negotiate several important trade agreements and to consolidate major bilateral ties across a broad range of issues. On a trip to Germany in June 2011, Prime Minister Wen Jiabao signed an agreement with German chancellor Angela Merkel "to establish special government consultations, which means representatives of the two countries will meet regularly and will discuss a wide range of topics, like trade, investment, education, environment, human rights, security and the rule of law." Simultaneously, trade agreements were signed as the Chinese sought to consolidate their exports to and investments in Germany. Wen used his country's new leverage to complain about Germany's decision to meet the Dalai Lama and sought to pre-

[103] Noble, "Is China Picking Euro Debt over US Treasuries?"

[104] "Asia buys 20% of EU Bond"; Liz Alderman, "Beijing, Tendering Support to Europe, Helps Itself," *New York Times*, 6 January 2011, http://www.nytimes.com/2011/01/07/business/global/07euchina.html?_r=1&ref=china (accessed 6 July 2011).

[105] "Chinese Investment in Europe: Streaks of Red," *Economist*, 30 June 2011, http://www.economist.com/node/18895430?story_id=18895430 (accessed 5 July 2011).

[106] Alderman, "Beijing, Tendering Support to Europe, Helps Itself."

empt German complaints about copying infringement and the theft of intellectual property. He called for "respect for China's system and China's territorial integrity."[107] There is some evidence that Chinese support of Portugal and Spain was also motivated in part by the access that those economies could provide to markets and investments in Latin America.[108] Subsequent Chinese investment in Italian bonds followed in the late summer of 2011 as contagion threatened. As Nicholas Zhu, a former World Bank economist commented, "It's a clear pattern of China's intention to help stabilize the euro area. . . . The benefit to China is that it will help in the perception of host countries if China is viewed as a responsible stakeholder in the global community."[109]

China now regularly links its financial support to broader economic and political issues. Six months earlier, Wang Qishan, a Chinese vice premier, met with EU officials in Beijing during the third annual China-EU High Level Economic and Trade Dialogue. He pledged that China would, if necessary, purchase European sovereign bonds. Qishan asked the EU to grant China "market economy" status and lift a long-standing arms embargo. The former had been a long-term goal of China in its efforts to avoid antidumping claims by European producers and governments.[110] The United States and the EU had consistently refused to recognize China as a market economy, but Merkel, with strikingly interesting timing, announced that Germany would actively push for China's recognition as a market economy within the EU.[111]

A WORLD AWASH IN CHINESE AID

China's growing custodial role in economic global finance is matched by a complementary emerging role in aid, trade, and foreign direct investment. While purchases of US Treasury bonds and European government bonds have bolstered the mature US and European economies,

[107] Judy Dempsey, "Chinese Leader's Visit to Germany Ends with Large Trade Deals," *New York Times*, 28 June 2011, http://www.nytimes.com/2011/06/29/business/global/29wen.html?_r=1&emc=eta1 (accessed 4 July 2011).

[108] Alderman, "Beijing, Tendering Support to Europe, Helps Itself."

[109] Shamim Adam and Lorenzo Totaro, "China Called On as Lender of Last Resort as Italy Faces Deepening Crisis," 13 September 2011, http://www.bloomberg.com/news/2011-09-13/china-called-on-as-lender-of-last-resort-with-italy-joining-morgan-stanley.html (accessed 14 February 2013).

[110] Jamil Anderlini and Peter Spiegel, "China Extends Help to Tackle Euro Crisis," 21 December2011,http://www.ft.com/intl/cms/s/0/4a1a7768-0cfa-11e0-ace7-00144feabdc0.html#axzz1R8HF6AwtChina extends help to tackle euro crisis (accessed 4 July 2011).

[111] "Germany to Push EU to Recognize China's Market Economy Status: Communique," *China Daily*, 16 July 2010, http://www.chinadaily.com.cn/china/2010-07/16/content_10118453.htm (accessed 4 July 2011).

Table 4.3.
US Official Development Aid, 2005–10 (US$ millions)

Year	Aid Budget
2005	27,934.74
2006	23,532.14
2007	21,786.9
2008	26,436.78
2009	28,831.34
2010	30,154.29

Source: Organisation for Economic Co-operation and Development, "Query Wizard for International Development Statistics," http://stats.oecd.org/qwids/#?x=1&y=6&f=4:1,2:1,3:51,5:3,7:1&q=4:1+2:1+3:51+5:3+7:1+1:2,24+6:2005,2006,2007,2008,2009,2010 (accessed 14 February 2013).

China's strategic expansion of overseas development aid (ODA) since the 2007 financial crisis has provided key capital injections for lesser-developed economies. By way of contrast, table 4.3 indicates that US official development aid fell by 20 percent in 2006 and only increased marginally in the following four years.[112]

Foreign aid giving is notoriously difficult to calculate and compare. America's stated ODA goals are vague and somewhat amorphous: peace and security, investing in people, governing justly and democratically, economic growth, and humanitarian assistance. American ODA figures are transparent, but much of what is grouped under the rubric of ODA includes military aid. The leading recipients of US foreign aid in fiscal year 2010 were Afghanistan, Israel, Pakistan, and Egypt, which together accounted for more than 50 percent of US bilateral aid. Since 2000, this percentage has been increasing; between 2006 and 2010, the aggregate amount spent on peace and security went up by approximately 27 percent to $10,380 million. A 2010 Congressional Research Service report notes that 21 percent of US aid was spent on civilian security and the military sector. By comparison, 25 percent was spent on political and strategic aid, 34 percent on bilateral development, and 13 percent on humanitarian relief.[113] While the United States remains the largest aid donor in the world, much of what constitutes

[112] Organisation for Economic Co-operation and Development, "Development Cooperation Directorate (DCD-DAC)," http://www.oecd.org/document/17/0,2340,en_2649_33721_38341265_1_1_1_1,00.html (accessed 5 July 2011).

[113] Curt Tarnoff and Marian Leonardo Lawson, *Foreign Aid: An Introduction of US Programs and Policy* (Washington, DC: Congressional Research Service, 2011), 5, 11–12.

aid is not directed at development. This makes comparisons with China difficult, despite American transparency.

We lack reliable data on China's aid.[114] What is clearly evident, however, is a remarkable shift in the course of the last ten years from China as a recipient of aid to a donor. The amount of Chinese ODA has surged; and that aid, in contrast to its American counterpart, is designed to foster a variety of nonmilitary goals. China's Department of Foreign Aid, located in its ministry of commerce, is largely responsible for the country's aid policy. Its aid takes many forms, not all with strict guidelines: grant programs, zero-interest loans, youth volunteer programs, and technical assistance. Under the ministry of commerce's direction, China's Export-Import Bank (Eximbank) administers the concessional foreign aid loan program using subsidies from the foreign aid budget. The Eximbank was set up in 1994, along with the China Development Bank (CBD) and the China Agricultural Development Bank, to allow the government to prioritize and organize its development goals. Aid is distinct from commercial trade or direct investments, although a variety of subsidies may be or have been applied. In effect, the Chinese now generally use their own companies, materials, and even their own labor to build infrastructure projects rather than simply handing out money, food, or other resources as aid.[115]

China's ODA is often highly strategic, intended to stimulate trade with developing markets, foster Chinese foreign direct investment, secure access to natural resources, and "export" Chinese labor when possible. The overwhelming proportion of Chinese imports from low-income countries consists of a variety of natural resources.[116] China's ODA gives preference to its own over indigenous labor whenever possible. It ignores more general human rights concerns and general labor standards, making it a target of criticism from Washington and elsewhere.[117] There is no evidence that Chinese aid money is awarded in the form of arms or political programs—such as democracy promotion—as in the case of the United States. China certainly trades in arms; it was embarrassingly caught transgressing a UN mandate barring arms sales

[114] Deborah Bräutigam, *China, Africa and the International Aid Architecture*, Working Paper 107 (Tunis-Belvedère, Tunisia: African Development Bank Group, 2010).

[115] Ibid., 6–7.

[116] International Monetary Fund, "New Growth Drivers for Low-Income Countries: The Role of BRICs," Figure A1.5, "Composition of LIC Exports to BRICs by Region, 2008," 12 January 2011, https://www.imf.org/external/np/pp/eng/2011/011211.pdf (accessed 4 June 2013).

[117] Scott Stearns, "Clinton Concerned by Chinese Trade Practices in Africa," 14 June 2011, http://www.voanews.com/english/news/asia/Clinton-Concerned-by-Chinese-Trade-Practices-in-Africa-123801939.html (accessed 4 July 2011).

to Libya.[118] But there is no evidence that arms are given as aid part of the ODA budget. Beyond immediate economic goals, much of the purpose of this ODA is to foster Chinese influence with countries desperate for its funds with "no strings attached" and at lower interest rates than loans offered by World Bank.

The huge upsurge in Chinese aid and loans has been welcomed in many parts of Latin America, Asia, and Africa, buying goodwill for China. Deborah Bräutigam reports that "China's grant aid and zero-interest loans usually promote broad diplomacy objectives, while the concessional foreign aid loans operated by China Eximbank mix diplomacy, development, and business objectives. . . . At the same time, China uses concessional lines of credit to promote exports of goods and services to creditworthy countries that can repay the loans, or for bankable projects in less creditworthy countries."[119] The Chinese government does not use standard World Bank reporting guidelines to account for its aid, nor does the broad swath of assistance and loans it offers all fall within strict definitions for aid, making comparison difficult and often resulting in exaggerated estimates.[120] Nonetheless, Chinese ODA showed a slow but unmistakable increase in absolute terms between 1995 and 2005, as is demonstrated in table 4.4.

China appears to have shifted from aid recipient to donor in 2005. That year it increased its overseas food aid by 260 percent, making it the third largest donor of food.[121] Unable to sustain this level of giving, aid soon declined as a major component of the budget. Foreign assistance nevertheless signaled China's intentions to increase its influence by linking its broader foreign policy to diverse aid initiatives. A second upswing in overseas aid came during the global financial crisis. Eximbank awarded loans of at least $110 billion to governments and companies in 2009 and 2010. This exceeded the $100.3 billion loaned by the World Bank.[122] Chinese assistance has become so important to developing economies that the World Bank sought ways to cooperate with China "to avoid escalating competition over loan deals."[123] As the CBD and Eximbank often offer better terms than the World Bank and, as

[118] Michael Wines, "China Says It Will Tighten Arms Sales Procedures," *New York Times*, 6 September 2011, http://www.nytimes.com/2011/09/07/world/asia/07china.html (accessed 17 September 2011).

[119] Bräutigam, *China, Africa and the International Aid Architecture*, 17.

[120] Ibid., 27.

[121] World Food Program, "China Emerges as World's Third Largest Food Aid Donor," 20 July 2006, http://www.wfp.org/node/534 (accessed 4 July 2011).

[122] Geoff Dyer, Jamil Anderlini, and Henny Sender, "China's Lending Hits New Heights," 17 January 2011, http://www.ft.com/intl/cms/s/0/488c60f4-2281-11e0-b6a2-00144feab49a.html#axzz1RFIPRpT0 (accessed 5 July 2011).

[123] Ibid.

TABLE 4.4.
Chinese Overseas Development Aid Expenditures,
1995–2005 (US$ millions)

Year	Total Aid
1995	682.4
1996	793.3
1997	923.4
1998	1,079.8
1999	1,318.8
2000	1,588.7
2001	1,890.3
2002	2,205.3
2003	2,465.0
2004	2,848.7
2005	3,393.0

Source: Compiled by Ji Jeong from multiple sources, and provided
to the authors by Barry Naughton.

noted, do not concern themselves with labor standards or human rights,
their appeal to developing countries is easy to understand. By 2013,
China was reputedly a larger source of loans to Latin America than the
World Bank and the InterAmerican Development Bank combined.[124]

Much of China's aid comes in the form of investment loans rather
than humanitarian aid. Not surprisingly, these loans are tied to the purchase of Chinese goods and services, and often the use of Chinese labor.
They are denominated, at least in part, in renminbi (RMB). A 2011 CDB
loan to Venezuela for improving infrastructure, for example, was half
denominated in RMB and half in US dollars, and was to be repaid in
oil.[125] This loan helped consolidate China's growing oil supplies from
Venezuela, enhance its relationship with then president Hugo Chávez
during a stressful time for the Venezuelan leader as his country was
caught in a credit crunch, and challenged American dominance as the
largest purchaser of oil from Venezuela.[126] Likewise, a 2009 loan to Brazilian state-controlled Petroleo Brasileiro SA for $10 billion included a
long-term supply contract as part of the deal.

[124] Ralph Atkins, "Global Capital Flows Plunge 60%," *Financial Times*, 28 February
2013, http://www.ft.com/intl/cms/s/0/aee926b8-80f6-11e2-9908-00144feabdc0.html#
axzz2eV8SyHkX (accessed 10 September 2013).

[125] Dan Molinski, "China's $20B Loan to Venezuela to Be Repaid in Oil," 23 April 2010,
http://www.rigzone.com/news/article.asp?a_id=91521 (accessed 6 July 2011).

[126] Simon Romero, "Chávez Says China to Lend Venezuela $20 Billion," *New York
Times*, 18 April 2010, http://www.nytimes.com/2010/04/19/world/americas/19venez
.html (accessed 6 July 2011).

China has been active on every continent. In 2010, as part of a consolidated effort to tie aid, investment and energy policy together, the SINOPEC Group, China's second largest energy company, paid $7.1 billion for a 40 percent stake in Madrid-based Repsol YPF SA's Brazil unit.[127] It has financed construction and infrastructural development in Algeria. In 2010, fifty Chinese firms benefitted from loan contracts amounting to $20 billion, and trade between the two countries climbed from $200 million to $4.5 billion within a decade. Much of China's interest in Algeria is to facilitate access to its oil and gas reserves. Beijing is also interested in exporting Chinese workers, and Chinese labor is often stipulated in such contracts. The 35,000 Chinese workers in Algeria make them the second largest foreign population in Algeria after the French.[128] This policy of exporting generally low-skilled labor is an important but understated part of China's ODA strategy. As one businessman with regular contacts with Chinese officials told one of the authors, "Senior government officials have often expressed the concern that the one-child policy will not address China's massive demographic problems. They believe that China is a country built for 900 million people but its population exceeds 1.3 billion. So what can they do with the remainder? The solution is to export people like they export manufactured products—everywhere and at low cost."[129]

The advantages and drawbacks associated with Chinese aid initiative are most evident in sub-Saharan Africa. Chinese aid is generally linked to "tied" expenditures designed to enhance Chinese investments and trade. Africa reportedly received 14 percent of Chinese investment in 2010, a sum that again surpassed the World Bank's contribution. Chinese government assistance has enhanced local market competitiveness, often displacing traditional protected producers. Criticism of Chinese exploitation, endemic corruption, a mercantilist focus on resource acquisition, and riding roughshod over labor and environmental norms are widespread, although evidence for these claims is often patchy.[130] The growing use of Africa as an industrial base by China has undoubt-

[127] Iuri Dantas, "Brazil Will Work with Obama to Counter Rising China Imports, Official Says," 2 February 2011, http://www.bloomberg.com/news/2011-02-02/brazil -wants-to-work-with-u-s-to-stem-chinese-import-flood-official-says.html (accessed 6 July 2011).

[128] "China Leads Algeria Construction Boom," *Washington Times*, 27 January 2010, http://www.washingtontimes.com/news/2010/jan/27/china-leads-algeria-construc tion-boom (accessed 6 July 2011). An estimate a year later put the figure at 40,000. James Kynge, Richard McGregor, Daniel Dombey, Martin Arnold, Helen Warrell, and Cynthia O'Murchu, "The China Syndrome," 3 March 2011, http://www.ft.com/intl/cms/s/0 /2ab8c5a8-45e1-11e0-acd8-00144feab49a.html (accessed 6 July 2011).

[129] Confidential interview with the authors, 4 January 2011.

[130] "Trying to Pull Together: Africans Are Asking Whether China Is Making Their

edly provided local benefits. This aid helped to increase employment and boost African exports, which had been negligible in value a decade before, with total trade reaching to over $120 billion.[131] Aid has been accompanied by other critical injections of finance through investments in local banks, such as the Chinese government–owned Industrial and Commercial Bank's purchase of 20 percent of South Standard Bank, the largest bank, measured by assets, in Africa.[132] Chinese aid and investments have bought Beijing considerable goodwill among Africa's political leadership.

The massive movements of Chinese funds into Africa have provided what one South African commentator described as "the single most important development of the previous decade for the continent. China is now Africa's largest trading partner. Sino-African trade now represents 10.4 percent of the continent's total trade, is more than 10 times what it was in 2000, having increased from $11-billion to $129-billion. By 2012, Chinese-African trade may rise to as much as $400-billion a year."[133] China and Africa have bypassed global multilateral institutions and effectively displaced the traditional influence of the World Bank, the United States, and the former European colonial powers. The same is true of Latin America.[134]

CHINA'S NEW SOVEREIGN WEALTH FUNDS

The third component of the growth in Chinese custodianship has been the notable expansion of Chinese portfolio and Overseas Direct Investment (ODI). This has taken the form of investment through government-owned or controlled sovereign wealth funds (SWFs) and corporations. Following two decades of relatively balanced inward and outward ODI accounts, there has been a steady pattern of growth in net Chinese ODI flows since 2005, as indicated in table 4.5.

Much of the post-2008 growth in overseas portfolio and direct investment can be explained by the activities of the Chinese Investment Cor-

Lunch or Eating It," *Economist*, 20 April 2011, http://www.economist.com/node/18586448?story_id=18586448 (accessed 23 May 2011).

[131] "Chinese in Africa: The Chinese Are Coming . . . to Africa," *Economist*, 22 April 2011, http://www.economist.com/blogs/dailychart/2011/04/chinese_africa (accessed 13 June 2011); "Trying to Pull Together."

[132] "Trying to Pull Together."

[133] Lloyd Gedye, "China's Boom Swells the Coffers of African Economies," *Mail and Guardian*, 6 May 2011, http://mg.co.za/article/2011-05-06-chinas-boom-swells-the-coffers-of-african-economies (accessed 23 May 2011).

[134] Ralph Atkins, "Europe's Debt Woes Put Squeeze on Cross Border Flows of Capital."

TABLE 4.5.
Chinese Overseas Direct Investment, 1990–2010
(US$ millions)*

Year	ODA Balance
1990	−830.0
1991	−913.0
1992	−4,000.0
1993	−4,400.0
1994	−2,000.0
1995	−2,000.0
1996	−2,114.0
1997	−2,562.49
1998	−2,633.81
1999	−1,774.31
2000	−915.777
2001	−6,885.4
2002	−2,518.41
2003	152.273
2004	−1,805.05
2005	−11,300.0
2006	−21,200.0
2007	−17,000.0
2008	−53,500.0
2009	−43,900.0
2010	−60,200.0

Note: * A negative sign signifies a net outflow of ODI.
Source: Data provided by Guonan Ma, based on Bank for International Settlements figures.

poration (CIC), created with assets of $200 billion at the outset of the financial crisis in 2007. The CIC's self-professed strategic goals are long-term and general rather than focused on reaping quick profits by exploiting market fluctuations.[135] This is eminently feasible in the absence of private shareholders demanding mandatory quarterly or yearly profits. The State Administration of Foreign Exchange (SAFE), which, in theory, is based in Hong Kong and privately owned, has Chinese government officials who serve on its board. Like many other sovereign wealth funds, this one is viewed as mercantilist and predatory by critics, concerned more with political than economic goals.[136]

[135] China Investment Corporation, *China Investment Corporation: Annual Report 2008*, http://www.swfinstitute.org/research/CIC_2008_annualreport_en.pdf, 26 (accessed 5 June 2013).
[136] "The Rise of State Capitalism," *Economist*, 18 September 2008, http://www.economist.com/node/12080735?story_id=12080735 (accessed 7 July 2011).

These investment funds have become major actors in the global economy. By June 2010, SAFE (with an estimated $347 billion in assets) and the CIC (with $289 billion) were the fourth and fifth largest SWFs in the world. Their total assets reputedly outstripped those of all hedge funds and private equity firms combined.[137] Their extensive array of assets include financial instruments such as treasury bills, mortgage-backed securities, and bonds. As noted earlier, they have been very active in the purchase of US Treasuries and European government bonds. Their mandate also provides for investments in individual stocks and real estate. These activities reveal another important aspect of China's growing custodial role.

In 2007, with the financial crisis unfolding, America's largest banks, investment houses, and financial services firms became the center of public attention as the paucity of their assets and deep involvement in the US subprime mortgage market became evident. The resulting bankruptcy of Lehman Brothers threatened the viability of the entire American banking system. As banking losses became evident, stock values plummeted and credit rating agencies devalued their ratings. Major investors withdrew their funds from large banks and other financial institutions. Governmental efforts to shore up the banking sector proved ineffective. Less vulnerable banks bought up some major companies, such as the Bank of America's purchase of Merrill Lynch.

At the epicenter of this meltdown was Morgan Stanley, among the world's largest global financial services firms (the second largest in the United States). It operated in thirty-six countries around the world, with over six hundred offices and a workforce of over 60,000. The bank was hemorrhaging cash in the winter of 2007 and reputedly lost $300 million in one day, in large part due to its involvement in Beazer Homes USA, a major victim of the bursting US housing bubble. With investors fleeing and the value of its assets falling precipitously, China's CIC took a large market position in Morgan Stanley. It provided a $5.6 billion capital infusion in the form of mandatory convertible securities as a passive investor in exchange for securities that would be convertible to 9.9 percent of the firm's total shares in 2010. This arrangement was similar to China's $3 billion investment in the Blackstone Group earlier that year.[138]

This investment was announced on the same day as Morgan Stanley reported a larger than expected fourth quarter loss of $3.61 billion, and

[137] Tina Aridas, "Largest Sovereign Wealth Funds in the World—2010 Ranking," *Global Finance*, http://www.gfmag.com/tools/global-database/economic-data/10300-largest-sovereign-wealth-funds-swf-2010-ranking.html#axzz1RPoOHB6A (accessed 7 July 2011).

[138] Megan Davies and Jessica Hall, "Beijing Fund to Hike Stake in Blackstone," *Reuters*, 16 October 2008, http://www.reuters.com/article/2008/10/16/blackstone-bwil-idUSN1640464920081016?sp=true (accessed 18 October 2011).

helped to cushion the blow. Chinese officials told reporters that the CIC "believes that Morgan Stanley has potential for long-term growth, particularly in its investment banking, asset management and wealth management businesses, as well as new business development opportunities in emerging markets."[139] The CIC's leadership subsequently came under severe attack in China when Morgan Stanley and Blackstone's values continued to decline. Blackstone's stock value halved within the year and the CIC lost heavily on its investment. It nevertheless retained its passive investor position.

If the motive for the CIC's investment had been "bottom-fishing"—the purchase of stock cheaply in a period of crisis—that strategy clearly failed. These two nonperforming investments incurred such large losses that they help explain the CIC's aggregate reported trading loss of 2.1 percent for the year.[140] To make matters worse, the Blackstone Group investment, aside from being financially damaging, provoked the hostility of numerous American commentators.[141] The CIC's response, in the face of Morgan Stanley's ailing fortunes, was to announce in March 2009 that it would invest a further $1.2 billion in the company, purchasing 44.7 million shares of common stock and thus raising its equity ownership to 9.86 percent. The CIC's total investment of $6.8 billion was only exceeded by that of the Mitsubishi UFJ Financial Group's purchase of $9 billion in convertible shares.[142]

Morgan Stanley trailed its major rival, Goldman Sachs, for six consecutive, disappointing quarters before posting a $1.96 billion profit in the second quarter of 2010.[143] Yet, even a year later, its stock still stood at less than half of its value in December 2007: $49.89 a share on 19 December 2007 versus $22.73 on 1 July 2011.[144] If the CIC's goal had been to profit directly from Morgan Stanley's misfortune, then it had failed miserably. A more plausible explanation is that as a representative of the Chinese government, the CIC recognized the critical importance of supporting a pivotal US financial institution. The effects of a Morgan

---

[139] "China Fund to Invest $5b in Morgan Stanley," *China Daily*, 20 December 2007, http://www.chinadaily.com.cn/bizchina/2007-12/20/content_6335134.htm (accessed 7 July 2011).

[140] China Investment Corporation, *Annual Report 2008*, 33.

[141] "Rise of State Capitalism."

[142] Wang Xu, "CIC Increases Stake in Morgan Stanley," *China Daily*, 3 March 2009, http://www.chinadaily.com.cn/china/2009-06/03/content_7978689.htm (accessed 7 July 2009).

[143] "Morgan Stanley's Earnings Take Off," *Wall Street Journal*, 22 July 2010, http://online.wsj.com/article/SB10001424052748704684604575380823427652984.html (accessed 7 July 2011).

[144] See "Morgan Stanley: Historical Prices," http://finance.yahoo.com/q/hp?s=MS&a=11&b=19&c=2007&d=06&e=7&f=2011&g=m (accessed 27 May 2013).

Stanley bankruptcy hard on the heels of the Lehman Brothers debacle for global capitalism and, inevitably, China's economic interests, would have been hard to overstate. Thus China as a lender of last resort proved critical in propping up this bastion of global capitalism.

CURRENCY STABILITY

The stabilization of currency exchange is key to custodial management. The Bretton Woods system, set up right after World War II, established the value of the dollar against gold at $35 an ounce. Since 1945, the US dollar has effectively been the global reserve currency. Gold, oil, and energy markets are generally denominated in dollars, and large transactions, such as mergers and acquisitions, are routinely paid in dollars. As of 2010, the US dollar still accounted for 61.5 percent of official foreign exchange reserves, although a decade earlier this figure had been 70 percent.

By 2010, global euro or euro-equivalent holdings had risen from 17.9 percent to over 26 percent.[145] Thus, while the dollar remained ubiquitous, it declined in value against other major currencies. In 1980, the US dollar bought 226 Japanese yen. By 2000, it only bought 107, and by the eve of the global financial crisis it purchased only 103. By 2011, it had reached a new postwar low of 76. By early 2013 there were mutterings of a possible "currency war."[146] A similar long-term decline took place against the euro; it increased in value against the dollar by over 65 percent between the summer of 2001 and 2011.[147]

Several factors were responsible for the dollar's drop in relative global significance. These include its diminishing use as a global reserve currency; declining value against other major currencies; the rapid emergence of China as the world's second largest economy and its contrasting growth trajectories; the US current account, trade, and budget deficits; the printing of dollars under the "quantitative easing" programs; and the persistently weak performance of the US economy. Chinese leaders at the time, among them Hu Jintao, went as far as to suggest that the current international currency system is a relic of the past and that China's long-term goal is for an alternative to be created

[145] "Currency Composition of Official Foreign Exchange Reserves," http://en.wikipedia.org/wiki/Pound_Sterling (accessed 15 July 2011).

[146] Tom Burgis, "Currency Wars: The Battle Lines Explained," 13 February 2013, http://www.ft.com/intl/cms/s/0/b543d370-75f5-11e2–9891-00144feabdc0.html#axzz 2Mgj1k04R (accessed 5 March 2013).

[147] European Central Bank, "Euro Exchange Rates," http://www.ecb.int/stats/exchange/eurofxref/html/eurofxref-graph-usd.en.html (accessed 15 July 2011).

to replace the dollar as a global reserve currency. China's central bank governor, Zhou Xiaochuan, made similar statements.[148] As an interim solution, China's leaders have suggested reverting to a long-discarded proposal of John Maynard Keynes: replacing the dollar-denominated system with a global system of international currency reserve using expanded special drawing rights administered by the International Monetary Fund.[149] In part, this proposal arises from the recognition by Chinese leaders of their country's vulnerability in being so dependent on dollar-based investments coupled with the inability of the RMB to assume that role.[150]

To facilitate a transition and reduce its dollar holdings, China has undertaken incremental efforts to make the RMB convertible and increase its value. In early 2011, the Bank of China offered its American customers the option of trading in the RMB, a sign of its promoted use in financial centers. The year before, the bank's US-based branches offered its customers limited currency exchange options.[151] The net effect was that trade settled in RMBs grew from 0.6 million RMB in 2009 to 60 billion RMB in only the second half of 2010.[152]

China has been comprehensively and consistently criticized for its currency exchange policy. Criticisms of the residual undervaluation of the RMB have some merit. According to some economists, much of the risk caused by asymmetric savings and consumption patterns between Asia and the United States could been mitigated by a free-floating rate of exchange between the Chinese RMB and the US dollar.[153] But, having depegged between 2005 and 2008, the Chinese government chose to

[148] "China's Hu Jintao: Currency System is 'Product of Past'," 17 January 2011, http://www.bbc.co.uk/news/world-asia-pacific-12203391 (accessed 16 July 2011); Richard MacGregor, "Hu Questions Future Role of US Dollar," 16 January 2011, http://www.ft.com/intl/cms/s/0/ae01a8f6-21b7-11e0-9e3b-00144feab49a.html-axzz1STBTrPeW (accessed 16 July 2011); Andrew Batson, "China Takes Aim at Dollar," *Wall Street Journal*, 24 March 2009, http://online.wsj.com/article/SB123780272456212885.html (accessed 17 July 2011).

[149] Jamil Anderlini, "China Wants to Oust Dollar as International Reserve Currency," 24 March 2009, http://www.ft.com/cms/s/0/be359094-1812–11de-8c9d-0000779fd2ac.html (accessed 17 July 2011).

[150] Steve LeVine, "China's Yuan: The Next Reserve Currency?" *Bloomberg Businessweek*, 26 May 2009, http://www.businessweek.com/globalbiz/content/may2009/gb20090522_665312.htm (accessed 18 July 2011).

[151] "Yuan Trading New York Signals More International Currency," *Shanghai Daily*, 13 January 2011, http://english.peopledaily.com.cn/90001/90778/7259215.html (accessed 18 July 2011); "Yuan-Based Trade to Increase," *Shanghai Daily*, 13 January 2011, http://www.chinadaily.com.cn/business/2011-01/13/content_11843902.htm (accessed 18 July 2011).

[152] "Yuan-Based Trade to Increase."

[153] Freund, "Adjustment in Global Imbalances and the Future of Trade Growth."

repeg the value of its currency to the US dollar, thereby limiting its up-ward appreciation rather than allowing markets to determine the ex-change rate. This policy allows Chinese producers to plan for produc-tion and exports on the basis of a stable exchange rate rather than having to take into account unpredictable fluctuations that would po-tentially hurt their competitiveness. A low-peg exchange rate also helped the Chinese obtain the two things they needed the most for al-most three decades: foreign currency earned from exports and foreign investment in China—and the technology transfer that often accompa-nies them.

Relatively few analysts have recognized that China has responded to foreign criticism by implementing an incremental rise in the value of the RMB and a greater internationalization of the currency. A notable exception is Steve LeVine, who describes how China began a series of currency swaps with other countries in 2009—providing RMB to other central banks for use in trade with China—thus allowing trade without the use of the dollar as an intermediary currency. Likewise, China has begun to denominate bilateral trade deals in local currencies, and Chi-nese bonds are being denominated in RMBs by authorized foreign banks. LeVine reports that Chinese officials have indicated that their goal is to make the RMB a reserve currency by 2020. Renowned Ameri-can economist and China expert Nicholas Lardy suggests that full con-vertibility could come earlier. As LeVine notes, the gradual shift in the Chinese government's dollar holdings from long-term treasuries to shorter terms bonds is consistent with a strategy of greater currency convertibility, as it presages a sale of dollar assets by the Chinese in favor of convertible RMB holdings.[154] Making the RMB fully convertible would lead to a sharp decline in the value of the dollar, further eroding its position as a reserve currency.

Despite these developments, American policy makers have persisted in focusing on the issue of incremental currency shifts as a source of America's problems rather than the variety of domestic sources of US deficits. This response echoes successive administrations' responses to the drug problem, which is to blame it on drug cartels and foreign sup-pliers rather than address the domestic demand for drugs. Policy mak-ers and critics have repeatedly pressed China to revalue the RMB more sharply against the dollar. It is a policy that, at least in principle, should reduce the demand for Chinese goods in the United States by making

---

[154] LeVine, "China's Yuan: The Next Reserve Currency?"; Nicholas R. Lardy and Pat-rick Douglass, *Capital Account Liberalization and the Role of the Renminbi*, Working Paper 11-6, Petersen Institute for International Economics, 2011, http://www.piie.com/publi cations/wp/wp11-6.pdf (accessed 4 June 2013).

them more expensive and increase the demand for US exports to China by making them correspondingly cheaper.

China's currency appreciated more than 21 percent against the US dollar between the reforms of 2005 (which increased the RMB's flexibility by depegging it from the dollar) and 2010. This increase did nothing to stem US criticism.[155] SAFE indirectly responded to this criticism in its annual report for 2010 when it declared that it would continue to make the RMB more flexible to better reflect market forces and diversify investment of the country's vast foreign reserves. China's central bank subsequently guided the currency to a series of new highs in the first half of 2011; it appreciated 5.59 percent in the twelve months after that.[156] By 14 January 2013, it briefly hit a record high rate of 6.2124 to the US dollar during intraday trading. In effect, the Chinese Central Bank implemented an orderly rise in the value of the RMB, ensuring incremental change in an attempt to address foreign concerns without destabilizing markets or giving Chinese manufacturers insufficient time to adjust. When coupled with the Chinese government's support for the dollar and euro through its investments in US Treasury bills and European government bonds, the net effect has been to help keep global exchange rates remarkably stable during, and in the aftermath of, the greatest financial crisis in over eighty years.

In sum, heavy Chinese support for the dollar and the euro, unprecedented aid and investment in the Global South, timely intervention through capital infusions to support American banks, record investments overseas, the stabilization of currency exchange, and the incremental convertibility of the RMB have all been essential to preserving global economic stability since 2007. China has acted this way because of its leaders' understanding of their economic interests and their recognition that intervention of this kind helps to expand their access to markets, raw materials, and foodstuffs and also increases their political influence. These policies have nevertheless invited accusations of hegemonic ambitions by those concerned with the possible political implications of their investments. However, the Chinese have not attempted to redesign the global system as the Americans did after 1945, nor have they signaled a serious interest in doing so despite their increased leverage. Rather, their behavior supports the view that they hope to preserve

[155] Mingyu Chen and Yi Wen, "RMB Appreciation and US Inflation Risk," *Monetary Trends*, June 2011; "Yuan Gained 24%, 14% against Dollar, Euro since 2005 Reform," *China Business News*, 28 December 2010, http://cnbusinessnews.com/yuan-gained-24-14-against-dollar-euro-since-2005-reform (accessed 18 July 2011).

[156] "Yuan Flat as Record-High Fixing Offset by Weak Dollar,"= *Economic Times*, 22 June 2011, http://articles.economictimes.indiatimes.com/2011-06-22/news/29689960_1_spot-yuan-yuan-non-deliverable-yuan-appreciation (accessed 2 July 2011).

this system *without* aggressively using their economic power to demand any quid pro quos. They are pursuing a strategy very similar to that of Germany and Japan, both of whom recognized the mutual advantages of preserving the existing system.

In this connection, it is worth considering some counterfactuals. Imagine the state of the global economy if China had not used SAFE and the CIC to buy billions of dollars worth of US Treasuries or billions of euros worth of European government bonds. Would national governments have defaulted on their debts because the IMF or EU did not have sufficient resources or market confidence to bail them out? What if the CIC had not intervened to support Morgan Stanley and the company had gone bankrupt? The US banking system would, arguably, have suffered a much more severe shock, and credit markets would have become frozen for consumers and banks alike, requiring the printing of even more money by the US government. Increasing unemployment and a rampant inflation would have been likely follow-on effects. Or, imagine a world in which a free-floating RMB massively increased in value while that of the dollar and euros plummeted, generating even lower global growth and exacerbating global imbalances. The Chinese government's custodial behavior did not save global capitalism, but it certainly played a significant role in preserving its contours and avoiding the kinds of economic depths visited in the Great Depression.

CONCLUSION

China's security policies give little indication of the threat envisaged by realists. Its economic policies come closer to meeting liberal expectations, but not for the reasons liberals provide. Both sets of policies reflect idiosyncratic Chinese goals and reasoned adaptations to the unique circumstances the country faces. These policies are nested in a larger understanding of China's conception of its place in the world. In the words of Joshua Cooper Ramo, "Chinese planners are already positing a new world order. The country's so-called New Security Concept, introduced in 1997 at an ASEAN meeting and refined in 2002, formalizes this Sino-US difference. Chu Shulong calls the heart of the NSC, which was endorsed publicly by Hu Jintao in April of 2004 'the Four No's,' which read like a manifesto for multi-polarity: no hegemonism, no power politics, no alliances and no arms races. It's like a Chinese Monroe Doctrine."[157]

[157] Ramo, *The Beijing Consensus*, 41.

These goals are readily achieved because they involve unilateral choices. China's influence in Asia, and in the world more generally, is a different matter; it depends on developments over which Chinese leaders have at best partial control. Most difficult in this connection is the maintenance of unprecedented growth rates at home and diplomatic engagements that avoid conflict in multilateral forums abroad. China's influence also depends on how others perceive its goals and accommodate them. Our argument suggests that China's current policies and longer-term goals do not pose the kind of threat that those of imperial Germany and the Soviet Union did. To the extent that Chinese leaders are interested in hēgemonia, not hegemony, and upholding, not overthrowing, the global international order, their goals are compatible with the security and economic interests of the United States and other developed countries. Real issues nevertheless remain, chief among them environmental concerns; Chinese adherence to human rights and international labor standards; and the avoidance of nasty, escalating competition for scarce resources. Improvements in all these areas, rather than rhetorical potshots, are the likely substance of negotiations as the Chinese continue to expand their influence and, with it, their access to resources.

Chapter 5

//

America and Security Sponsorship

Markets will rise and fall. But this is the United States of
America. . . . No matter what some agency may say, we've
always been and always will be a triple-A country.
— President Barack Obama, White
House speech, 8 August 2011

Sigmund Freud devised the concept of *projection* to describe the psychological defense mechanism by which people subconsciously
deny their desires and emotions and ascribe them to others. Projection
reduces anxiety and guilt by allowing the expression of unwanted im-
pulses, desires, or behavior without letting the conscious mind recognize them. Toward these ends, the people on whom attributes are projected are often demonized or punished. Freud described projection as
a primitive form of paranoia.[1] Projection has a long history in politics
and international relations, where religions, ethnic groups, and nations
have been demonized for reasons that have little to do with their char-
acteristics and behavior and more to do with the psychological needs of
their tormentors.

We suspect that many members of the American national security
community, some politicians, and some academics engage in projection.
They look for evidence that China's leaders seek hegemony and assert
that they are not beyond resorting to force to attain this end. This devil
image is maintained, as are all stereotypes, by outright falsehoods, selective use of evidence, and assimilation of that evidence to existing
schemas. Equally revealing, the key attributes projected on to China
arguably describe American foreign policy goals in the postwar era.
Further evidence for projection might be adduced from the fact that
those who are the strongest advocates of American hegemony, and the

[1] Anna Freud, *The Ego and the Mechanisms of Defense* (London: Hogarth Press and Institute of Psycho-Analysis, 1937).

use of force to "maintain" it, make the most vocal charges about China's alleged quest for international dominance.

A more honest assessment suggests that the United States has behaved in a more cavalier fashion than its Asian rival with regard to military intervention and global economic policies. The United States in recent years has invaded countries far from its homeland and, in the case of Iraq, on a pretext that was subsequently exposed as unwarranted. Its military spending as a percentage of national wealth is a multiple of every other country's, and has increased proportionately since the end of the Cold War.

China, as we documented in chapter 4, has increasingly become a lender of last resort. It made record amounts of investment in the Global South in key development projects, kick-starting bilateral trade without resort to the kind of predatory corporate "asset-stripping" measures— dismantling a corporation, selling off its prime assets, and firing the remainder of the staff—for which American entrepreneurs have been famous in the past. The United States, by contrast, has increasingly disregarded its managerial role by abandoning what we have referred to as custodial economic functions. Despite the continued importance of the dollar as a reserve currency, the United States no longer acts as the lender of last resort. It now borrows an unprecedented amount of money rather than lending it. Washington's foreign aid contributions have leveled out after a period of decline, but much of that aid takes the form of the provision of arms. The humanitarian aid budget has been slashed, undermining the US Department of State's "smart power" strategy.[2]

American officials and the press repeatedly decry China's abuse of human rights, and especially the imprisonment and persecution of political dissenters and minorities who complain about their ill treatment as well as violence directed against specific ethnic groups. These are the same officials who introduced, supported, and in some cases continue to support the internment without legal recourse of so-called terrorists at Guantanamo Bay, the use of waterboarding and other forms of extreme interrogation, the "rendition" of suspects to countries where they are routinely tortured; and they provide military and other forms of aid to some of the world's most repressive regimes. In 2011, President Obama signed a defense-spending bill that included a clearly unconstitutional provision for indefinite detention without trial of terrorism sus-

---

[2] Steven Lee Myers, "Foreign Aid Set to Take a Hit in US Budget Crisis," *New York Times*, 4 October 2011, http://www.nytimes.com/2011/10/04/us/politics/foreign-aid -set-to-take-hit-in-united-states-budget-crisis.html?pagewanted=all (accessed 4 October 2011).

pects. His administration has expanded—and continued to justify—the use of drones to kill suspected terrorists even though the collateral damage of these kinds of strikes is high.[3]

Since 9/11, the United States is arguably in the grip of the same kind of paranoia as in the early years of the Cold War. Politicians seeking to advance their careers propagate ridiculously inflated estimates of internal and external threats, supported in some cases by those who stand to reap economic rewards from fear arousal. Other politicians ride this bandwagon, or fail to speak out against it, for fear of electoral punishment. There are, however, cooler heads in Washington, the media, academe, and the public at large. Our chapter is addressed to them. We offer conceptual tools for rethinking the US role in the world. This includes our relationship with China, but also with our allies in Europe and the Pacific Rim and developing countries around the world.

Toward this end, we suggest that the United States should recognize this changed environment and reframe American foreign policy in terms of *sponsorship* in lieu of hegemony. We offer Iraq and Libya as contrasting multilateral cases in this regard, and review and compare the lessons of both interventions as examples of respective hegemonic and sponsorship strategies. We also provide a counterfactual analysis of American unilateral foreign policy toward Mexico, arguing that a policy of sponsorship might have succeeded in limiting the effects of the drug war there. In the conclusion, we briefly reflect on a second counterfactual case—concerning nonproliferation and North Korea—and reflect on the general lessons to be drawn from these cases.

THE AMERICAN CULTURE OF NATIONAL SECURITY

In chapter 4 we argued that China's foreign policy had to be understood in historical context. The same is true of the United States, whose foreign policy and national security elites generally operate in terms of deep-seated traditions about the US role in the world. They reflect and have been reinforced by America's extraordinary military economic and cultural dominance since 1945. Americans have become conditioned to view their country as the appropriate model for others to emulate, which in turn provides an ideological rationale for American

[3] Charlie Savage and Peter Baker, "Obama in a Shift, to Limit Targets of Drone Strikes," *New York Times*, 22 May 2013, http://www.nytimes.com/2013/05/23/us/us-acknowl edges-killing-4-americans-in-drone-strikes.html?pagewanted=all&_r=0 (accessed 3 June 2013); Mark Mazzetti and Declan Walsh, "Pakistan Says US Drone Killed Taliban Leader," *New York Times*, 29 May 2013, http://www.nytimes.com/2013/05/30/world/asia/drone -strike-hits-near-pakistani-afghan-border.html?pagewanted=all (accessed 3 June 2013).

leadership. This vision is increasingly at odds with dominant economic, political, and ideological realities. Despite optimistic claims of hegemonic renewal, Washington is having a hard time coping with a much-changed world in which others states reject the claim, in the words of Joseph Nye Jr., that the United States is "bound to lead." This is a principal—but by no means the only—reason why many policy makers and academics try to cast China as a "pantomime villain."[4]

America's security culture is based on three widely shared myths. These are American exceptionalism, messianism, and indispensability. All three are supported by a striking parochialism that blinds Americans to others' accomplishments and goals and perception of their country, its leaders, and policies.

Political scientist Louis Hartz first coined the term *exceptionalism* nearly six decades ago.[5] Focusing on America's unique road to modernity, he argued that the American Lockean liberal consensus—and with it, the absence of any socialist tradition—could be explained by the fact that America was "born new" and thus avoided the feudal conflicts that stimulated revolutionary movements in Europe. Hartz's influential thesis was adapted and exploited by later generations of American scholars and policy makers to justify their claim that America was a beacon, lighting the way forward for other countries. A stunning example is the well-received book of Walter Russell Mead, which describes American foreign policy as the product of "special providence."[6] His more recent writing dismissively rejects the notion of American decline as simply the product of the "international chattering classes" and that "Washington will remain the chairman of a larger board."[7] This self-congratulatory view makes American policy makers sensitive to the frailties and failings of other states but not their own. When France and Germany opposed US intervention in Iraq, President George W. Bush's defense secretary Donald Rumsfeld scornfully contrasted tired "old Europe" with the vigorous "new America."[8]

[4] One example is the US debate over the introduction of a currency law targeted at China for its purported currency manipulation. See "US Senate Delays Vote on Currency Bill amid Differences," 7 October 2011, http://www.bbc.co.uk/news/mobile/business -15209902 (accessed 7 October 2011).

[5] Louis Hartz, *The Liberal Tradition in America: An Interpretation of American Political Thought since the Revolution* (New York: Harcourt, Brace, 1955).

[6] Walter Russell Mead, *Special Providence: American Foreign Policy and How It Changed the World* (New York: Routledge, 2002).

[7] Walter Russell Mead, "The Myth of America's Decline," *Wall Street Journal*, 9 April 2012, http://online.wsj.com/article/SB10001424052702303816504577305531821651026.html (accessed 17 August 2012).

[8] "Outrage at 'Old Europe' Remarks," 23 January 2003, http://news.bbc.co.uk/2/hi /europe/2687403.stm (accessed 8 August 2011).

American exceptionalism was buttressed by a succession of unprecedented achievements, all of which were understandably played up in contrast to failures that were ignored or later seen to be erased by successes. America's expansion across the continent, victory over Spain, and acquisition of colonies was followed by its pivotal role in determining the outcome of the First World War. Triumph over Germany and Italy in World War II, the invention and use of nuclear weapons to end the war with Japan, the Bretton Woods Agreement, and the Marshall Plan all consolidated Americans' sense of themselves as technological and organizational visionaries. The landing of the first man on the moon served to overcome the shock of Sputnik just as the successful occupation of Guadalcanal had demonstrated American resolve in response to Pearl Harbor almost a generation earlier. Many liberals would later join conservatives in proclaiming that President Ronald Reagan "won" the Cold War, an utterly fatuous claim, but one now firmly embedded in America's psyche.

Failures like General Douglas MacArthur's push north in the Korean War; the Bay of Pigs Invasion; the Vietnam War; and more recently, failed interventions in Lebanon, Somalia, Afghanistan, and Iraq were reconceived of as "victories" (Korea), inconsequential (the Bay of Pigs), or part and parcel of strategies that were, or will be, successful in the longer term. Bush "hawks" now hail the Iraq invasion as the necessary prelude to the Arab Spring.[9]

The messianic component of American foreign policy conceives of the nation as embodying a set of political, economic, and social values that should be emulated by others. A sense of superiority is common to dominant powers and empires. The British spoke of "the White Man's burden," a term formulated by Rudyard Kipling in an 1899 poem intended as a cautionary warning about American imperialism. The reading public missed the satirical nature of the poem, which was widely interpreted as an exhortation for their compatriots to bring civilization, culture, and Christianity to "less-developed" peoples.

Postwar American hegemony never took the form of empire, although neoconservatives like Niall Ferguson garnered widespread publicity when they urged that the United States become one.[10] In his laundry list defending British and American messianism, Ferguson associated it with competition, science, democracy, modern medicine,

---

[9] Ben Armbruster, "Condi Rice Credits Bush for Arab Spring: We Had a Role in That," 1 November 2011, http://thinkprogress.org/security/2011/11/01/358037/condi-rice-bush-arab-spring/?mobile=nc (accessed 6 March 2013).

[10] Niall Ferguson. "Welcome to the New Imperialism," *Guardian*, 31 October 2001, http://www.guardian.co.uk/world/2001/oct/31/afghanistan.terrorism7 (accessed 8 August 2011).

consumerism, and the Protestant work ethic, all of which he described as critical components of freedom.[11] Richard Haass, former director of policy planning in the George W. Bush administration and current president of the Council on Foreign Relations, authored a similar call for an imperial America. He advocated a foreign policy "that attempts to organize the world along certain principles affecting relations between states and conditions within them. The U.S. role would resemble 19th century Great Britain." Countries that conform to democracy and capitalism would be welcome. Force would be used against those who resisted.[12] Haass's promotion of empire did not win the support of the Bush White House, and he left office early in the president's first term. The administration's doctrine of preemptive intervention nevertheless reflected a similar, sustained, zealous, messianic, and military approach to problems that has been a consistent element of American foreign policy since the war against Spain in 1898.[13]

The third element of the culture of national security is an abiding faith in America's indispensible role in providing peace, order, and, by extension, democracy. Toward this end, American leaders constructed a security architecture based on a series of regional alliances and bilateral agreements. Beginning with the 1944 Bretton Woods Agreement, the United States also sought to construct an economic order modeled on its values, institutions, and practices. According to G. John Ikenberry:

> During the decades after World War II, the United States did not just fight the Cold War, it created a liberal international order of multilayered pacts and partnerships that served to open markets, bind democracies together, and create a trans-regional security community. The United States provided security, championed mutually agreed upon rules and institutions, and led in the management of an open world economy. In return other states affiliated with and supported the United States as it led the larger order. It was an American-led hegemonic order with liberal characteristics.[14]

The end of the Cold War and disappearance of the communist enemy led many to question the continuing relevance of these traditional alliances. When new and different security threats emerged—notably, those

[11] Niall Ferguson, *Civilization: The West and the Rest* (London: Allen Lane, 2011); Niall Ferguson, *Colossus: The Rise and Fall of America's Empire* (London: Allen Lane, 2004).

[12] Richard Haass, "What to Do with American Primacy?" *Foreign Affairs* 78, no. 5 (September/October 1999): 37–50.

[13] Simon Reich, "The Evolution of a Doctrine: The Curious Case of Kofi Annan, George Bush and the Doctrines of Preventative and Preemptive Intervention," in William Keller and Gordon Mitchell, eds., *Hitting First: Preventive Force in US Security Strategy* (Pittsburgh: University of Pittsburgh Press, 2006).

[14] G. John Ikenberry, "Grand Strategy as Liberal Order Building," paper prepared for the conference "After the Bush Doctrine: National Security Strategy for a New Administration," University of Virginia, 7–8 June 2007.

associated with ethnic conflict and terrorism—American policy makers reasserted the importance of these mechanisms as part of the appropriate platform for expanded cooperation, now enlarged to incorporate the former communist states of Eastern Europe into NATO. Their rationale behind alliance expansion remains the claim that America stands as indisputable leader in the fight against global chaos and disorder.[15]

These several components of America's national security culture encouraged its militarization, readily apparent in the Bush administration's response to the terrorist attacks of 9/11. These attacks offered a rationale to sell the Congress and public on invasions of Afghanistan and Iraq, and subsequently more limited military actions in Pakistan and Yemen. The alternative, favored by most Europeans, was treating terrorism as a criminal offense and developing limited and closely calibrated responses directly against its perpetrators.[16]

The United States may have eschewed formal empire, but nonetheless shares the parochialism of great empires. During the Cold War, one of the authors of this book, Richard Ned Lebow, briefly served as a scholar in residence at the Central Intelligence Agency (CIA) and can report that vast assets and hundreds of analysts throughout the intelligence community were devoted to collecting and analyzing information about Soviet strategic and conventional military capabilities. A couple of analysts, at most, worked—and only part-time—on Soviet nationality problems and a relatively small number on understanding the country's political culture. American intelligence is still overwhelmingly focused on the military capabilities and intentions of adversaries—state and nonstate actors alike. The CIA remains notably lacking in personnel who know much about the Arab world—let alone those who can speak Arabic—even as it has ramped up its counterterrorism capabilities and operated on a significantly expanded budget since 9/11.[17] The government has increased funding for area studies programs about the Arab and Muslim world, just as it did for the Soviet Union and Eastern Europe in the 1950s and '60s. The Congress nevertheless slashed funding for the Title VI and Fulbright-Hays programs that form the foundation

[15] Michael Mandelbaum, *The Frugal Superpower: America's Global Leadership in a Cash-Strapped Era* (Philadelphia, Public Affairs, 2010), 3–10.

[16] See, for example, Didier Bigo, "The Emergence of a Consensus: Global Terrorism, Global Insecurity and Global Security," in Ariane Chebel d'Appollonia and Simon Reich, eds., *Immigration, Integration and Security: America and Europe in Comparative Perspective* (Pittsburgh: University of Pittsburgh Press, 2008), 67–94.

[17] See National Commission on Terrorist Attacks Upon the United States, "The 9/11 Commission Report" (DC: GPO, 2004): 92; Matt Bennett and Jonathan Morgenstein, *Modernizing Our Intelligence Force* (DC: The Third Way National Security Program, April 2008); "US Spy Agencies 'Struggle with Post-9/11 Languages,'" *The Telegraph*, 20 September 2011, http://www.telegraph.co.uk/news/worldnews/september-11-attacks/8775550/US-spy-agencies-struggle-with-post-911-languages.html, (accessed 6 September 2013).

for language training and faculty and student exchange programs.[18] If Americans learn a second language, it is far more likely to be Spanish.

Most college graduates who embark on intelligence careers are not required to learn a strategically important language for national security or global commerce such as Arabic, Mandarin, or Urdu. Access to foreign languages is complicated by the fact that many US-based native Arabic or Urdu speakers have a very difficult time being awarded the national security clearances necessary to work in sensitive jobs because of the rigorous screening rules introduced by the Bush administration and retained by the Obama administration. As a result, many capable candidates for intelligence jobs are therefore either denied a clearance or deterred by the process.

Parochialism extends well beyond the learning of languages. The US military fights foreign wars with a dearth of interpreters or knowledge of local conditions, down to such basics as adequate maps. As noted, American international relations (IR) theorists downplay culture as a determinant of behavior. Many consider knowledge of foreign cultures, history, geography, or language unnecessary because "they" think and act just like "us," or at least that they would do so if "they" just had the chance or were shown the benefits of doing so. Alternatively, these theorists stress so-called structural factors as determinants of foreign policies and depict policy makers as rational beings who respond in predictable ways to these opportunities and constraints. A well-known realist at Ohio State University famously tells his students that they never need to leave Ohio to understand international relations.

Consistent with this view are the strategies of deterrence and compellence developed during the Cold War. They required no knowledge about Soviet leaders or the foreign and domestic context in which they formulated policy. They assumed that they viewed the world the way these theories assumed and applied the same rationalist principles as Americans, despite ample evidence that policy making in Washington bore little relationship to this logic. Deterrence and compellence, and their American theoreticians, also assumed that emotions were irrelevant to foreign policy and that success depended on a mutual signaling of commitments and intentions, which could be treated as technical problems.[19]

[18] Sheila A. Smith, *America's Global Future on the Chopping Block* (New York: Council on Foreign Relations, 2011), http://blogs.cfr.org/asia/2011/06/09/americas-global-future-on-the-chopping-block (accessed 15 September 2011).

[19] Robert Jervis, Richard Ned Lebow, and Janice Gross Stein, *Psychology and Deterrence* (Baltimore: John Hopkins University Press, 1984); Richard Ned Lebow and Janice Gross Stein, *We All Lost the Cold War* (Princeton, NJ: Princeton University Press, 1994); Ted Hopf, *Peripheral Visions: Deterrence Theory and American Foreign Policy in the Third World, 1965–1990* (Ann Arbor: University of Michigan Press, 1994).

Perhaps the most disturbing manifestation of parochialism is the emphasis on military force as a mechanism of foreign policy, something widely shared within the national security elite. A powerful and confident America, in contrast to Europe's limited military capability, can supposedly rely on the instruments of hard power to justify America's leadership and secure its goals, oblivious to the limitations of this view despite all evidence to the contrary.[20] This view plays out well at home. But it neither worked in varied multilateral forums nor the battlegrounds of the Middle East, Asia, or Africa.

Sponsorship

In what Yuen Foong Khong recently described as the "American Tributary System," postwar American leadership has relied on extensive foreign aid and an enormously powerful military to buy or coerce support for its alliances and foreign policies.[21] As noted in this volume's preface, this approach is increasingly at odds with post–Cold War realities. President George W. Bush's invasions of Afghanistan and Iraq antagonized allies, leading to two costly and unsuccessful wars. Other major security and economic initiatives, many of them unilateral in nature, such as the covert drug wars in Latin America, were not as catastrophic but can hardly be considered successful. In his most recent book, Ikenberry acknowledges these developments, but suggests that it is evidence of the successful functioning of the liberal international order that the United States created.[22] We disagree.

It is time to create a new framework and rethink foreign policy goals. Our alternative framing is based on the assumption that less is often more. Sponsorship strategies entail the endorsement, support, and enforcement of multilateral initiatives proposed by other state and nonstate actors who receive wide international support and become codified in the protocols of supranational and global organizations. This does not require any undermining of American sovereignty because Washington would decide which policies to support based on its leaders' understanding of the nation's interests. While sponsorship eschews

[20] Robert Kagan, "Power and Weakness," *Policy Review* 113, http://www.newamericancentury.org/kagan-20020520.htm (accessed 16 February 2011); Robert Kagan, *Paradise and Power: America and Europe in the New World Order* (New York: Knopf, 2003).

[21] For an interesting perspective on this issue, see Yuen Foong Khong, "The American Tributary System," *Chinese Journal of International Politics* 6 (2013): 1–47.

[22] G. John Ikenberry, *Liberal Leviathan: The Origins, Crisis, and Transformation of the American World Order* (Princeton, NJ: Princeton University Press, 2011).

hegemony, it has the virtue of remaining faithful to other elements of America's culture of national security. It is activist, engaged, robust, and, at times, muscular. Yet it is also prudent.

Sponsorship is a form of *hēgemonia*, a concept we described in earlier chapters. It sharply differs from the conventional definition of hegemony that assumes American leadership, relies on a foundation of coercion to assert that leadership, and entails the projection of American values. Hēgemonia draws on social and material power by utilizing resources in ways that increase legitimacy through the enhancement of collective interests and values. It has the potential to increase American influence while minimizing accusations of aggression and pursuit of narrow self-interest at the expense of the community at large. Sponsorship's defining characteristic is action on behalf of the larger community with the official backing of that community. It does sometimes involve coercion or the use of force, but is legitimated and given credibility by broad support, often entailing official authorization, from supranational organizations like NATO and the UN. When force is used, it is within a multilateral framework in which costs are shared and the United States does not appear to lead.

Sponsorship is entirely different from "soft" or "smart" power, which aspires to build support for American foreign policies through the export of American cultural and material products. Sponsorship advances or enforces more universal values, not specifically American ones, although the two must be consistent to attract American participation. There is wide support in the United States and abroad for humanitarian policies that protect civilians in zones of warfare or ethnic conflict. However, US intervention appears fundamentally different to foreign audiences when it is the result of a sponsorship strategy—a striking contrast to US intervention in Central America and the Caribbean during the Cold War or in Iraq in this century.[23]

Sponsorship links social and material power in ways consistent with hēgemonia that hegemony does not, thereby enhancing American legitimacy abroad and expanding its influence. Sponsorship and hegemonic strategies are largely incompatible. The former entails modesty. It rejects chauvinism and with it the American claim to being a universal role model. It emphasizes American values, particularly those associated with democracy, peace, and prosperity, but not merely rhetorically to mobilize domestic support for policies that undercut these values. It advocates civil liberties, democracy, and free

[23] Stephen Zunes, "The US Invasion of Grenada," *Global Policy Forum*, October 2003, http://www.globalpolicy.org/component/content/article/155-history/25966.html (accessed 29 December 2011).

trade and sees these goals as compatible with, if not essential to, international order.

Sponsorship strategies offer real advantages for America globally, as we shall demonstrate. For a start, they are relatively cheap in blood and treasure in contrast to leadership strategies. The war in Iraq—a quintessential example of a leadership strategy—is conservatively estimated to have cost in excess of $800 billion. By late 2011, the war in Afghanistan had cost another $467 billion.[24] Other estimates suggest the eventual long-term costs will approach $4 trillion.[25] The sponsorship strategy in Libya cost a small fraction of that amount, and was notably successful in orchestrating civilian protection and regime change. This comparison is not intended to suggest that sponsorship would have succeeded in removing Saddam Hussein from power in Iraq. However, it is not at all evident that this objective was on any way critical to US security or economic or reputational interests. A commitment to sponsorship could have forestalled a foolhardy adventure when it failed to gain support in the UN Security Council or backing from key American allies.

Sponsorship strategies generally avoid the engagement of US forces in combat, a welcome contrast for an American public weighed down by the casualties resulting from a decade of war in Afghanistan and Iraq. For reasons we will discuss, they generally provide for easier exit strategies. They also retain flexibility because fewer resources are committed by the United States when it is not leading the initiative.

Sponsorship strategies confer another significant advantage: prospectively restoring American legitimacy. Since the end of the Cold War, the absence of legitimacy, more than any other factor, has rendered American initiatives problematic and unsuccessful. American policy makers, journalists, and scholars routinely assert that foreigners long for America to take a central role. There is little evidence in support of this assertion in many, if not most, conflict situations. The struggles among Israel, the Arab states, and the Palestinians is a case in point. Indeed, distrust of the United States is so great and widespread that any American initiative has met serious opposition merely by virtue of its association with Washington. Hegemonic strategies will continue to generate accusations of imperialism from America's most avowed opponents, but also from states and regimes that have been friendly in the past. Sponsorship strategies—like the fight against human trafficking or

---

[24] David R. Francis, "Iraq War Will Cost More Than World War II," *Christian Science Monitor*, 25 October 2011, http://www.csmonitor.com/Business/new-economy/2011/1025/Iraq-war-will-cost-more-than-World-War-II (accessed 29 December 2011).

[25] Watson Institute, Brown University, "Costs of War," http://costsofwar.org/article/economic-cost-summary (accessed 5 April 2013).

protection of civilians in Libya—offer the possibility of the rebuilding of American legitimacy.

Sponsorship is a relatively new approach to policy, at least in conception, so it is difficult to find historic evidence concerning security issues from the United States. We nevertheless offer three cases. The first and second cases are the invasion of Iraq and intervention in Libya, contrasting a leadership and a sponsorship strategy. The third, which relies on counterfactual reasoning, is a study of the United States, Mexico, and the drug problem. This became a major issue in the 1970s, in the administration of President Richard Nixon, and is even more important today. The pairing of counterfactual with so-called factual methods is an effective means of contrasting the use and consequences of hegemonic and sponsorship strategies. All three cases shed light on different ways of framing American foreign policy goals and their consequences for American legitimacy and the achievement of prescribed policy goals.

IRAQ VERSUS LIBYA

No pair of cases better contrasts the comparative processes, implementation, costs, and benefits of leadership strategies associated with the goal of hegemony, and sponsorship strategies associated with that of hēgemonia than the invasion of Iraq and the intervention in Libya.

By any assessment, the Iraq invasion led to a long and costly war that in no way served American interests. Saddam is gone but was not replaced by any regime that might be called pro-American and stable. US influence in the region has weakened rather than strengthened. The war further destabilized Pakistan and encouraged Iran to push ahead with its nuclear program. Terrorism against US allies and Americans overseas has arguably increased since the invasion. The avowed goal of military intervention—to forestall Iraq's acquisition of nuclear weapons—did not require military action because Saddam's regime had already abandoned its nuclear program. It is well to remember too that there was no compelling evidence beforehand that Saddam was anywhere close to developing a nuclear device. The costs of eight years of war have been considerable. Over 4,500 Americans lost their lives; 30,000 more were wounded and over $800 billion was wasted. Estimates vary, but there is a general consensus that at least 120,000 Iraqis were killed in the course of the fighting.[26]

[26] Michael E. O'Hanlon and Ian Livingston, "Iraq Index: Tracking Variables of Reconstruction and Security in Post-Saddam Iraq," 28 October 2011, http://www.brookings.edu/iraqindex (accessed 24 December 2011).

Most foreign policy analysts would not dissent from our negative assessment of the war. The more interesting question is why it all happened. Here too there is something of a consensus: much of the answer lies in bad planning and execution by the Bush administration. Articles, books, and memoirs have documented the extent to which the administration made the decision to intervene on the basis of false or doctored intelligence, refused to consider the possibility that the failure to discover any sign of weapons of mass destruction (WMDs) was evidence that there were none, failed to plan for a postwar occupation, and never considered the possibility that they would meet resistance after occupying Baghdad.

All of these criticisms are on target, but too narrowly focused on the performance of the Bush administration. They leave open the possibility that, at least in theory, a more skillful set of American leaders could have done better. On one level this is certainly true. A more thoughtful and better-elaborated occupation policy—one that did not disarm the Iraqi Army and made plans beyond the occupation of the oil ministry— might have reduced some of the support for the insurgency. But it is doubtful if any American invasion and occupation of a Middle Eastern country could succeed in an era of nationalism. Even a supremely capable administration would have failed by the very nature of the goal and the United States would have lost prestige by the mere fact of the near-unilateral nature of its military intervention. The goal of regime change and of reconstituting Iraq as a loyal ally, led by a secure puppet regime, was nothing short of delusional.

Military intervention might still have been justified if the threat posed by Saddam Hussein to regional and world security was sufficiently severe. There is no evidence to support this proposition. Saddam was undeniably a bloodthirsty tyrant, a rather common phenomenon in the Middle East. He had invaded Iran and Kuwait, but had been repulsed from both, the latter by an international coalition led by the United States. He had used poison gas against Kurdish civilians and had tried to develop atomic weapons. Iraq's defeat in the Gulf War had dramatically reduced Saddam's military assets, although it left him with enough forces to reassert his authority within Iraq. Saddam's air force and air defense network were in a shambles and no-fly zones had been imposed over the Shi'a and Kurdish regions of Iraq and enforced by frequent NATO aerial sorties. The UN maintained economic sanctions and interdicted any strategic materials that could assist in the development of WMDs. Saddam repeatedly limited inspections and expelled UN weapons inspectors, but there was never credible evidence indicating that he had recommenced his prewar efforts to acquire a nuclear arsenal. A degree of uncertainty nevertheless remained, and it was reasonable, even prudential, to compel Saddam to readmit UN inspection teams and give them unrestricted access. The US military buildup accomplished this goal, and the UN inspectors found no evidence to support American claims that Iraq was attempting to acquire WMDs.[27]

In the absence of WMDs and a usable air force, and with a poorly equipped and trained army, Saddam was more a nuisance than a threat to his immediate neighbors. At conferences sponsored by the American Enterprise Institute and in op-ed pieces and articles published in the *Weekly Standard*, neoconservatives nevertheless charged Saddam with supporting terrorism around the world. After 9/11, they accused him of being the guiding hand behind al-Qaeda, an allegation that Vice President Dick Cheney repeatedly referred to as an established fact. There was never any evidence for this connection, as Cheney himself must have realized. So terrorism was even more transparent a rationalization than WMDs for an invasion that high-ranking policy makers and their neoconservative supporters wanted to carry out for other reasons.

Neither was there any compelling economic interest at stake. Despite frequently voiced claims by Noam Chomsky and others that the invasion was driven by the desire to control Middle Eastern oil, such an explanation is unpersuasive.[28] The United States has traditionally allowed oil companies, interested only in the flow of reasonably priced oil, to make deals with all kinds of authoritarian regimes in the Middle East.[29] If the administration wanted access to Iraqi oil all it had to do was end sanctions, as many people were urging on humanitarian grounds. Saddam would have been happy to sell oil to all comers as he was desperate for income, and the price of oil would have dropped as Iraq's production reentered the international market. The Republican Party's right wing would not consider ending sanctions and buying

---

[27] National Commission on Terrorist Attacks, *The 9/11 Commission Report: Final Report of the National Commission on Terrorist Attacks upon the United States* (New York: Norton, 2004): 61, 161, 334–35; Iran Study Group, United States Institute of Peace, *The Iraq Study Group Report*, http://www.usip.org/programs/initiatives/iraq-study-group (accessed 11 February 2013). For the pre- and postinvasion nondiscovery of WMDs, see Joseph Cirincione, Jessica T. Matthews, and George Perkovich, *WMD in Iraq: Evidence and Implications* (Washington, DC: Carnegie Endowment for International Peace, 2004).

[28] Noam Chomsky and David Barsamian, *Imperial Ambitions: Conversations in the Post-9/11 World* (New York: Metropolitan, 2005); Noam Chomsky, "Imperial Ambitions," interview by David Barsamian, *Monthly Review*, May 2003, http://www.monthlyreview.org/0503chomsky.htm; (accessed 27 May 2013); Alex Callinicos, *New Mandarins of American Power: The Bush Administration's Plans for the World* (London: Polity, 2003).

[29] Edward Ingram, "Pairing off Empires: The United States as Great Britain in the Middle East," in Tore T. Petersen, ed., *Controlling the Uncontrollable? The Great Powers in the Middle East* (Trondheim, Norway: Tapir, 2006): 1–32.

Iraqi oil. Invasion and occupation were their preferred strategy. The war and subsequent occupation cost the United States an estimated $100 billion in the first year alone and the total cost of invasion and occupation weighs in at well over a trillion dollars, far exceeding any conceivable economic benefit.[30]

At the outset, the administration maintained that the invasion would pay for itself with Iraqi oil revenues, a "break even" estimate that can be construed as additional evidence that its primary goal was not material gain.[31] This unrealistic but well-publicized claim was almost certainly politically motivated, like another that Saddam had—or was about to possess—weapons of mass destruction. Both assertions were calculated efforts to undercut opposition to an invasion motivated by completely different goals.

In the first weeks of the Bush administration, high-ranking officials indicated to foreign officials and the media that they were deeply offended by the survival of Saddam's regime and on the lookout for a pretext to invade Iraq.[32] They confided to friendly listeners that Saddam's removal would allow Washington to remake the map of the Middle East and dramatically increase its influence worldwide. They assumed Iraqis would welcome their American "liberators" with open arms and accept émigré puppet Ahmed Chalabi as their new ruler. A pro-American regime in the heart of the Middle East was expected to provide significant leverage over Saudi Arabia, Iran, and the Palestinians.

Administration officials also reasoned that a high-tech military campaign that would later be referred to as "shock and awe" would paralyzed Iraqi forces at the outset with precision bombing and missile attack and overthrow Saddam with few American casualties and thus would intimidate North Korea and Iran. "Iraq is not just about Iraq," a

---

[30] Christian Reus-Smit, "Unipolarity and Legitimacy: On the Relative Cost of the Iraq and Persian Gulf Wars," unpublished manuscript; Martin Wolk, "Cost of War Could Surpass One Trillion," 17 March 2006, http://www.msnbc.msn.com/id/11880954; Watson Institute, "Costs of War."

[31] Bob Davis, "Bush Economic Aide Says Cost Of Iraq War May Top $100 Billion," *Wall Street Journal*, 16 September 2002; Elisabeth Bumiller, "White House Cuts Estimated Cost of War with Iraq, *New York Times*, 31 December 2002, http://www.nytimes.com/2002/12/31/us/threats-responses-cost-white-house-cuts-estimate-cost-war-with-iraq.html?pagewanted=all&src=pm (accessed 2 September 2012).

[32] Seymour M. Hersh, *Chain of Command: The Road from 9/11 to Abu Ghraib* (New York: Harper, 2004), 163–71; James Mann, *Rise of the Vulcans: The History of Bush's War Cabinet* (New York: Penguin, 2004), 294–310; Stefan Halper and Jonathan Clarke, *America Alone: The Neo-Conservatives and the Global Order* (New York: Cambridge University Press, 2004), 28–35; Michael Isikoff and David Corn, *Hubris: The Inside Story of Spin, Scandal, and the Selling of the Iraq War* (New York: Crown, 2006), 16.

senior official confided, but about Iran, Libya, and North Korea.[33] Victory was expected to encourage widespread bandwagoning, making countries around the world more intent on currying favor from the United States while allowing Washington to put more pressure on countries like France that opposed its vision of a world order.[34] In effect, the Bush administration sought unsuccessfully to "lock in" American hegemony and to make friends and foes alike more pliant. These goals were a natural, if utterly unrealistic, expression of America's national security culture.

Now, we must consider the counterfactual of what might have happened if the Bush administration had continued the policy of the administration of President Bill Clinton. When George W. Bush assumed office in January 2001, his secretary of state, Colin Powell, cheerfully admitted to reporters that his predecessor's Iraq policy was successful: "We have kept Saddam contained, kept him in a box."[35] There is no reason to suppose that he could not have been kept in this box for the next eight years. Evidence that came to light after the invasion indicated that Saddam had given up his nuclear program. Sanctions had been effective, as had the cost and difficulty of independent efforts to develop weapons of mass destruction. Iraqis would have continued to suffer under Saddam's rule, but no more so than other people of the region under other rulers. And Washington in any case seemed happy to do business with oppressive dictators, as it had with Saddam prior to his invasion of Kuwait. So it is reasonable to assume that Saddam would have held on to power for some time to come and that Iraq's economy, crippled by sanctions, would have continued to decline. His regime, while unpalatable, would not have posed any serious threat to the peace of the region. It is even possible that he would have become another victim of the so-called Arab Spring of 2011, facing an internal uprising of the kind that Bashar al-Assad confronted in Syria. Either way, US prestige would not have suffered, and Washington would have avoided the entire array of human, financial, and political costs brought about by its ill-considered invasion.

[33] David E. Sanger, "Viewing the War as a Lesson to the World," *New York Times*, 6 April 2003, http://www.nytimes.com/2003/04/06/world/a-nation-at-war-policy-viewing-the-war-as-a-lesson-to-the-world.html?pagewanted=all&src=pm (accessed 2 September 2012).

[34] David Frum and Richard Perle, *An End to Evil: How to Win the War on Terror* (New York: Random House, 2003): 33, 212–13, 247–66.

[35] Colin Powell, "Press Briefing Aboard Aircraft en Route to Cairo Egypt," 23 February 2001, http://2001-2009.state.gov/secretary/former/powell/remarks/2001/931.htm (accessed 4 June 2013).

In contrast, the NATO intervention in Libya lasted only five months, from the late spring to the autumn of 2011. It cost approximately a billion dollars, produced no American casualties, and achieved its policy goals by protecting civilians and orchestrating regime change. America's reputation abroad was enhanced as a responsible and responsive global citizen. Obama's domestic critics charged that he committed the cardinal sin of depriving America of its sovereignty by deferring to the UN and NATO. Picking up on the ill-considered words of a loose-lipped Obama administration official, they pilloried his approach as "leading from behind."[36] Other critics insisted that it was all a waste of money, given—they insisted—the absence of any serious national interest.[37] These criticisms did not erode public support for the intervention, even in the maelstrom of an American presidential campaign. Among academics, some rejoiced, albeit perhaps prematurely, declaring that it signaled the resurrection of the UN's responsibility to protect initiative, while realists remained uncharacteristically mute.[38]

Press pundits suggested that Libyan policy was motivated by a desire to avoid the mistakes of Iraq: the commitment of troops with over-ambitious goals and no defined exit strategy. But it would be a mistake to explain the difference only with respect to "lessons learned."[39] American policy in these two conflicts represents more than a tactical contrast. It is symptomatic of a more profound difference, between leadership and sponsorship strategies.[40]

[36] David Remnick, "Behind the Curtain," *New Yorker*, 5 September 2011, http://www .newyorker.com/talk/comment/2011/09/05/110905taco_talk_remnick (accessed 24 December 2011); Zach Carter, "Lindsey Graham Criticizes Obama on Libya Days after Gaddafi's Death," *Huffington Post*, 23 October 2011, http://www.huffingtonpost.com/2011 /10/23/lindsay-graham-criticizes_n_1027098.html (accessed 22 December 2011).

[37] Zach Carter, "Richard Lugar Questions US Costs Of Libya Conflict," *Huffington Post*, 27 March 2011, http://www.huffingtonpost.com/2011/03/27/libya-lugar-ques tions-us-costs_n_841136.html (accessed 23 December 2011).

[38] Tim Dunne and Jess Gifkins, "Libya and the UN Security Council," 19 April 2011, http://uq.academia.edu/TimDunne/Blog/14229/Libya-and-the-UN-Security-Council (accessed 22 December 2011); Tim Dunne and Jess Gifkins, "Libya and the State of Intervention," *Australian Journal of International Affairs* 65, no. 5 (2011): 515–29. For a realist reaction, see Peter Feaver, "Giving Obama Credit—When He's Followed Bush's Footsteps," *Foreign Policy*, 31 October 2011, http://shadow.foreignpolicy.com/posts/2011/10/31 /giving_obama_credit_when_hes_followed_bushs_footprints (accessed 24 December 2011).

[39] Fareed Zakaria, "How the Lessons of Iraq Paid Off in Libya," *Time*, 5 September 2011, http://www.time.com/time/magazine/article/0,9171,2090374,00.html (accessed 6 March 2013).

[40] Mark Lander, "Iraq, a War Obama Didn't Want, Shaped His Foreign Policy," *New York Times*, 17 December 2011, http://www.nytimes.com/2011/12/18/us/politics/iraq -war-shaped-obamas-foreign-policy-white-house-memo.html?pagewanted=all&_r=0 (accessed 10 February 2013).

Characteristic of a sponsorship strategy, the initial requests for intervention began with local participants, and were considered by states in the region and then by the United Nations Security Council. The outcome was a UN resolution that authorized intervention to protect the lives of civilians.[41] Although the United States was fully supportive of intervention, its fingerprints were not in evidence in the formulation or implementation of policy.

Emboldened by political change in Libya and Egypt, protests broke out in the eastern Libyan city of Benghazi on 15 February 2011. Dictator Muammar Gaddafi responded with a violent crackdown that involved indiscriminate firing on residents. Violence quickly spread to other cities in the east—notably, Misrata. A largely disorganized resistance force sprung into being, later named the National Transitional Council (NTC). It proved itself to be surprisingly durable despite its lack of resources or a coherent strategy; it was able to evade the government's heavy artillery and tanks sent into the streets of Libyan cities.[42]

The response of the European Union (EU) and the UN was surprisingly swift; within weeks, resolutions were passed that imposed sanctions against Gaddafi and his small coterie of advisers, freezing assets, limiting their travel, and referring the matter to the International Criminal Court.[43] The African Union met and declined to follow suit but, critically, the Arab League took a different approach, agreeing to suspend Libyan membership. By the second week in March, twenty-two members of the Arab League endorsed a no-fly zone over Libyan airspace to protect local resistance. This cleared the way for a similar UN resolution, increasing the pressure on what the *New York Times* characterized as "a reluctant Obama administration" to act.[44]

Sanctions against Gaddafi took effect and the rebels began to advance from the east. After 10 March 2011, debate in France focused on recognition of the NTC, prompted in part by the very public remonstrations of noted French philosopher Bernard-Henri Lévy.[45] His private

[41] Ian Williams, "Resolution 1973: Responsibility to Protect, Not Humanitarian Intervention in Libya," *Washington Report on Middle East Affairs* 30, no. 4. (2011), 42.

[42] C. J. Chivers, "Pinned Down in Battered City, Libyan Rebels Endure With Grit and Dirt," *New York Times*, 17 April 2011, http://www.nytimes.com/2011/04/17/world/africa/17misurata.html?pagewanted=all (accessed 8 January 2012).

[43] Edward Wyatt, "Security Council Calls for War Crimes Inquiry in Libya," *New York Times*, 26 February 2012, http://www.nytimes.com/2011/02/27/world/africa/27nations.html?hp (accessed 10 January 2012).

[44] Ethan Bronner and David E. Sanger, "Arab League Endorses No-Flight Zone over Libya," *New York Times*, 12 March 2011, http://www.nytimes.com/2011/03/13/world/middleeast/13libya.html?scp=1&sq=Arab%20League%20Endorses%20No-Flight%20Zone%20Over%20Libya&st=cse (accessed 8 January 2012).

[45] Steven Erlanger, "By His Own Reckoning, One Man Made Libya a French Cause,"

campaign to commit the United States to intervention began by him organizing a secret meeting on 14 March 2011 between Mahmoud Jibril, the leader of the Libyan rebels, and Secretary of State Hillary Rodham Clinton. According to Michael Hastings, "Coached by Lévy, Jibril had urged Clinton to support a no-fly zone, arm the rebels and launch attacks on Gaddafi's army. If the U.S. failed to intervene, he warned, there would be mass killings, just as there had been after Bill Clinton failed to take action in Rwanda and the Balkans in the 1990s."[46] Rebel pleas for NATO intervention to protect them from aerial bombardment intensified the pressure on the international community.

The initially reticent Obama came to accept the need for intervention in response to the crescendo of developments and pressures in this direction. These included the Arab League's decision to support intervention through the UN, the United Arab Emirates' indication that it would participate in an intervention force, the back-door efforts of Lévy and Jibril to influence the administration and perhaps, most important, the support for intervention by Secretary of State Clinton. The president asked for military options, which Admiral Mike Mullen, chairman of the Joint Chiefs of Staff, hand delivered to the White House the following day. The president had two caveats: American involvement should be finite—"days, not weeks," a senior White House official reported—and no ground troops would be committed.[47]

On 17 March 2011, Russia presented a resolution to the UN advocating a ceasefire.[48] Aware that an interventionist American resolution would generate opposition, France, with the support of the Arab League, presented a resolution calling for UN authorization of a no-fly zone over Libya.[49] The resolution authorized member states, acting uni-

New York Times, 1 April 2012, http://www.nytimes.com/2011/04/02/world/africa/02 levy.html?pagewanted=all (accessed 10 January 2012); Jacob Heilbrunn, "Beware the French Poseur Bernard-Henri Levy," *National Interest*, 5 April 2011, http://nationalinter est.org/blog/jacob-heilbrunn/beware-the-french-poseur-bernard-henri-levy-5116 (accessed 10 January 2012).

[46] Michael Hastings, "Inside Obama's War Room: How He Decided to Intervene in Libya—And What It Says about His Evolution as Commander in Chief," *Rolling Stone*, 13 October 2011, http://www.rollingstone.com/politics/news/inside-obamas-war-room -20111013 (accessed 10 January 2011).

[47] Helene Cooper and Steven Lee Myers, "Obama Takes Hard Line With Libya After Shift by Clinton," *New York Times*, 18 March 2012, http://www.nytimes.com/2011/03/19 /world/africa/19policy.html?scp=2&sq=Inside%20Obama%27s%20War%20Room%20 How%20he%20decided%20to%20intervene%20in%20Libya&st=cse (accessed 8 January 2012).

[48] United Nations Security Council, 6498th Meeting, S/PV.6498, 17 March 2011, http://www.un.org/ga/search/view_doc.asp?symbol=S/PV.6498 (accessed 4 June 2013).

[49] Cooper and Myers, "Obama Takes Hard Line with Libya after Shift by Clinton"; Bronner and Sanger, "Arab League Endorses No-Flight Zone over Libya."

laterally or through regional organizations, to take all necessary measure to protect civilians and civilian populated areas under threat of attack in the Libyan Arab Jamahiriya. It also authorized the no-fly zone and requested the states concerned to coordinate their actions closely with the UN secretary general.[50] China and Russia abstained. The United States remained very much in the background, although engaged in extensive private bilateral discussions with undecided council members prior to the vote. "On the political front," one observer noted, "in sharp contrast to the 2003 invasion of Iraq, the U.S. has not forced everyone else's hand with a 'you're either for us, or against us' approach. Instead, European powers have taken the lead, given their military capabilities and the fact that the trouble is in Europe's own backyard."[51]

After the vote, Obama made it clear that any intervention would have to be an international effort, with the burden shared among multiple countries.[52] France launched a string of air attacks against Gaddafi's forces two days after the passage of the UN resolution. The UK commitment of air forces was soon followed by the United States, Canada, and, of great symbolic importance, Qatar. NATO assumed formal control of the intervention. Eighteen countries eventually contributed forces to what was now called Operation Unified Protector. Jordan and the United Arab Emirates eventually joined Qatar as Arab participants, contributing to a portion of the over 26,500 sorties, though they were not a party to the over 9,700 air strike sorties eventually reported by NATO.[53]

The coalition campaign soon expanded beyond the narrow UN mandate of civilian defense in Benghazi as air forces attacked Gaddafi's tanks and antiaircraft systems. While media reports initially suggested that Washington's role was only supportive, it soon became evident that the United States was responsible for the overwhelming percentage of Tomahawk missile strikes against Libyan government forces as well as playing a critical logistical role.[54] By the end of the first week, the United States had flown nearly 900 sorties while the French forces, which had garnered most of the public attention, had carried out only 110.[55]

---

[50] Williams, "Resolution 1973."

[51] "West Had to Act, but Needs a Plan," *Aviation Week and Space Technology* 173, no. 11 (2011): 58.

[52] Cooper and Myers, 'Obama Takes Hard Line With Libya after Shift by Clinton."

[53] North Atlantic Treaty Organization, Public Diplomacy Division, "Operation UNIFIED PROTECTOR Final Mission Stats" (Brussels: North Atlantic Treaty Organization, 2011).

[54] "Libya: The Coalition Campaign Begins," *Stratfor*, 19 March 2011, http://www.stratfor.com/sample/analysis/libya-coalition-campaign-begins (accessed 4 June 2013).

[55] "NATO Operations in Libya: Data Journalism Breaks Down Which Country Does

As the conflict unfolded, Washington played an increasingly important role in coordinating bombing attacks while allowing France and the United Kingdom to conduct most of the actual sorties, leading much of the media to conclude that the costs were reasonably shared.[56] Aggregate figures seem to support this appraisal. The United States provided the most personnel (8,507 of the total force of approximately 13,000 troops), a little more that half the aircraft, and launched 228 of the 246 cruise missiles. The United States is reported to have dropped only 455 bombs out of 1,256, only 25 percent more than Denmark, while France and the United Kingdom flew the majority of air strike missions.[57]

The financial cost of the war was reasonably shared. Washington spent approximately $1 billion, France $400 million, Britain $333 million, and Canada $50 million. The remaining fourteen participants in military operations contributed substantially less, but overall sharing across the coalition stood in stark contrast to the previous actions in Iraq. Consistent with a sponsorship strategy, the United States shouldered a large percentage of the burden of enforcement without assuming the mantle of leadership, which was left to the French and their British allies.[58]

The United States also pursued the pattern anticipated by a sponsorship strategy: it followed rather than led. In contrast to France, Washington did not recognize the TNC until the second week in July, three months after the NATO campaign against Gaddafi had begun and at a point where the military tide had turned against his forces. Secretary

---

What," https://docs.google.com/spreadsheet/ccc?key=0AonYZs4MzlZbdFY5dFNsZD dfamdPQUdfbW5HcVR6eUE&hl=en_US#gid=0 (accessed 16 January 2012).

[56] Jay Solomon, "US, France Seek Balance on Mideast," *Wall Street Journal*, 24 December 2011, http://online.wsj.com/article/SB10001424052970204336104577094500038099554.html (accessed 12 January 2012).

[57] "NATO Operations in Libya;" Elisabeth Bumiller, "Libyan War Goes a Long Way to Improve the Pentagon's View of France as an Ally," *New York Times*, 26 August 2011, http://www.nytimes.com/2011/08/27/world/africa/27military.html?_r=2 (accessed 17 January 2012).

[58] Kevin Baron, "For the US, War against Qaddafi Cost Relatively Little: $1.1 Billion," *Atlantic*, 21 October 2011, http://www.theatlantic.com/international/archive/2011/10/for-the-us-war-against-qaddafi-cost-relatively-little-11-billion/247133 (accessed 17 January 2012); Thomas Penny, "Libya Operation Cost U.K. $333 Million, Defense Ministry Says," *Bloomberg Businessweek*, 8 December 2011, http://www.businessweek.com/news/2011-12-08/libya-operation-cost-u-k-333-million-defense-ministry-says.html (accessed 17 January 2012); "La guerre en Libye a coûté 300 millions d'euros à la France," *Le Parisien*, 23 October 2012, http://www.leparisien.fr/intervention-libye/la-guerre-en-libye-a-coute-300-millions-d-euros-a-la-france-23-10-2011-1681579.php (accessed 17 January 2012); Mark Dunn, "Libya Mission Cost Canadians $50 million," *Toronto Sun*, 29 October 2011, http://www.torontosun.com/2011/10/29/libya-mission-cost-canadians-50-million (accessed 17 January 2012).

Clinton declared that American recognition had been contingent on the TNC's assurances that it would pursue democratic reforms through a transparent process. The TNC announced its plan for elections within a year.[59]

As part of a broad coalition, Washington achieved the goal of regime change in Libya in a few months. Success in Libya and failure in Iraq were attributable to different conditions in the two countries but also President Obama's adherence to a sponsorship strategy. He insisted on four conditions before he would commit the United States to any military operations. First, there had to be a local opposition movement that was willing and able to wage war against the dictator. Any international action had to be requested by the locals. Second, given the sensitivity of Arab opinion, it was important to gain regional legitimacy to undercut the allegation that outside intervention in Libya was another example of Western imperialism. Toward this end, several Arab countries were drawn into the coalition. Third, broader legal legitimacy was successfully sought through the UN. Finally, European allies who were pressing for intervention were put on notice that the operation would have to be genuinely multilateral, and that they would have to bear significant costs. In every respect, this was very different from Iraq, where the Bush administration—either through arrogance or incompetence—met none of these conditions.[60]

The consequences of the initial assault were overwhelmingly positive. American goals of civilian protection and regime change were achieved at a relatively low cost and without incurring US military casualties. Washington's exit strategy was uncomplicated and did not require, as it did in Iraq, the smokescreen of patriotic rhetoric and the unfounded declarations of achievement. More important, intervention helped to improve the US image among allies and at the UN, much needed in the aftermath of the Iraq War. In contrast to the staged welcoming of American troops into Baghdad, unprompted Libyans waved American flags in the streets of Benghazi following Washington's recognition of the Libyan rebel forces.[61] Furthermore, when a militia

[59] Scott Peterson, "US Recognition of Libya Rebels Could Bring More Funds," *Christian Science Monitor*, 15 July 2011, http://www.csmonitor.com/World/Middle-East/2011/0715/US-recognition-of-Libya-rebels-could-bring-more-funds (accessed 12 January 2012).

[60] Zakaria, "How the Lessons of Iraq Paid Off in Libya"; Shadi Hamid, "After Libya," 14 September 2011, http://www.brookings.edu/interviews/2011/0914_libya_hamid.aspx (accessed 28 December 2011).

[61] David Zucchino, "Libyan Rebels Embrace US and Its Flag," *Los Angeles Times*, 5 August 2011, http://feb17.info/news/libyan-rebels-embrace-u-s-and-its-flag (accessed 28 December 2011).

named Ansar al-Sharia attacked the US Consulate in Benghazi two months later, resulting in the death of four Americans including US ambassador Christopher Stevens, Libyans expressed their outrage at the attack. Thousands took to the streets to express their sorrow and solidarity. The protestors then drove the militia out of the city. A further attack by protestors on an allied militia group resulted in three deaths and twenty injuries in arguably unprecedented demonstrations of solidarity with the United States in the Middle East.[62]

Not surprisingly, positive public opinion about the United States in the aftermath of Libyan intervention was most evident in Europe. The Libyan intervention appears to have brought Americans and Europeans closer together in terms of legitimizing cooperative security policy. The 2011 German Marshall Fund's *Transatlantic Trends* survey found that while an opinion gap still existed on some security topics, there was a degree of policy convergence between EU and US pubic opinion. American and Europeans overwhelmingly agreed that the best way forward in Libya was humanitarian intervention led by an international force. Notably, this poll was conducted before the rebel victory in Libya.[63]

The European Council on Foreign Relations also perceived an improvement between the Europeans and the United States. The council noted, "The Arab Awakening reinforced Europe's role as a partner for the US, especially in the common intervention in Libya." Their annual "scorecard" gave the United States higher grades. "Cooperation on European Security Issues" went from a C to a B-, with the highest scores going to the Libyan operation. "Cooperation on regional and global issues" rose from a C to grade B, with the second highest scores going to the administration's response to the Arab Spring.[64] James Joyner, the managing editor of the Atlantic Council, noted, "Libya clearly demonstrates that any future U.S. military involvement under the auspices of 'global policing' will be dependent on the contribution of other countries, most notably from Europe."[65]

On a bilateral basis, the Libyan war had a major impact on the relationship between the United States and its French, British, and Italian allies. In a strongly worded speech following the November 2011 Group

---

[62] Wyre Davies, "Libya: Islamist Militia Bases Stormed in Benghazi," 22 September 2012, http://www.bbc.co.uk/news/world-africa-19680785 (accessed 5 April 2013).

[63] German Marshall Fund, *Transatlantic Trends 2011*, http://www.gmfus.org/publica tions_/TT/TT2011_final_web.pdf. (accessed 27 May 2013).

[64] European Council on Foreign Relations, "European Foreign Policy Scorecard 2012," http://www.ecfr.eu/scorecard/2012/usa (accessed 12 February 2013).

[65] James Joyner, "The Future of EU-US Security and Defense Cooperation: What Lies Ahead?" http://www.iss.europa.eu/publications/detail/article/q-the-future-of-eu-us -security-and-defence-cooperation-what-lies-ahead-4 (accessed 12 February 2013).

of Twenty (G20) Summit, former French president Nicolas Sarkozy affirmed his commitment to the transatlantic relationship and praised the joint contribution of US and French forces in the Libyan intervention.[66] British Prime Minister David Cameron made equally encouraging comments during his official state visit to the United States in March 2012.[67] According to then prime minister Mario Monti, the Libyan intervention also improved US-Italian relations.[68]

Just as predictably, the response in the Arab and wider Muslim world was mixed. A Brookings Institution poll of October 2011 found that 59 percent of Arabs interviewed continued to regard the United States unfavorably, but that favorable views of the United States had increased 16 percentage points over the prior twelve months.[69] The report attributes this increase to America's handling of the Arab Spring as 24 percent of its sample—drawn from Egypt, Jordan, Lebanon, Morocco, and the United Arab Emirates—described the United States, along with Turkey and France, as the countries that played the most constructive role.[70] In a Zogby poll, a majority of Saudis and a plurality of Lebanese regarded the US contribution to enforcement of a no-fly zone over Libya positively.[71] Decades of suspicion in the Arab and Muslim worlds about American motives were not about to be redressed by one episode, but the episode indicates that change is possible.

THOUGHT EXPERIMENTS

Sponsorship strategies are too recent to evaluate en masse, so our case study on US-Mexican relations is an historical "what-if," or counterfac-

[66] Nicholas Sarkozy, "Discours du Président de la République à l'occasion de la cérémonie franco-américaine, à Cannes," 4 November 2011, http://www.elysee.fr/president/les-actualites/discours/2011/discours-du-president-de-la-republique-a.12382.html (accessed 4 November 2011).

[67] David Cameron, "Press Conference by David Cameron and Barack Obama," 15 March 2012, http://www.number10.gov.uk/news/press-conference-by-david-cameron-and-barack-obama (accessed 12 February 2013).

[68] Barack Obama, "Remarks by Obama, Italian Prime Minister Monti after Meeting," http://iipdigital.usembassy.gov/st/english/texttrans/2012/02/20120209190044su0.5858119.html#axzz1qdAZSRxl (accessed 12 February 2013); Ruth Santini, "The Libyan Crisis Seen from European Capitals," http://www.brookings.edu/papers/2011/0601_libya_santini.aspx (accessed 12 February 2013).

[69] Shelby Telhami, "The 2011 Arab Public Opinion Poll," http://www.brookings.edu/reports/2011/1121_arab_public_opinion_telhami.aspx, 3 (accessed 12 February 2013).

[70] Ibid.

[71] James Zogby, "Arab Attitudes, 2011," http://www.aaiusa.org/reports/arab-attitudes-2011, 2, 8 (accessed 12 February 2013).

tual, that explores the potential of sponsorship versus leadership strategies in American foreign policy. *Counterfactual* means contrary to fact and accordingly describes an event that did not occur.[72] Counterfactual thought experiments vary some aspect of the past to change a feature of the present.[73] They often do so to probe the causes and contingency of the actual historical outcome.

In international relations, counterfactual experiments are often evidence-rich but inevitably involve speculation because, as Stephen J. Gould observes, we cannot rerun the tape of history to see what would actually have happened. This is equally true of so-called factual or normal history. If we assert that Adolf Hitler was responsible for the Holocaust we really have no way of knowing if this is a valid inference unless we can know what would have happened if he had never become the dictator of Germany. Of course, we cannot do this. So almost any causal claim rests on unproven counterfactuals.

The most plausible counterfactuals employ minimal rewrites of history.[74] They also imagine outcomes close to the changes they introduce into the fabric of history and connect an antecedent (one small change in the fabric of reality) to the consequent (the major change we expect to result) through a chain of logic that appears consistent with available evidence. A small and credible rewrite of history has the potential to bring about a very different world. Consider the survival of the young Elián Gonzalez. In November 1999, Elián fled Cuba with his mother and twelve others in a small boat with a faulty engine; Elián's mother and ten other passengers died in the crossing. Floating in an inner tube, Elián was rescued at sea by two fishermen who handed him over to the US Coast Guard. The subsequent decision by Attorney General Janet Reno to return Elián to his father in Cuba rather than letting him stay with his paternal great-uncle in Florida infuriated many Cuban Americans. As a result, many fewer Americans of Cuban descent voted Democratic in the 2000 presidential election. If Elián had drowned—not that we personally wish him any ill fortune—Al Gore would have carried Dade County (Miami and vicinity) with a sufficient majority to have won the state of Florida and have become president of the United States.

---

[72] Neal J. Roese and James M. Olson, "Counterfactual Thinking: A Critical Overview," in Roese and Olson, eds., *What Might Have Been: The Social Psychology of Counterfactual Thinking* (Mahwah, NJ: Erlbaum, 1995), 1–56.

[73] For protocols for conducting counterfactual thought experiments in history and international relations, see Richard Ned Lebow, *Forbidden Fruit: Counterfactuals and International Relations* (Princeton, NJ: Princeton University Press, 2008), chap. 2.

[74] Max Weber, "Objective Possibility and Adequate Causation in Historical Explanation," in *The Methodology of the Social Sciences* (Glencoe, IL: Free Press, 1949), 164–88.

His election would not have prevented 9/11, but almost certainly would have prevented the invasion of Iraq.

The overall American approach to foreign policy and national security cannot be untracked by even multiple minimal rewrites of history. Throughout the Cold War and its immediate aftermath, the worldview of the American leaders and their advisers—and indeed, the national foreign policy and security establishments—was inconsistent with the adoption of sponsorship strategies and the understanding of national self-interest on which it was based. To shift that worldview so it would be supportive of sponsorship strategies would require reshaping the lessons Americans learned from their history and the deeper-rooted beliefs—exceptionalism, messianism, and indispensability—that we have described.

The following case study accordingly rests on a "miracle counterfactual" that introduces inherently implausible changes in reality. It violates our understanding of what is "realistic" or even conceivable, but is valuable when it allows us to reason our way to the causes and contingency of real events, or the dynamics that govern them. Alexis de Tocqueville hypothesized that America developed differently from Europe because it had no history of a landed aristocracy governing a society in which one's status at birth was all but determining. To make his case, he had to imagine what an aristocratic America would have been like—or, alternatively, prerevolutionary France without an aristocracy. Neither condition can be created with minimal rewrites of history; they must be assumed for the sake of argument. The goal here is not to argue that either world could have come about, but rather to use these admittedly unrealistic worlds as tools for developing and evaluating historical interpretations and social science theories. In this case, we use this approach to compare a hegemonic strategy with a prospective sponsorship one.

The United States, Mexico, and the Drug Problem

In the 1970s, Mexico became an increasingly attractive place to grow and process drugs. By 1975, 87 percent of the heroin and 95 percent of the marijuana entering the United States was thought to come from Mexico.[75] Drug lords effectively controlled the so-called critical triangle of Sinaloa, Durango, and Chihuahua through violence and bribery. The Mexican government was aware of the problem, and sought to develop

---

[75] Mathea Falco, *Winning the Drug War: A National Strategy* (New York: Priority Press, 1989), 36.

a joint strategy with Washington for suppressing the production and transport of drugs.[76] Mexico rejected an American plan for joint border operations in favor of an extensive eradication program. Under Operation Condor, American agents and technical advisers worked with their Mexican counterparts and soldiers to eradicate fields of marijuana and other drugs and to confiscate cocaine. By 1980, Mexico's heroin exports to the United States had declined from 87 percent to 25–30 percent of the total, and Operation Condor was judged a huge success.[77]

The relative success of Operation Condor was dependent on Mexico's willingness to cooperate with the United States. President Carlos Salinas nevertheless imposed limits to this cooperation when it abrogated Mexican sovereignty. The Northern Response Force was a relatively successful program consisting of rapid response teams of helicopters and aircraft acting on the basis of intelligence supplied by the US military to intercept illicit flights carrying drugs across the border. Mexico halted the program when American tactical teams and P-3 aircraft consistently violated Mexican airspace.[78]

The success of Operation Condor and the Northern Response Force confirmed American officials in their belief that drug importation from Mexico could be seriously curtailed. It encouraged the Nixon, Reagan, and, to a degree, the Clinton administrations to consider more interventionist, unilateral initiatives when Mexico began imposing restraints. These initiatives had frustrating and generally counterproductive results.

Operation Intercept was launched by the Nixon administration in September 1969 with the avowed goal of preventing any drugs from crossing the border from Mexico. It assumed that the Mexicans had been dilatory in their interdiction efforts and were unreliable. Officials pressured Mexico to allow the United States to conduct aerial surveillance over coca and marijuana growing areas and to use newly developed and largely untested herbicides to destroy crops they discovered.[79]

[76] Gregory F. Treverton, "Narcotics in US-Mexican Relations," in Riordan Roett, ed., *Mexico and the United States: Managing the Relationship* (Boulder, C. O.: Westview, 1988), 215.

[77] Richard Craig, "Operation Condor: Mexico's Anti-Drug Campaign Enters a New Era," *Journal of Interamerican Studies and World Affairs* 22, no. 3 (August 1980): 345–63; Maria Celia Toro, "The Internationalization of Police: The DEA in Mexico," *Journal of American History* 86, no. 2 (1999): 623–40; Kate Doyle, "The Militarization of the Drug War in Mexico," *Current History* 92, no. 571 (1993): 83–88.

[78] Peter Reuter and David Ronfeldt, *Quest for Integrity: The Mexican-US Drug Issue in the 1980s* (Santa Monica, CA.: RAND, 1992).

[79] "Narcotics, Marihuana and Dangerous Drugs Task Force," *Report of the Presidential Task Force Relating to Narcotics, Marihuana and Dangerous Drugs*, 6 June 1969 (mimeographed), cited in Richard B. Craig, "Operation Intercept: The International Politics of Pressure," *The Review of Politics* 42, 4 (1980); 556.

Not surprisingly, the Mexicans resisted the American pressure, and repeated meetings failed to lead to any agreement. One drug expert at least recognized that the "key American requests touched the very sensitive nerve of Mexican sovereignty, for they involved US participation in exclusively Mexican internal affairs."[80]

Nixon was undeterred, ordering the task force to proceed in implementing its border control operations. The US Defense Department placed Tijuana off limits to military personnel and required all civilian planes entering the United States from Mexico to file flight plans and periodically report their positions. Temporary roadblocks were set up in Brownsville, El Paso, and San Diego. Over a three-week period, at the cost of some $30 million and involving thousands of US military personnel and border agents, 4.5 million individuals and their vehicles or planes were inspected. Very few drugs were intercepted, but business on both sides of the border dropped off by some 70 percent in the communities most affected.[81] G. Gordon Liddy—one of the Watergate conspirators—nevertheless considered it a huge success: "It was an exercise in international extortion, pure and simple and effective, designed to bend Mexico to our will. We figured Mexico could hold out for a month; in fact, they caved in after two weeks, and we got what we wanted."[82]

Mexican border towns and the federal government alike were outraged. One Mexican official described the impact on the Mexican psyche as "equaled only by the assassination of President Kennedy. The whole affair is still so sensitive, so painful to most Mexican people that they literally avoid discussing it."[83] President Gustavo Diaz Ordaz publicly condemned Operation Intercept as discriminatory and insulting, noting the deep resentment it had provoked among Mexicans. Nixon hastened to issue an apology for the "frictions" and "irritations" it had caused, and promised to work in a more cooperative manner in future ventures.[84] US negotiators were compelled to accept that any accelerated antidrug campaign would have to be conducted "exclusively by Mexican personnel under Mexican direction."[85] A joint working group was established but came up with no new initiatives.

[80] Quoted in Craig, "Operation Intercept," 560.
[81] "FAA Proposes Restraints on Drug Traffic," *Aviation Week and Space Technology*, 18 August 1969, 112; Craig, "Operation Intercept"; Peter Andreas, *Border Games* (Ithaca, NY: Cornell University Press, 2009), 41.
[82] G. Gordon Liddy, *Agency of Flair* (New York: St. Martin's, 1980).
[83] Quoted in Craig, "Operation Intercept," 568.
[84] Craig, "Operation Intercept"; José Manuel Jurado, " 'Un Error Burocratico' Dana las relaciones con EU: Diaz Ordaz," *Excelsior*, 30 September 1969.
[85] Craig, "Operation Intercept."

In the absence of an agreement with Mexico, the US Drug Enforcement Administration (DEA) began sending undercover agents to Mexico without alerting the Mexican government. Washington's concerns intensified when one of the agents, Enrique Camarena Salazar, was murdered in February 1985. Ten days after his disappearance, the Reagan administration put Operation Intercept II into motion, which entailed stricter inspections and partial closure of the border. In 1985, as in 1969, the United States used the border as a high-profile stage from which to signal disapproval of Mexico's antidrug performance.[86] The Mexican government made little headway in bringing Camarena's murderers to justice, as they appeared to have close connections to the country's federal police force. In March 1986 the administration escalated its pressure on Mexico with Operation Leyenda, closing the border for eight days. They bribed Mexican police to kidnap a drug lord thought to be responsible for Camarena's murder, and to smuggle him across the border for arrest and trial.[87] These actions accelerated negotiations and led to the February 1989 Agreement on Cooperation in Fighting Drug Trafficking and Drug Dependency. Mexico compelled Washington not to undertake any actions on its territory, which is "reserved by national laws or rules exclusively to the authorities of the other country."[88]

The United States ignored the agreement from the outset. In April 1990, DEA agents kidnapped Humberto Alvarez-Machain, a prominent obstetrician thought to be involved in the Camarena affair, and brought him to trial in the United States, where he was acquitted. Supported by other foreign governments, the Mexicans challenged the legality of the kidnapping, arguing that it violated Mexican sovereignty and the 1978 US-Mexico Extradition Treaty.[89] The Mexican government halted all American antidrug operations in the country, and allowed—or possibly encouraged—the news weekly *Processo* to publish the names of forty-nine DEA agents operating undercover there.[90] These actions brought

[86] Andreas, *Border Games*, 47.

[87] William O. Walker III, "After Camerena," in Bruce M. Bagley and William O. Walker III, eds., *Drug Trafficking in the Americas* (Miami, FL: North-South Center Press, 1995): 395–421; Elaine Shannon, *Desperados* (New York: Penguin, 1989).

[88] Walker, "After Camerena."

[89] Mark S. Zaid, "Military Might versus Sovereign Right: The Kidnapping of Dr. Humberto Alvarez-Machain and the Resulting Fallout," in *El Papel Del Derecho Internacional en America* (Mexico City: Universidad Nacional Autonoma de Mexico/American Society of International Law, 1997), 429–450.

[90] Raymundo Riva Palacio, "Los 57, distribuidos en seis centros de operaciones," *Proceso*, 21 April 1990; Philip Shenon, "US Agents in Mexico, Listed, Are on Alert," *New York Times*, 24 April 1990.

the United States to the negotiating table where it accepted the 1991 Mutual Assistance Treaty, which established stricter guidelines for DEA agents in Mexico. It also had to make concessions in another treaty on extradition and agree to a bilateral agreement that prohibited cross-border abductions.[91]

The Clinton administration, motivated by a shared stake in the North American Free Trade Agreement, abided by its agreements for a few years. But it became increasingly concerned about the laundering of drug money by Mexican banks. On 16 May 1998, as part of Operation Casablanca, twelve Mexican bankers were lured to Las Vegas and arrested by DEA agents. Criminal indictments were brought against three of Mexico's largest banks and prominent bank officials.[92] Mexicans were angered by the sting operation, conducted without their knowledge. President Ernesto Zedillo refused to extradite five Mexican bankers, wrote a letter of protest to the US State Department, and complained bitterly to President Clinton by telephone.[93]

Unilateral policies by the Nixon, Reagan, George H. W. Bush, and Clinton administrations consistently backfired over the course of four decades; they provoked harsh and public reactions by Mexican officials, who resented US infringement on their country's sovereignty, secrecy about undercover operations, the gaining of cheap political capital from well-publicized but generally ineffective border operations, and the consistent violation of treaties and agreements. Periodically the Mexican government would placate the United States and arrest major drug figures, usually at critical moments in the certification process, when the administration had to inform the Congress if Mexico had made serious efforts to arrest and try traffickers and corrupt public officials. But this was reciprocal politicking and not effective cooperation.

The administration of George W. Bush made a real effort to improve relations with Mexico, but cooperation soon foundered. Two important causes of this deterioration both trace back to the American conception of its leadership role and of its national interest, which peaked in the

---

[91] Toro, "The Internationalization of Police"; US Senate Committee on Foreign Relations, *Mutual Legal Assistance Cooperation Treaty with Mexico*, S. Treaty Doc. 100-13, 100th Congress, 2nd session, 16 February 1988.

[92] Tim Padgett, "Banking On Cocaine," *Time*, 1 June 1999, 12–17; J. Carreno and C. Ferreyra, "Detuvo EU a 22 Ejecutivos: Decomisados 157," *El Universal*, 9 May 1998.

[93] Padgett, "Banking on Cocaine"; Tim Golden, "Mexican General Off-Limits to US Agents in Drug Sting," *New York Times*, 16 March 1999; Marco A. Garcia and Sofia Miselem, "Violo Nuestra Soberania la Operacion Casablanca," *Excelsior*, 26 May 1998; Jose Luis Ruiz, "Presentara Mexico a EU 'Codigo de Etica' para Reglamentar la Cooperacion Bilateral," *El Universal*, 29 May 1998.

aftermath of 9/11. In each case, the issues—the Iraq War and drug interdiction, and domestic security and immigration—were framed primarily in terms of the rhetoric of US leadership. Policies were perceived and evaluated in both the United States and Mexico accordingly. In the United States, the idea of border security was redefined in light of the newly felt threat of terrorism. Many Americans conflated the perceived threat to homeland security posed by a porous southern border with the need for a "tough" immigration policy.[94] Meanwhile, the Mexican government refused to endorse or participate in the Iraq War, in part because it resonated too closely with precisely the brand of American arrogance that had fostered resentment for generations.

After 9/11 there was a widespread backlash in the United States against the influx of immigrants across the southern border. President Bush and Congress grew more interested in strengthening border controls in response to public concerns over illegal immigration, which became markedly more pronounced as immigration and homeland security became linked. Responding to recommendations of the 9/11 Commission, the Intelligence Reform and Terrorism Prevention Act of 2004 clamped down on the border in the name of national security.

The ensuing spate of legislation angered Mexicans in its substance and execution. During border policy negotiations in 2002, Mexican officials signaled their willingness to work out a comprehensive antiterrorism border security agreement, but only on the condition that it also addressed immigration policy. Washington flatly refused to address the issue.[95] Mexico routinely denied American requests for the extradition of drug lords because of its own prohibition against life sentences and the death penalty. Congress retaliated with the Foreign Operations Appropriations Act of November 2005. This barred economic aid to any country that refused to extradite people accused of killing American law enforcement officers unless the secretary of state issued a waiver. In December 2005, the Mexican foreign ministry issued a press release asserting that legislation that focused on security in the absence of comprehensive immigration reforms was bound to fail. In January 2006, the Mexican government protested shootings of undocumented Mexicans by a border patrol agent in California and a police officer in Texas. Generally speaking, once immigration was reframed as a unilateral issue of national defense, there was no room for bilateral compromise with

---

[94] Tony Payan, *The Three US-Mexico Border Wars: Drugs, Immigration and Homeland Security* (Westport, CT: Praeger Security International, 2006).

[95] Edward Alden, *The Closing of the American Border: Terrorism, Immigration, and Security since 9/11* (New York: Harper Perennial, 2008): 259–60.

Mexico. Border policy was dictated by the imperatives of US homeland security, and Mexican concerns and priorities were set aside.[96]

The rhetoric of unilateralism embraced, encouraged, and exploited by the Bush administration in support of unilateral policy ventures was in part responsible for the undoing of its cooperative venture with Mexico. The US government consciously and deliberately emphasized its right, even its obligation, to pursue narrow unilateral interests to generate support for the Iraq War and other policies that were generally opposed by the global community. The Bush administration lost control of public opinion with respect to immigration. When the administration tried to pursue multilateral policies with Mexico, the right wing of the Republican Party, primed by the Iraq War to think unilaterally, turned on and defeated its own political leadership. Conservatives who framed illegal immigration as a security issue saw no room for compromise. Those who had opposed immigration reform for other reasons jumped on the bandwagon. With approval ratings in 2006 at or near record lows, Bush's big push for immigration reform failed to win over what had hitherto been his steadfast political base.

The implicit agreement between US president Bush and Mexican president Vicente Fox—immigration reform in exchange for cooperation on narcotics interdiction and border security—was dead. "It's a shame," said a member of the opposition serving on Mexico's Senate Foreign Relations committee, "because Mexico has been permanently supporting the United States on security and drug trafficking."[97] In an interview at the very end of his term, Bush cited the failure of comprehensive immigration reform as one of the biggest disappointments of his administration.[98]

US drug policy had unexpected implications for the Iraq War. Since losing half of its territory in its 1846–48 war with the United States, Mexico has been especially sensitive to American condescension and continental dominance, and correspondingly prone to resisting Washington's authority. This sensitivity was exacerbated by a long history of American unilateral policies toward Mexico, lack of respect for Mexican sovereignty, and a casual disregard of previous agreements, all of which were manifest in US drug interdiction policy. Mexicans considered US policy consistently selfish, hypocritical, and imperious. Only half the Mexican population expressed sympathy for the United States after the

---

[96] Andreas, *Border Games*, 156.

[97] Alistair Bell, "Bush Immigration Failure Hurts Mexico's Calderon," 10 June 2007, http://www.reuters.com/article/idUSN1035847620070610 (accessed 12 February 2013).

[98] Lauren Sher, "Bush: 'I Did Not Compromise My Principles.' President Says He Will Leave Office with 'Head Held High,' " 1 December 2008, http://abcnews.go.com/WN /Politics/story?id=6354012&page=1 (accessed 12 February 2013).

terrorist attacks of 9/11. Suspicion of the US government deepened with the Iraq war.[99]

Mexican foreign minister Jorge Castañeda backed the United States in the UN, consistent with the Fox administration's efforts to prove a reliable ally, only to be excoriated by domestic audiences. Fox felt compelled to distance himself from his foreign minister. In late 2002, when it became increasingly evident that the Bush administration was gearing up for an invasion of Iraq, Mexican ambassador to the UN Adolfo Aguilar Zinser worked behind the scenes in support of the French effort to deny UN Security Council backing to the Americans. What really infuriated President Bush was President Fox's decision to give a nationally televised address to explain why Mexico would have voted against the United States at the UN. The address was broadcast on Spanish language networks in the United States within hours of Bush's speech justifying his decision to wage war without UN backing.[100] Fox's speech "created a rare moment of national unity, one without parallel in recent . . . history."[101]

Conventional interpretations of immigration consider it to be essentially a unilateral American issue, whereas drug smuggling is bilateral.[102] This misses the unavoidable political connection between these issues. If narcotics interdiction and border security dominated Washington's agenda with Mexico, the Mexicans framed their relationship with the United States in terms of immigration above all else. In the hotly contested 2006 Mexican election, both presidential candidates spoke out against a border fence, defended Mexican autonomy, and voiced strong support for US immigration reform favorable to Mexican interests. Both candidates implicitly predicated further cooperation with the United States on acceptable immigration reform.

On the strength of his stance against US unilateralism, Felipe Calderón went on to win the Mexican presidential election. Shortly after taking office in December 2006, he sent federal troops into the state of Michoacán to combat violent drug traffickers. This intervention began an escalating conflict between the government and the drug cartels. Forty-seven thousand or more people died in the ongoing "Mexican drug war" in the ensuing half dozen years.[103] It has become the central issue

---

[99] Leticia G. Juárez, "Mexico, the United States and the War in Iraq," *International Journal of Public Opinion Research* 16, no. 3 (2004): 331–43.

[100] Pamela K. Starr, "US-Mexico Relations," *Hemisphere Focus* 12, no. 2 (2004), csis.org /files/media/csis/pubs/hf_v12_02.pdf (accessed 4 June 2013).

[101] Juárez, "Mexico, the United States and the War in Iraq."

[102] Andreas, *Border Games*, 14.

[103] Damien Cave, "Mexico Updates Death Toll in Drug War to 47,515, but Critics Dispute the Data," *New York Times*, 11 January 2012, http://www.nytimes.com/2012/01/12

in domestic Mexican politics, and exacts a serious toll on the country's political, economic, and social institutions. The drug war has now overshadowed illegal immigration as the primary political issue between the United States and Mexico.

The drug war has ushered in the most violent period in Mexican history since the revolution. Extremely aggressive and highly organized terrorist groups pose a mounting threat to the central institutions of Mexican political and social life. Corruption is pandemic, and those entities responsible for maintaining order in many regions have either been co-opted or have ceased to function. Mexican journalist Ricardo Ravelo estimates that half his nation's police force is on the payrolls of the drug cartels.[104] Many local officials or journalists courageous—or foolish—enough to attempt to challenge the cartels are murdered, often along with their families. Assassinations and kidnappings, many of which end with merciless beheadings, have become the norm. Parts of Mexico have become ungovernable. The military should be the government's leading weapon in the fight against the cartels, but it may be part of the problem. It stands accused of human rights violations and of acting as another cartel. In July 2009, Human Rights Watch noted, "Mexican military courts . . . have not convicted a single member of the military accused of committing a serious human rights violation."[105] Critics allege that former Mexican president Calderón, who took office with a razor-thin electoral victory, used the drug war as an excuse to weaken his political opposition.

For the United States, the drug war means an ongoing influx of drugs, spillover of violence and corruption over the border, and the looming, if exaggerated, possibility of a "failed state" to the south. This unprecedented crisis precipitated a rapid shift in Mexican-American relations and with it a movement in the United States toward a strategy of sponsorship. In 2008, President Bush and the United States reached an agreement with Mexico (the Mérida Initiative) to provide roughly $1.4 billion in assistance to Mexico to continue the fight against the drug cartels. It provided for an increase in aid to Mexico from $65 million in 2007 to $406 million in 2008.[106] The total aid package reached $1.5 billion

/world/americas/mexico-updates-drug-war-death-toll-but-critics-dispute-data.html?_r=0 (accessed 6 March 2013).

[104] Patrick Corcoran, "Focus on US-Mexico Cooperation Ignores Differing Interests in Drug War," *World Politics Review*, 26 March 2008, http://www.worldpoliticsreview.com/articles/1838/focus-on-u-s-mexico-cooperation-ignores-differing-interests-in-drug-war (accessed 12 February 2013).

[105] Human Rights Watch, "Mexico: US Should Withhold Military Aid: Rights Conditions in Merida Initiative Remain Unmet," 13 July 2009, http://www.hrw.org/en/news/2009/07/13/mexico-us-should-withhold-military-aid (accessed 12 February 2013).

[106] Clare Ribando Seelke, *Mexico-US Relations: Issues for Congress*, Congressional Research Service, 3 June 2010, http://fpc.state.gov/documents/organization/145101.pdf.

in Mérida's first three-year phase.[107] This is the largest foreign aid package in the Western hemisphere since Plan Colombia a decade beforehand. The Mérida Initiative met with broad support from both governments and marks a high-water mark in mutual cooperation. The current crisis has engendered recognition on both sides of the border of the serious and shared nature of the problem and the need for cooperation. The Obama administration has continued to aid Mexico in its struggle with drug trafficking. There is widespread recognition that the Calderón administration showed an unprecedented willingness to increase narcotics control cooperation with the United States.[108] It is too early to tell how his successor, Enrique Peña Nieta, will manage this relationship.

Let us now consider the sponsorship counterfactual. By the time of the Bush administration, we have seen, cooperation was severely constrained by political forces in both countries. More important, the drug cartels were by now powerful enough to undermine efforts by the Mexican federal government to restrain them. To alter the course of history in a meaningful way, we must go back to the Nixon administration and the era in which Mexican-American efforts to interdict drugs met with initial success. What would have happened if the Nixon administration had been content to work with the Mexican government rather than alienating it through unilateral initiatives that infringed on Mexican sovereignty? This is admittedly a miracle counterfactual because that administration broke domestic and international laws in pursuit of its internal and external adversaries. It nevertheless allows us to contrast the possible consequences of sponsorship and leadership strategies.

As noted at the beginning of this section, the Northern Response Force was a relatively successful program in eradicating drug crops and interdicting drug transport, but one where American tactical teams and P-3 aircraft consistently violated Mexican airspace. If the Nixon administration had been able to restrain itself, the program would have continued to the mutual advantage of both countries. Some marijuana would still have been grown and harvested and some traffickers would still have transported drugs through Mexico into the United States. However, there is good reason to believe that intelligence, surveillance, and Mexican police and military action could have kept this flow limited. In the absence of the major trafficking that developed in the aftermath of the collapse of Mexican-American cooperation, profits grew to

[107] Mark P. Sullivan and June S. Beittel, *Mexico-US Relations: Issues for Congress*, Conressional Research Service, 13 May 2009, http://fpc.state.gov/documents/organization/125501.pdf (accessed 3 June 2013). See also Clare Ribando Seelke and Kristin M. Finklea, *US-Mexican Security Cooperation: The Mérida Initiative and Beyond*, Congressional Research Service Report R41349 (Washington DC: Congressional Research Service, 2011), 8.

[108] Ribando Seelke, *Mexico-US Relations*, 11.

the point where drug cartels formed, acquired the weapons they needed to intimidate or kill local authorities and to bribe those at every level of the civilian and military authorities. Once this tipping point was reached, the ability of the Mexican government to win the war on drugs was severely curtailed.

Mexican-American cooperation would not have solved the drug problem because that required addressing the "demand" as well as the "supply" side of the problem. It would have required more miracle counterfactuals to reduce the appeal of drugs to significant segments of the American population, including an administration prepared to initiate programs to provide better living conditions and job prospects to the underprivileged. So let us assume that American demand for drugs is undiminished. The Mexican conduit would still have been active, but costly enough to encourage the Colombian cartels and their American collaborators to have found other, safer routes. At the very least, the Mexican government would have been spared the domestic crisis that threatens its political order and civil society. We can go a step further and reason that if successive American administrations cooperated the way we have described with Mexico they would have been more open to similar collaborative arrangements with Colombia and other Latin American countries. Here, too, policies that built on common interests rather than imposing American will by fiat, would have had greater chances of success.

The case of Mexico—like the Iraq War case—suggests that self-interest framed in narrow, egoistic leadership terms is myopic and often self-defeating. In Mexico, as in Iraq, American foreign policy ignored the binds of constraints that would have better served American interests. They arise from international law, institutional and alliance obligations, norms of consultation, and policy by agreement or consensus. With regard to its southern neighbor, the United States felt free to try to impose its will by fiat, frame international issues in unilateral terms, and ignore the perspective of the Mexican people and government. It continued to do so even when unilateral initiatives repeatedly failed to achieve their goals. The leadership mind-set became more pronounced in the aftermath of the Cold War and the collapse of the Soviet Union. America's self-understanding as the only remaining superpower encouraged far-reaching and ultimately unrealistic ambitions, as evidenced by its intervention in Mexico—and in Iraq.

Accommodation to power must always be rationalized in the mind of the subject.[109] There are many ways of doing this, including legitimi-

---

[109] Hans J. Morgenthau, *Scientific Man vs. Power Politics* (London: Latimer House, 1947), 145.

zation of its exercise so that actors who must comply, or decide to do so, can interpret their response as conformity to accepted norms and principles of justice. Effective use of power must accordingly be for purposes close enough to such norms and principles as to allow those who comply to "normalize" this behavior in this manner. Naked power, and power exercised in contradiction of widely accepted norms—as in Mexico and Iraq—is likely to arouse opposition, have unintended undesirable political consequences and generate "blowback."

CONCLUSIONS

Was Libya a special case of sponsorship? Without doubt, it had many features that made a sponsorship strategy particularly suitable. But the 2013 case of American support for French intervention in Mali suggests sponsorship has effective application in intervention cases, as the United States provided intelligence, transportation, and financial assistance to the French- and African-led force mission without any commitment of its own ground troops. America's extensive support for the campaign against human trafficking and against piracy substantiates the view that a trend of sponsorship strategies is emerging. It is increasingly becoming an American global function, as it evolves away from hegemony. Furthermore, sponsorship might have worked in other situations as a more general strategy had it been tried, as the Mexican drug case illustrates.[110] Another important example in our view is North Korean nuclear proliferation.

For almost two decades Washington has taken the lead on this issue, turning it into an eyeball-to-eyeball confrontation with Pyongyang, epitomized by crisis of 2013. As one news report tellingly commented, "Quotes from unnamed Pentagon officials suggest Washington is now questioning whether some of its actions may have contributed to the tension, with CNN quoting one official as saying the US would try to 'turn the volume down' on its rhetoric."[111] By singling out its regime as a renegade, by making frequent public demands that North Korea halt its nuclear and missile programs, and by seeking to cobble together an

[110] Julian Pecquet, "Obama OKs $50 Million to Support French Operation in Mali," *The Hill*, 11 February 2013, http://thehill.com/blogs/global-affairs/terrorism/282297-obama-oks-50-million-to-support-french-operation-in-mali (accessed 11 February 2013); Claudette Roulo, "Mali Lessons Inform Future Partnership Efforts, Official Says," 14 February 2013, http://www.defense.gov/news/newsarticle.aspx?id=119300 (accessed 14 February 2013).

[111] Lucy Williamson, "North Korea Warns Foreign Embassies to Prepare Escape," 5 April 2013, http://www.bbc.co.uk/news/world-asia-22045245 (accessed 5 April 2013).

international coalition against it, Washington transformed the nature of what was at stake. By giving in, North Korea would have lost substantial face in addition to appearing weak, even craven, in the face of threats. The US invasion of Iraq also had the effect, one can reasonably infer, of convincing those already in favor of going nuclear in North Korea and Iran that these weapons were all the more necessary as a deterrent. In effect, Washington acted in ways that guaranteed the outcome opposite to the one it desired.

Sponsorship would have started from the twin assumptions that public confrontation should be avoided and that others should take the leading role in dealing with North Korea. The obvious leader was China, the state in the region with the most influence in Pyongyang. Successive American presidents had tried, without seeming success, to convince China to pressure North Korea to halt its quest for nuclear weapons. Beijing certainly desires stability in North Asia, and would regard another war on the Korean Peninsula as a disaster, as it would the collapse of the North Korean regime—a view it made clear as tensions mounted in the spring of 2013.[112] At the same time, Chinese leaders have no desire to give the appearance to their own people or other states that they are taking orders from Washington. They have walked a fine line on the Korean issue given the cross pressures they face. In our counterfactual sponsorship scenario, Presidents Clinton or Bush suggest to China that this is an issue on which they can demonstrate their leadership capability and commitment to peace in the region. Washington promises to provide whatever quiet support might be helpful but, most important, to refrain from its usual confrontational rhetoric. In these circumstances, Beijing would have had a strong incentive to take the initiative, and backed diplomatically by Japan, South Korea, and possibly, Russia, might have persuaded the Kim Il-Jong regime to accept some agreement that offered positive rewards for not pursuing a nuclear option without the cost of external—and possibly internal—humiliation of those who signed the accords. China would have strengthened its diplomatic position in Asia, something unpalatable to the anti-China lobby in Washington, but the United States would have resolved a serious security threat. In the aftermath, Sino-American relations might also have improved. As the rhetoric escalated and the North Koreans announced it was restarting its mothballed nuclear reactor, it became clear that the United States had not achieved its policy goals.

[112] Zhang Yuwei, Joseph Boris, Cheng Guangjin, and Pu Zhendong, "Beijing Calls for DPRK Talks," *China Daily USA*, 3 April 2013, http://usa.chinadaily.com.cn/epaper/2013-04/03/content_16373505.htm (accessed 5 April 2013).

The contrast between Iraq and Libya, and the Mexican and North Korean counterfactuals, point to the superiority of sponsorship strategies. Persuasion and common action is generally a more effective means of achieving and maintaining genuine influence, both domestically and internationally, than the exercise of power through threats, bribes, unilateral action, and coercion. That said, there are situations where persuasion will not work. Saddam Hussein, Iranian officials, and North Korean leaders appear to have been equally unresponsive to carrots and sticks. In dealing with such leaders or countries, the choices are limited and often ineffective. Hence there is a temptation to resort to brute force, which often risks making matters worse unless conducted multilaterally and applied through institutions that are sufficiently fine-tuned to be up to their task. Our counterfactual case study of North Korea nevertheless suggests that there was some possibility that a sponsorship strategy implemented by China, South Korea, and Japan might have been effective in restraining North Korea's nuclear program. If it had failed, the situation would not have been any worse, and US prestige would not have suffered as much as it has through an unsuccessful policy of confrontation.

Another lesson emerges from these cases, which harks back to Thucydides and his account of the Peloponnesian War. Great powers routinely exaggerate threats to their security or standing and feel the need to act aggressively in response. Great powers are even more aggressive and, not content with their advantages, routinely seek hegemony. They start wars they lose. Thucydides teaches us that great powers can often be their own worst enemy. American policies in Afghanistan and Iraq are the latest example of this phenomenon. In search of security and hegemony, the United States damaged both.[113]

Closely related to great power hubris is the tendency to export domestic threats. When these threats are politically difficult to confront at home, great powers project the problems onto others. The American drug problem was consistently understood by successive administrations as more the result of supply than of demand. The lion's share of Washington's efforts went into reducing the supply from Afghanistan, South and Central America, and Mexico with little success. Even if the Mexican government is moderately successful in dealing with the cartels, it is unlikely that there will be much of a long-term reduction of the flow of drugs across the border as long as high drug demand exists in the United States. This is the ultimate source of the trafficking problem and of the violence in Mexico.

---

[113] See Richard Ned Lebow, *A Cultural Theory of International Relations* (Cambridge: Cambridge University Press, 2008), chap. 9.

It is an open question as to whether Libya is an exception to US aspirations to hegemony or the sign of a shift in policy aspirations and practices. In prior work, Simon Reich has shown that its principles have been applied to other policy areas—notably, the fights against human trafficking and piracy.[114] So there are signs of a trend as the United States assumes these functions in a posthegemonic world. Policy learning is difficult, especially in the realm of foreign policy. Europe is illustrative of this truth. It took two catastrophic wars for its leaders to change their thinking about the world and their role in it. Their reeducation was facilitated by defeat and decline and also by the positive role the United States played in restoring their economies and providing a security umbrella for them. But Western Europeans have undeniably undergone a revolution in thinking about the ways in which they relate to themselves and others. We now turn to this shift to understand it in its own right but also to look at the lessons it might have for the United States.

[114] Simon Reich, *Global Norms, American Sponsorship and the Emerging Patterns of World Politics* (Basingstoke, England: Palgrave Macmillan, 2010).

Chapter 6

///

The Future of International Relations

> At our best, America has led. . . . We have led by our example, as a shining city on a hill. . . . The demand for our leadership in the world has never been greater. People don't want less of America. They want more.
>
> —Senator John McCain, address to
> Republican Party Convention, August 2012

We have made a series of related conceptual and empirical arguments in this book. First, and foundational, is our interrogation of the concept of hegemony. Second is our contention that the United States has not been a hegemon for a very long time. Third is our finding that the United States often behaves in ways that undermine rather than enhance international stability. Fourth is our claim that the world is shifting toward a division of functions based on contrasting notions of the relationship between power and influence, and that a hegemon is unnecessary for international stability and inappropriate in any case in today's interdependent—and what we characterize as an increasingly multipowered—world. In this chapter, we review these arguments, elaborate some of the most important connections among them, and assess their implications for both US foreign policy and international relations (IR) theory.

THE DECLINE OF HEGEMONY AS A USEFUL CONCEPT

American IR theorists make unwarranted assertions about American leadership, its attractiveness as a model, and the organic nature of hegemonic functions. They assume American legitimacy where in fact little exists. To evaluate the conventional wisdom about hegemony, we broke the concept down to identify the functions realists and liberal expect hegemons to perform and asked the extent to which the United States performs them. We identified three distinct but related functions. The first, *agenda setting*, is a form of social power. It relies heavily on persuasion, generally in an institutional context. Arguably, it constitutes the most important form of leadership, just as it does in the domestic politics of democratic states.[1]

The second function is *custodianship*. It entails being the "lender of last resort," thus adding liquidity to the global system in times of economic crisis, addressing economic imbalances and stabilizing currencies.[2]

The third element of hegemony is *sponsorship*. It includes sponsorship of rules, norms, agreements, and decision-making processes as well as the provision of security to sustain peace and enhance finance and trade.[3] Liberals and realists maintain that only hegemons can provide such enforcement because of their preponderance of material power. They assert that hegemony is legitimate in the eyes of other important actors who welcome American leadership and enforcement as beneficial to global stability and their national interests.

We raise empirical, conceptual, and normative objections to the American hegemonic discourse. The claim of hegemony is historically false. The partial American hegemony of the immediate postwar period eroded quickly. It was based on the extraordinary and short-lived economic and military power of the United States in comparison to the rest of the noncommunist world. America's share of global GDP steadily declined in the decades after World War II, stabilized at around 25 percent for the four decades, and has again declined in the last few years to just over 21 percent. It currently ranks below that of the European Union.[4] If the next ten years look like the last ten, that percentage decline will continue, to below 15 percent.[5] Western Europe and Japan not only rebuilt their economies in the first decades after the war but also

---

[1] John W. Kingdon, *Agendas, Alternatives, and Public Policies*, 2nd ed. (New York: HarperCollins, 1995).

[2] Charles P. Kindleberger, *The World in Depression, 1929–1939* (Berkeley and Los Angeles: University of California Press, 1973), 305; Robert Gilpin, *War and Change in World Politics* (Cambridge: Cambridge. University Press, 1981): 173–75.

[3] Simon Reich, *Global Norms, American Sponsorship and the Emerging Pattern of World Politics* (Basingstoke, England: Palgrave, 2010) 62–63.

[4] Angus Maddison, *Monitoring the World Economy, 1820–1992* (Paris: Organization for Economic Cooperation and Development, 1995); Mark Perry, "Charting World Shares of GDP," 18 November 2011, http://seekingalpha.com/article/308958-charting-world-shares-of-gdp (accessed 5 April 2013); Gilpin, *War and Change in World Politics*, 173–175, acknowledges that US global dominance was fleeting.

[5] "US Share of World GDP Has Fallen 32% Since 2001," *Ecominoes*, 29 November 2012, http://www.ecominoes.com/2012/11/us-share-of-world-gdp-falls-32–since.html (accessed 5 April 2013).

regained much of their self-confidence, developments that reduced the need and appeal of American leadership. The recent surge in economic development in Asia, accelerated by the 2008 Great Recession, sustained that trend away from American leadership.

American policies demonstrated the limits of would-be hegemony in the Korean War stalemate in the early 1950s, the strategic failure and economic cost of the Vietnam War in the 1960s and the delinking of the dollar from the gold standard in the early 1970s. More recently, the costly interventions in Afghanistan and Iraq have further eroded American standing and influence. In each intervention, America's capacity was found wanting, its strategic objectives were frustrated, and its standing declined among friend and foe alike. The US' drone policy has been greeted with enormous hostility abroad, a perspective that American policy makers either ignore or fail to fathom. The supposed "unipolar moment" of US power in the early 1990s was accompanied by a decline in the number of interstate wars (the only type of wars that realists and liberals focus on in their analysis). But the number of intrastate wars rapidly expanded and killed millions, as the example of the civil war in the Democratic Republic of the Congo—with four million deaths—amply demonstrates.[6] These wars often proved as destabilizing as interstate wars, and the United States was unable to maintain the stability that a hegemon should provide. On the contrary, America's interventions often proved the precursor to instability.

By the 1980s, the limits of US hegemony was just as evident in terms of the global economy when it systematically reneged on its own liberal trading rules, introducing a variety of tariffs and quotas against new cheaper Asian and Latin American producers, rather than bearing the costs of adjustment. Until the 1960s, when the dollar was the world's undisputed reserve currency, the US current account balance ran at zero or a small surplus. That position dramatically eroded in the 1980s, and the US current account deficit peaked at 6 percent in 2006, just before the financial crisis.[7] These imbalances were in part the result of deliberate American efforts to foster greater financial integration among advanced industrial economies in the 1980s. They were subsequently associated with efforts to integrate emerging markets, including China. This all took place at a time when there was a consistent decline in net

---

[6] Andrew Mack, "The Changing Face of Global Violence (Part 1)," in *The Human Security Report 2005* (Oxford: Oxford University Press, 2005), 15–16, 18, 31–32.

[7] Joshua Aizenman, "On the Causes of Global Imbalances and Their Persistence: Myths, Facts and Conjectures," in Stijn Claessens, Simon Evenett, and Bernard Hoekman, eds., *Rebalancing the Global Economy: A Primer for Policymaking* (London: Centre for Economic Policy Research, 2010): 23–30.

US public and private savings.[8] The American public was no longer prudent. Successive US administrations abandoned fiscal discipline in favor of consumption and defense expenditures. American policies accordingly had the effect of making the US government and consumers increasingly reliant on foreign capital to finance their expenditures. Runaway expenditure by Americans and their government, reflected in low personal savings rates coupled with increased government deficits, became important causes of global imbalances.[9]

The growth in American personal debt has been unmistakable. It reached a low of –0.5 percent in 2005, a negative rate not seen since the Great Depression.[10] As savings plummeted, debt increased. By 2005, total US household debt, including mortgage loans and consumer debt, stood at $11.4 trillion.[11] This growth in personal debt finds a parallel in the US federal budget deficit. Since the end of President Bill Clinton's second term, the annual deficit of the US government has increased every year. It went from an annual figure of $186.2 billion inflation-adjusted dollars in 2002 to over an estimated $1,500 billion by 2011.[12] By the time this book went to press in February 2013, these figures had ballooned to over $16.5 trillion in total, at an average of just under $52,500 per citizen.[13]

US trade deficit figures, a third indicator, provide supplementary evidence of this trend, having consistently run a deficit since 1969. Comparable to the budget deficit, these figures have worsened over time and have grown since the turn of the century, peaking in 2006 on the eve of the financial crisis. The growing trade imbalance has been exacerbated by US policy and a lack of regulatory mechanisms. Significant tax cuts introduced by the administration of President George W. Bush, liberal policies designed to attract foreign funds, unregulated credit markets (that then made personal credit easier to obtain and led to a housing

[8] Ibid., 24.

[9] The personal savings rate is calculated by taking the difference between disposable personal income and personal consumption expenditures and then dividing this quantity by disposable personal income.

[10] Massimo Guidolin and Elizabeth A. La Jeunesse, "The Decline in the US Personal Saving Rate: Is It Real and Is It a Puzzle?" *Federal Reserve Bank of St. Louis Review* 89, no. 6 (2007): 491–514; see 492, fig. 1.

[11] Board of Governors of the Federal Reserve System, Federal Reserve Statistical Release, 9 March 2006, http://www.federalreserve.gov/releases/Z1/20060309/data.htm, 8, 102 (accessed 29 January 2011).

[12] Lori Montgomery, "CBO Projects US Budget Deficit to Reach $1.5 Trillion in 2011, Highest Ever," *Washington Post*, 26 January 2011, http://www.washingtonpost.com/business/cbo-projects-us-budget-deficit-to-reach-15-trillion-in-2011-highest-ever/2011/01/26/ABKue3Q_story.html (accessed 28 June 2011).

[13] "The US National Debt Clock," http://www.brillig.com/debt_clock (accessed 1 July 2011); Treasurydirect, http://www.treasurydirect.gov/NP/BPDLogin?application=np (accessed 5 April 2013).

bubble) combined with low savings rates to dramatic effect. In several decades, the United States has gone from being the bulwark of the international economy to the principal source of its instability.

Liberals and realists contend that hegemony is legitimate in the eyes of other important actors who welcome American leadership and enforcement as beneficial to global stability and their national interests. The only foreign support for these claims comes from conservative politicians and authoritarian leaders, the latter direct beneficiaries of US military and economic backing. There has been a noticeable decline in pleas for US leadership since the end of the Cold War, and as noted earlier, a corresponding increase in opposition to US military and economic initiatives. President Barack Obama's personal popularity, even at its zenith soon after taking office, didn't translate into multilateral leadership and his efforts proved embarrassing when rebuffed. Since the Iraq War, the United States has undergone a shift in its profile from that of a status quo to that of a revisionist power. Germany, Canada, and Japan now top the list of respected countries, followed by France, Britain, China, and India. Even pariah countries such as North Korea score better than the United States on some surveys. More recent surveys reflect a sustained theme: the United States is rarely perceived as acting in the interests of the international community, and that whatever legitimacy its leadership once had has significantly eroded.[14]

ORDER AND DISORDER

The United States has not been a hegemon for some time, and no other state aspires to the role. In contrast to the expectations of many realists and liberals, the world has not became correspondingly more disorderly, only more complex. Most of the disorder that currently plagues the world has nothing to do with the presence or absence of a hegemon, but is the consequence of the breakup of communism, ethnic conflict, uneven economic development, kleptocratic and theocratic regimes, clashing visions of justice, and desires of people everywhere for a better life. Had the United States been stronger militarily and economically, it would have not been able to prevent or dramatically influence such events as the Iranian proliferation, the euro crisis, the Arab spring, or the civil war in Syria. "Power" as we know it simply doesn't equate with that kind of control.

[14] Pew Survey, "Obama More Popular Abroad Than at Home, Global Image of US Continues to Benefit," 17 June 2011, http://www.pewglobal.org/2010/06/17/obama-more-popular-abroad-than-at-home (accessed 26 September 2011).

In the aftermath of the Cold War and the collapse of the Soviet Union, realist Cassandras predicted increasing, if not acute, conflict among the great powers. One famously urged Germany and Japan to develop nuclear weapons in the expectation that they would be needed to deter great power adversaries.[15] These fears proved absolutely groundless. There have been no war-threatening crises among the great powers in the two decades since the end of the Cold War. Relations among them remain relatively stable. Sino-American relations, which realists worry have the potential to lead to a war of power transition, are relatively tranquil despite periodic rhetorical excesses on both sides. In terms of interstate war, the first two decades of the post–Cold War world have proven at least as peaceful as the two that preceded it. This continuity is only surprising to those who, misled by their emphasis on power and its relative distribution, expected major changes in conflict and threat levels in the aftermath of bipolarity. But, as we have argued, power is rarely, if ever, determining. Far more significant is the nature of the society in which states interact. Embedded in an increasingly "thick" regional order, the once antagonistic great powers of Europe have developed a pattern of peaceful relations as their influence has increased. This success has led to an even greater commitment to maintain the peace and to stress a common European identity. Most of the continent has become what Karl Deutsch referred to as a "pluralistic security community," a region of independent states among whom war has become all but unthinkable.[16] Much of the Pacific Rim is slowly moving in this direction, with North Korea being an outlier. There is reason to believe that China, now increasingly part of the global economic system, is committed to a peaceful foreign policy and even prepared to exercise restraint on the question of Taiwan as long as its leaders make no move to declare their independence.

The concept of hegemony is neither accurate nor suited to the post–Cold War world. For reasons we have made evident, the United States is incapable of leading or managing either security or economic affairs along the lines envisaged by nostalgic realists and liberals. New transnational forces, coupled with US loss of legitimacy and abandonment of its traditional economic management responsibilities, have hastened the fragmentation of those functions commonly associated with hegemony. Networks of actors in Asia, Europe, and the United States attempt to implement all three functions in order to maximize their power

[15] John G. Mearsheimer, "Back to the Future: Instability in Europe after the Cold War," *International Security* 15, no. 1 (1990): 5–56.

[16] Karl W. Deutsch, "Supranational Organizations in the 1960s," *JCMS: Journal of Common Market Studies* 1, no. 3 (1963): 212–18.

and influence while recognizing that self-interest entails some degree of policy coordination. States in different regions have made different choices about their appropriate roles in this connection. European actors increasingly and consciously focus on expanding their normative influence by advocating a series of global reforms in a variety of policy areas. China, by contrast, has focused more on custodial functions designed to sustain a system that may have been constructed by the United States, but from which it and its Asian partners are now among the primary beneficiaries. The United States, however, does retain its role in the provision of the security architecture. It is for American policy makers to decide if it will try and pursue a self-defeating hegemonic strategy or a sponsorship one, thereby rebuilding the lost legitimacy which is key to reestablishing a modicum of leadership.

Many Americans, and quite a few Asians, debate whether we are shifting toward a multipolar world reliant on the vocabulary of traditional realists. To describe the debate in those terms would be both an analytical and an empirical misnomer. It suggests that we are simply witnessing a shift in material resources, one in which a degree of symmetry operates, common to other historical periods—horse for horse, tank for tank, nuclear weapon for nuclear weapon. The implication of our argument is that this is not the case. In fact, we are witnessing a shift toward a world in which actors have differing forms of influence, contrasting balances between material and social resources that they use to effect in differing domains.

Such a perspective concedes that we cannot rely on the intellectual or analytic simplicity, generality, or parsimony that lies at the heart of realism and, to a lesser degree, liberalism. The world is messy and getting messier, much to the discomfort of realists and liberals. Hegemony is even less suited to such a world than it was to the Cold War. This does not mean that America has no role to play in a more pluralist world; most state and nonstate actors recognize that it can provide important, indeed at times indispensible economic and military resources and technical expertise in addressing global problems—from providing the logistics for UN peacekeeping operations to addressing the smuggling of fissile materials. Indeed, America's contribution to the campaign against piracy has proved to be a stunning success—to its own benefit. Any claims that America has no role to play are premature. However, it can only exercise influence effectively to the extent it pursues and supports policies that reflect a broader consensus among key actors. It must be careful to offer selective support for important initiatives of others that suit its interests as well as advancing policies of its own. It is the only way that it can rebuild the credibility and thus retain the leadership for which it yearns.

Our counterfactual case studies of Mexico and drugs and North Korea and nuclear weapons suggest that self-restraint can be more productive than bullying. With Mexico, US adherence to any of its negotiated pacts about drugs would have maintained Mexican participation in efforts to reduce cross-border trafficking, and could have prevented a Mexican federal loss of control and the near civil war that country now faces. In dealing with North Korea, the United States might have been more successful if it had played a quiet, backseat, and supportive role. Washington should have encouraged China to take the lead in restraining North Korea, displaying regional leadership, which is something Beijing is keen to do. Washington would have avoided making the conflict over nuclear proliferation and rocket delivery systems into an eyeball-to-eyeball US–North Korean confrontation, making it that much more costly—and less likely—for Pyongyang to back down, dating from the 1950s to the spring of 2013.

Agenda setting, custodianship, and sponsorship are domains that involve considerable competition and jockeying for influence among state and nonstate actors. We neither suggest nor imply that there is a conscious division of labor in the global system. Rather, the focus on distinct functions is driven by domestic cultural conceptions of self-interest. Within limits, actors attempt to exert what degrees of control or influence they can. There are considerable differences in how effectively actors pursue these objectives. Their efforts vary in effectiveness not only according to their material resources but also as a result of the priorities they establish and their legitimacy in the eyes of other actors. Influence, as we noted earlier, is a complex outcome that cannot be reduced to any simple formulation of power based on material capabilities. Actors subjectively construct their notions of interest: they are not objectively defined. They are embedded in national cultural and historical factors, as well as the boundaries imposed by both domestic politics and international constraints.

REFLECTIONS ON POWER AND INFLUENCE

Power, we have observed, is difficult to define or measure with any precision. For this reason, some IR theorists either measure it in terms of its consequences, which is tautological, or, like Kenneth Waltz, attempt to reduce it to a single component. Hans Morgenthau attempted to develop a nuanced description of power that was built not only on its material bases but also on national character, popular morale, and the quality of leadership. He recognized that power was relational and thus context dependent; physical or moral resources that allowed leaders to influence one government might not work when deployed against another. Morgenthau's definition of power as "anything that establishes and maintains the control of man over man" is all but impossible to operationalize.[17] But he was right in directing our attention to influence, and with it, the thoroughly context dependent nature of the application of power.

In practice, material capabilities and power are related in indirect, complex, and problematic ways. Material capabilities are a principal source of power, but critical choices must be made about which capabilities to develop and how to use them effectively. The relationship between power and influence is malleable and fluid. Attempts to translate power directly into influence, even when successful, consume resources—often at a prodigious rate. They succeed only so long as threats are available, credible, and effective. This is equally true of bribes. Egypt and Israel illustrate this political truth; they have been major recipients of US aid over many decades, assistance that has not often translated into political influence. Israel built and expanded settlements on the West Bank, complicating US relationships with Arab countries, and has consistently threatened military action against Iranian nuclear facilities. Egypt's Hosni Mubarak stonewalled American pressures to reform his regime, yet the United States was powerless to influence the choice of either of his successors.

Joseph Nye Jr.'s concept of soft power, which we critiqued in chapter 2, is motivated by a reasonable concern over a broader understanding of power and its use in other than coercive ways. It is nevertheless conceptually vague and empirically questionable. Nye describes "soft power" as a form of influence, thus running together these two very different concepts. He assumes that foreign policy influence somehow derives from the appeal of a country's products and culture but offers no mechanisms or convincing examples. In the case of the United States, its products and culture are just as likely to arouse hostility abroad as they are welcomed. The insistence on women returning to wearing traditional garb in most of the Muslim world is just one notable example of this backlash. Soft power is, alas, a very soft concept.

The most effective form of influence is persuasion. It consists of efforts to convince others that it is in their interest to do what you want them to do. If successful, these other actors are often willing to contribute resources of their own toward the common goal. Persuasion must be build on shared values and advocate policies that involve widely accepted practices. If a state asks others to accept its leadership, a seri-

---

[17] Hans J. Morgenthau, *Politics in the Twentieth Century: The Impasse of American Foreign Policy* (Chicago: University of Chicago Press, 1962), 141.

ous effort must be made to convince them that they will have meaningful input and that the initiatives in question will not go beyond commonly agreed upon goals. Material capabilities may be critical, but so is political skill, as coalition building and maintenance is an art. Persuasion and coalition building is an iterative process, one greatly assisted by past successes in cooperation and leadership that create a degree of trust and propensity to cooperate again. Of equal importance, cooperation helps to build partially shared, if not common, identities that make cooperation and persuasion more likely in the future. Material capabilities are usually essential to the implementation of common policies, but coalition building depends on what is best described as political and moral power. Depending on the nature of the initiatives, it also benefits from institutional and technical expertise.

Persuasion is founded on the bedrock of legitimacy. Legitimacy is a long-run, low-cost means of social control as compliance becomes habitual when values are internalized. Where an actor accepts a rule because it is perceived as legitimate, that rule assumes an authoritative quality. The rule is then in some sense hierarchically superior to the actor, and partly determinate of its behavior. Over time, it contributes to the actor's definition of its interests. An organization that is perceived as a legitimate rule maker has authority vis-à-vis its members. The character of power accordingly changes when it is exercised within a framework of legitimate relations and institutions. The concepts of power and legitimacy might be said to come together in the exercise of "authority."[18]

From Thucydides to Morgenthau, there is a tradition of scholarship that has understood that the exercise of power is likely to provoke resistance because it compels those who bend their wills in face of it to recognize their inferior status. Subordination is an uncomfortable mental state, and an increasingly unacceptable one in an age in which equality and justice are dominant political values. For this reason, power has to be masked in order to be effective. Even in circumstances involving coercion or bribery, leaders have to pretend that they are acting on the basis of consensus and conspire with those they coerced or bribed toward this end. This might be accomplished by making some face-saving concessions to others, using language that appeals to mutually shared values and implementing policies through institutions in which others have representation and some real chance of influencing policy.

Politics is therefore as much about efforts to shape language and beliefs as it is about coercing behavior. One of the most important forms of power, as Karl Marx and Antonio Gramsci recognized, is the ability

---

[18] Ian Hurd, "Legitimacy and Authority in International Politics," *International Organization* 53, no. 2 (1999): 400–401.

to create and sustain particular discourses.[19] Marx and Gramsci thought this was dependent on, and an expression of, control over the means of production. Although far from being Marxists, realists also insist on the centrality of material capabilities. The numerous cases in this volume indicate this relationship is not nearly so straightforward.

Those with power do indeed attempt to foster and maintain discourses commensurate with their interests. Realism developed and was propagated during the early postwar years when Washington required a justification for its hegemonic strivings. Neoliberalism offers another primarily American example. It justifies tax cuts for the rich and cuts in services for the poor, legitimizing greed. Discourses that work domestically can work against influence abroad, as the rhetoric of John McCain quoted at the beginning of this chapter illustrates. It is delusional. The "war on terror" and the justification of the invasions of Afghanistan and Iraq in the name of national security and local democracy sold well in the United States but eventually struck much of the world as duplicitous. The Bush administration's behavior and rhetoric accelerated the sharp decline in respect and sympathy for the United States from its heights in the days after 9/11. The Obama administration arrived on a tide of foreign popularity, but frittered much of it away through the use of drones and a refusal to pay the domestic political costs of closing the prison at Guantanamo Bay. These phenomena are indicative of the extent to which discourses surrounding the legitimate uses of military force underwent significant evolution during the course of the twentieth century. Discourses, like influence, arise from a complex interplay of ideas and capabilities, and any theory of international relations or foreign policy must take both into account.

The invasion of Iraq offers dramatic evidence that power does not necessarily produce influence, and that its use at odds with prevailing norms and practices can seriously erode a state's influence. For the United States, it has led to the seeming paradox that the most powerful

---

[19] Antonio Gramsci, *Selections from the Prison Notebooks of Antonio Gramsci*, ed. Geoffrey Nowell Smith (London: ElecBook, 1999), 131–34; Robert W. Cox, "Gramsci, Hegemony and International Relations: An Essay in Method," *Millennium—Journal of International Studies* 12, June 1983, 162–75; Stephen R. Gill and David Law, "Global Hegemony and the Structural Power of Capital," *International Studies Quarterly* 33, no. 4 (1989): 475–99. For non-Marxist applications to international relations, see Friedrich V. Kratochwil, *Rules, Norms and Decisions: On the Conditions of Practical and Legal Reasoning in International Relations and Domestic Affairs* (Cambridge: Cambridge University Press, 1991); Craig Murphy, "Understanding IR, Understanding Gramsci," *Review of International Studies* 24, no. 3 (1998): 417–25; Neta C. Crawford, *Argument and Change in World Politics: Ethics, Decolonization, and Humanitarian Intervention* (Cambridge: Cambridge University Press, 2002); and Martha Finnemore and Stephen J. Toope, "Alternatives to Legalization: Richer Views of Law and Politics," *International Organization* 55, no. 3 (2001): 743–58.

state the world has ever witnessed is increasingly incapable of translating its power into influence. The obverse is also true. We have shown how European nations have led the way in instigating significant economic, environmental, military, and social reforms that were often opposed by the United States. And China, with a much smaller economy than that of the United States, has adroitly used its limited resources to serve its interests and cultivate influence around the globe. Both of these outcomes are anomalies for most realist and liberal understandings of power, but not for an understanding of power that disaggregates influence from power and directs our attention to the social construction of both and the ways in which they interact. Our cases indicate that international relations theory would greatly benefit from focusing on influence rather than power. Such a shift, while not ignoring material capabilities, would link social and material aspects of power and would ground the study of influence in the shared discourses that make influence possible. It would return to and build on Thomas Hobbes's understanding in *Behemoth*, cited at the outset of this book, that "the power of the mighty hath no foundation but in the opinion and belief of the people."[20] Europe and China, in their different ways, implicitly recognize the distinction between hegemony and *hēgemonia*, and aspire to the latter. Their respective foreign policies have proved quite effective in today's multipowered world. The United States has, meanwhile, pushed a two-tracked approach in the last decade—both hegemonic and sponsorship strategies. One is expensive in blood and treasure and the other relatively cheap: one drains legitimacy and the other enhances it; one is a barrier to leadership and the other helps reclaim it.

Our most optimistic take on the United States is that it is the process of a gradual transition from leadership to sponsorship. We believe that it serves American interests. Many influential Americans nevertheless believe that their country is the world's natural leader and must rely on, if not increase, its military capability. They remain committed to a traditional conception of hegemony and a belief in hegemony in a unipolar world. If this trend toward sponsorship continues, American academics and policy makers alike will come to understand that power and influence are diffused in today's world and that hegemony is an impossible and counterproductive goal. Europeans focus their efforts toward influence by relying preponderantly on normative or social power. The Chinese prefer to do so mostly through a combination of material economic power and bilateral diplomacy. Sponsorship increasingly offers a third formulation of the relationship between normative

---

[20] Thomas Hobbes, *Behemoth, or the Long Parliament*, ed. Paul Seaward (Oxford: Oxford University Press, 2010), 59.

power and material military and technical power, with a tilt toward the latter.

Ultimately, hegemony is difficult to reconcile with democracy. Leading intellectuals and political leaders have frequently proclaimed that democracy and pluralism in government and decentralization in economics are not only more effective means of governing than hierarchy and centralization but are important ends in their own right. The commitment to democracy and pluralism is equally applicable to international relations. This makes it enigmatic and indefensible for scholars and policy makers to embrace hegemony and the undemocratic hierarchies it aspires to impose and maintain.

Many American IR theorists and foreign policy and national security analysts have a normative commitment to American world leadership. They have developed the concept of hegemony to justify and advance this project, and the former have incorporated it into the very heart of their research programs. We have shown that it is empirically unsupported, rests on a flawed understanding of power and its superordinate importance in world politics, and encourages the United States to behave in ways counterproductive to its interests and those of the world community. It is incumbent upon IR scholars to cut themselves loose from this concept. We must say good-bye to hegemony as a theoretical and policy guide as the first step toward pragmatism and restoring America's global standing in both domains.

Index